LATINO AND MUSLIM IN AMERICA

AMERICAN ACADEMY
of RELIGION

RELIGION, CULTURE, AND HISTORY

SERIES EDITOR
ROBERT A. YELLE, LUDWIG-MAXIMILIANS-UNIVERSITÄT MÜNCHEN

A Publication Series of
The American Academy of Religion
and
Oxford University Press

AMERICAN ACADEMY
of RELIGION

LATINO AND MUSLIM IN AMERICA

RACE, RELIGION, AND THE MAKING OF A NEW MINORITY

HAROLD D. MORALES

OXFORD
UNIVERSITY PRESS

OXFORD
UNIVERSITY PRESS

Oxford University Press is a department of the University of Oxford. It furthers the University's objective of excellence in research, scholarship, and education by publishing worldwide. Oxford is a registered trade mark of Oxford University Press in the UK and certain other countries.

Published in the United States of America by Oxford University Press
198 Madison Avenue, New York, NY 10016, United States of America.

© Oxford University Press 2018

Library of Congress Cataloging-in-Publication Data
Names: Morales, Harold D., 1981– author.
Title: Latino and Muslim in America : race, religion, and the making of a new minority / By Harold D. Morales.
Description: New York, NY : Oxford University Press, [2018] |
Includes bibliographical references and index.
Identifiers: LCCN 2017042782 (print) | LCCN 2017043638 (ebook) |
ISBN 9780190852610 (updf) | ISBN 9780190852627 (epub) |
ISBN 9780190852603 (hardcover) | ISBN 9780190852634 (online content)
Subjects: LCSH: Muslims—United States. | Hispanic Americans—Religion. |
Muslim converts—United States. | Alianza Islámica.
Classification: LCC BP67.A1 (ebook) | LCC BP67.A1 M67 2018 (print) |
DDC 305.6/9708968—dc23
LC record available at https://lccn.loc.gov/2017042782

CONTENTS

ACKNOWLEDGMENTS

On January 25, 2009, I drove to the Los Angeles Latino Muslim Association for the first time. I was a graduate student seeking in part to better understand the Latino religious communities I had grown up within. My parents were born and raised in Guatemala, *la tierra de la eterna primavera*. They followed my grandfather to the United States, who, after founding many churches there in the land of eternal spring, accepted an invitation to start a Spanish-speaking religious community in Los Angeles. I was born in L.A., raised bilingual, and the majority of my Spanish and my *Latinidad* (Latino or Latinx ways of being) were performed at home and in church. By the time I began my graduate education in religious studies at the University of California, Riverside, my own bilingual, religious, and multicultural experiences had become an inseparable aspect of my academic projects.

As part of my graduate training, I was assigned a project requiring ethnographic fieldwork. My professors and mentors encouraged me to visit the Latino Muslim community in Los Angeles regularly and to develop meaningful relationships. When I first visited the group, they were meeting at the Omar ibn al Kittab mosque, a white building with a large green dome nestled between the University of Southern California and Exposition Park. Nearby were the various museums and the Colosseum that I visited regularly as a child. There were many other elements during those early trips that seemed very familiar to me like the use of Spanish, the close reading of sacred texts, the prominence of matriarchal leaders, and the warm *pan dulce* before and *Pollo Loco* after. There were also elements that were not so familiar like the use of Arabic, the tonal quality of communal recitation, the smell of rugs while prostrating, and the gendered segregation during prayer. As a Latino born to immigrants from Guatemala, I felt welcomed into the community. As a non-Muslim researcher, however, I experienced a distance that I hoped to bridge. To help me navigate a sort of experiential vertigo between the familiar and unfamiliar during these times, I could not have asked for a more adept, caring and critical guide than Marta and the LALMA community. They welcomed me and my family into their sacred spaces and community events, opened themselves up to us as we did to them, and exchanged stories about each other's experiences.

To Marta and LALMA, Juan and LADO and so many others from various Latino Muslim communities across the United States who entrusted me with their stories for this monograph, I am indebted and grateful. To Vero, Jakob, and Max who often joined me and even more often listened to me enthusiastically talk about the work, I owe more than I can ever describe or repay. I also owe a special debt to Jennifer Hughes who helped me engage religious communities as partners and guides and who poured her own time and energy into carefully and critically engaging the work. Her close and careful research, depth of understanding, and captivating writing continues to be a principle source of inspiration for my own. I am also indebted to several other scholarly mentors who helped encourage, shape, and refine the work, including Jonathan Walton, Muhamad Ali, Gaston Espinosa, June O'Conner, Reza Aslan, Ryan Falcioni, Jeanette Reedy Solano, and Christina Schwenkel. I am grateful for input from Hisham Aidi, Patrick Bowen, Kambiz GhaneaBassiri, Julian Hammer, Rosemary Hicks, Terry Smith, Charles Townsend, Leo White, Homayra Ziad, Michael Monahan, and many others. Thank you to Brandon Berrios and Luis Soria for the cover art. I am also grateful for generous research grants from the department of religious studies at University of California, Riverside, the American Academy of Religion, and the department of philosophy and religious studies at Morgan State University. Finally, to my parents, Esther y Rene Morales, *por dedicar sus vidas a las de nosotros, gracias.*

H.D.M.

LATINO AND MUSLIM IN AMERICA

INTRODUCTION

THE EXPERIENCE AND MEDIATION
OF RACE-RELIGION

After almost two years of learning about Islam, brother Ismail had finally decided to take his *shahadah*, the Islamic proclamation of faith that would initiate him into the Muslim community. Mariela, who had only been introduced to the teachings and practices of Islam three months prior, had also decided to make the proclamation that there is no god but God. Ismail had migrated from Guatemala, was now in his late forties, and had adult children living on the other side of the country. Mariela had been born in the United States to immigrant parents; she was in her early twenties and was single with no children. Ismail spoke only a few words in English; Mariela was fluent in both English and Spanish. Ismail relied almost entirely on face-to-face conversations and printed writings to learn about Islam. Mariela would do the same but would also look up information from websites and ask questions on blogs and social media. The two were joining a community of Muslims that, like them, had diverse backgrounds and experiences and who nevertheless all identified as both Latino and Muslim, or rather, as Latino Muslims.

The director and *imam* of the Omar ibn al Khattab mosque in South Central Los Angeles had prepared a certificate for Ismail and Mariela. The document would verify their Islamic identity to Saudi officials if they were to ever undertake the *Hajj* pilgrimage to Mecca where only Muslims are allowed to enter. The Latino Muslim community had been welcomed into this mosque located between university buildings and museums, and had been allowed to congregate and hold meetings in a room on the second floor. While the *imam* prepared for the official business of the *shahadahs*, the community of Latino Muslims prepared a welcoming potluck to be held after the ritual proclamations. For all the alienation the new converts would experience from Latinos who might interpret the act as a rejection of Latino heritage and from Muslims who might identify Latino culture as incompatible with Islam, the Latino Muslim community would do its best to make Ismail and Mariela feel welcome. Together, they would not only learn to cope with such alienation but also would come to celebrate their Latino Muslim identity in their daily lives and in their mass-mediated representations.

At the last minute and in an almost whispered statement, Ismail had a change of heart; he would not go through with his *shahadah*. Mariela showed no such signs of doubt and moved forward with a determination that prompted everyone else to follow her. Before anyone had any time to reflect on Ismail's rejection of Islam, the group left the meeting room where the upcoming *fiesta* had been prepared and headed down the building's stairs to the prayer hall. Ismail quietly spoke about his interest in studying other religions to a friend, took off his shoes along with everyone else, and entered the main prayer hall for one last time. Mariela, the *imam*, and a representative from the Latino Muslim community, stood at the front of mosque, which pointed toward Mecca, the direction of prayer. They faced the rest of group, a body of witnesses to the public proclamation. Mariela repeated the words in Arabic first, *lā ilāha illallāh, muhammadur-rasūlu-llāh*. Then in Spanish, *No hay más dios que Alá y Muhammad es su profeta*. And for a third time, now in English, *There is no god but God, and Muhammad is the messenger of God*.

Latino Muslims have emerged in an American religious landscape that is both "very diverse and extremely fluid."[1] Distinctive immigration patterns and laws, urban spaces, and new media technologies have increasingly brought Latinos and Muslims into contact with one another. The mass exodus out of the Catholic Church, the digitization of religion, and the growth of Islam have also played significant roles as has the prominence of American media politics, information economies, and the hyper-racialization of individuals and their religious identities. The historically specific character of groups like Latino Muslims with complex and intersecting identities increasingly compel us to approach the categories of race, religion, and media as inextricably intertwined. Latino Muslim identities emerge through complex and historically specific processes, through competing and dominant narratives that are mediated in newspapers and on the Web, and in relation to broader categories and histories regarding race and religion in America. At stake, is the manner in which we relate to and engage with so-called minorities.

At a 2010 presentation given in southern California titled "Is the United States Becoming Islamophobic?" public intellectual Reza Aslan proclaimed that the two groups most negatively stereotyped in American media today are Muslims and Latinos, adding, "and God help you if you happen to be both!" The reference to Latino Muslims was not merely an improvisational hypothetical; it was a very real warning regarding the discrimination and marginalization that individuals face in America at the dawn of the twenty-first century. The United States, we are told, is currently poised to become the first nation whose collective minorities will outnumber the dominant population, and Latinos play no small role in this world-changing demographic shift.

It is important to keep in mind at this juncture that not only is "America" constructed through narratives about immigration and diversity but also that "Latinos are made in the USA;" that is, both the "Latino" and "Hispanic" labels are unstable constructs produced within a racialized American public discourse.[2] Beyond being treated as a homogeneous group in the United States, very little if any shared class, immigrant, religious, cultural, and other identity markers exist to unify all the people placed within this umbrella term. Instead, most individuals prefer to identify with their family's country of origin, Mexican-American or Chicano, Puerto Rican, and so on, than with a pan-ethnic label like "Latino."[3] Given broad doctrinal, legal, and ritual differences between various Sunni, Shi'a, Ahmadiyya, and uniquely American Muslim groups, there is also very little that unifies Muslims across the globe and in the United States. Instead, so-called minorities

3

(i.e., identity categories like "Latino," "Muslim," and "Latino Muslim") are complex, diverse, and dynamic.

Given the unstable significance of the "minority" category and the existence of minorities within minority groups, it is imperative that we ask how the term "minority" has been used to dominate, negotiate, and liberate in order to envision a more democratically egalitarian future.[4] In *What Is an American Muslim? Embracing Faith and Citizenship*, Abdullahi Ahmed An-Na'im maintains that to identify as a Muslim is to identify as a religious "minority" in the United States. However, individuals have many different and overlapping or intersecting identities, and all Americans, whether Muslim or not, are part of the majority as American citizens.[5] Rather than engage in America's democratic processes as so-called minorities, I agree that those who identify or are identified as Latino, Muslim, both, or neither, should do so as full agents seeking to live out their complex, diverse, and dynamic identities.

Even as many people view Latinos and Muslims as growing threats, Latino Muslims celebrate their intersecting identities in their daily lives and in their mass-mediated representations. By following the lives of individuals who participate in the mediation of Latino Muslim identity, including Marta Galedary from the Los Angeles Latino Muslim Association, Juan Galvan from the Latino American Dawah Organization, and others, this book provides historically specific and thick descriptions of diverse Latino Muslim groups while offering a cultural studies analysis of race-religion (or ethnic religious groups), media, and the making of a new American "minority."

A DEMOGRAPHIC SKETCH

"Religion in the United States," we are told in a seminal PEW report on America's religious landscape, "is often described as a vibrant marketplace where individuals pick and choose religions that meet their needs, and religious groups are compelled to compete for members."[6] Migration to America has been a vital source of the nation's diversity and formation of a "vibrant religious marketplace." Although various

Christian groups abound, some larger and better known than others, Jewish, Buddhist, Hindu, Sikh, Muslim, and other religious communities have also taken root in the United States. Even though changes in immigration law and migration patterns have greatly contributed to this diversity, conversion or religious switching has also played a significant role.

Roughly 37 percent of all Americans abandon the religion they were raised in.[7] Individuals are increasingly identifying with no religion and as spiritual but not religious.[8] The Catholic Church in America has experienced the biggest loss of membership due to disassociation but has also gained just as many members, not through conversion but through immigration.[9] A significant number of Catholic immigrants are Latinos, who currently make up about one-third of all American Catholics.[10] Latinos are not only adding to the community's membership, however, they are also converting out of the church. Pew's 2014 findings estimated that nearly one-third (32%) of Latinos leave the religion they were raised in and nearly 77 percent of these are former Catholics.[11] The report finds Latinos switch out of the religion they were raised in because they started questioning (8%), because they disagreed with the "worship" of saints (6%), because of the sex abuse scandal (3%), because they wanted to be closer to God (3%), because of family/relatives (5%) and because of marriage/spouse/partner (2%). More broadly, the report also found that "just gradually drifting away" (55%), unbelief in the tradition's teachings (52%), finding another community that helps more (31%), and a "deep personal crisis" (23%) played "an important role for why they are no longer affiliated with their former religion."[12] A previous report not only asked about why Latinos leave the religion in which they were raised but also how they first came into contact with the new religion they embraced. 48 percent of Latino converts reported having come into contact with their new religion through relatives, 26 percent through friends, 14 percent from members of the religion they converted to, and 2 percent through mass media such as radio or television.[13]

The US Muslim population is also significantly impacted by immigration and conversion patterns. At roughly 1.8 billion adherents across the globe in 2015, Islam is the second largest religion in the world.[14] Although Islam is the fastest growing religion in the United States, less than 1 percent of the total US population (roughly 3.3 million out of 322 million) identify as Muslims.[15] According to a Pew report, nearly one-quarter of Muslims in the United States are converts, and most identified as Christians prior to their embrace of Islam. More than half of the American-born Muslim population identify racially as black, some of whom additionally describe themselves as ethnically Latino. Latinos represent 4 percent of all Muslims in America and 8 percent of African American Muslims. Although immigration has played an important role in the Muslim American landscape, there has also been a prominent domestic American Muslim presence in the United States and a growing convert population. 58 percent of converts to Islam cite religious reasons such as "the truth or appeal of Islam's teachings, the belief that Islam is superior to Christianity, or that the religion just 'made sense' to them," as prompting their decision to embrace Islam while another 18 percent cited relational factors such as marriage.[16]

With regard to Latino Muslims specifically, the 2017 report "Latino Muslims in the U.S.: Reversion, Politics, and Islamidad" found that:

> Approximately 62 percent of the [Latino Muslim survey] sample was born in the U.S. and 38 percent was born in Latin America or elsewhere . . . eighty-four percent were U.S. citizens, 4 percent permanent residents, and 12 percent undocumented or something else . . . the states with the highest concentrations of Latino Muslim participants were California (19%), Texas (15%), New York (12%), New Jersey (11%), Florida (7%), Illinois (5%), Georgia (4%), and Pennsylvania (3%). . . . The majority of Latino Muslim participants traced their Latino ancestry to either Mexico (31%) or Puerto Rico (22%) . . . 12 percent to South American countries, and 9 percent to Central American countries. Participants also traced their Latino ancestry to the Dominican Republic (5%) and to Cuba (3%). With regard to race, 28 percent of the [Latino Muslim survey] sample identified themselves as white, 23 percent as brown, 6 percent as black, and

3 percent as American Indian or Alaska Native. . . . The overwhelming number of Latino Muslim participants (73%) were women and only 27 percent were men . . . 93 percent of respondents reported that both their father and their mother were not Muslims, indicating that they were not raised as Muslims.[17]

The report provides a more detailed demographic sketch of Latino Muslims than had previously been available. Nevertheless, current estimates of the total Latino Muslim population are based on studies that approach the group either as an ethnic subgroup of Muslims or as a religious subgroup of Latinos. A 2015 Pew study estimates there are 198,000 Latino Muslims in the United States. However, given the low number of Spanish-language mosques and Latino Muslim clergy, it is more likely that the number of Latino Muslims in the United States is much lower and closer to a Hispanic Churches in American Public Life study, which estimates there are 52,000 when updated to reflect census data from 2015.[18] The question of who is counted as a Latino and who is counted as a Muslim directly influences how and by whom Latino Muslims are studied and the conclusions that are drawn from such studies.[19] Are scholars of Latino religions or Islamic studies scholars best suited or prepared to understand the nuances of Latino Muslims and their complex and intersecting identities?

The difficulty with estimating the number of Latino Muslims derives not only from the lack of resources and studies conducted specifically on the group but also and importantly precisely because Latino Muslims reveal ethnic and religious categories to be fluid sites of contestation. What term is more appropriate, Latino or Hispanic, or are they synonymous and interchangeable? Must someone self-identify as a Latino to be counted as one or can Latino identity be ascribed based on other factors? Can Muslims be identified as such by simply having ties to Muslim majority nations? Is there a minimum level of religious commitment necessary to be counted as a Muslim and if so, how are such boundaries determined? Such questions present crippling difficulties for survey studies in general, and for those who make incidental observations on Latino Muslims in particular. Given the current lack of scholarly attention given to Latino Muslims and the difficulty in attempting to fix the fluid categories of "Latino" and "Muslim," this study proceeds through an interdisciplinary approach while remaining critical of the relationship between power and the production of knowledge.

METHODS AND SCOPE OF THE STUDY

This study of Latino Muslims and the formation of identity groups draws on and engages central categories, theories, and issues in the fields of critical race theory and ethnic studies, religious studies, and media studies. The field of ethnic studies in the United States was prompted by post–civil rights critiques of ethnocentrism in academia. The dismal number of nonwhite scholars in universities and the privileging of certain worldviews in the production of scholarship on so-called minorities were of particular concern. Ethnic studies draws from various disciplines in the examination of how individuals and groups are racialized and how these formulations aid in the discursive, political, legal, and economic domination of one group over another. While critiquing histories that support privileged positions of power, ethnic studies scholars often seek to produce alternative and liberating histories of so-called minority groups. This study examines the colonial construction of Latino and Muslim identities, the racialization of Latino and Islamic religions, the historical degradation of popular practices, and the alternative histories produced by Latino Muslims.

Religious studies is also an interdisciplinary academic field that critically engages with definitions of its central category, religion. Although some definitions narrowly focus on God or gods, beliefs and scriptures, or on rituals, symbols, and social structures, 'religion' is also approached as a broader set of dimensions. Some formulations of religion reduce the category to other phenomena, including religion as an aspect of culture or politics. Other formulations take seriously the view of practitioners and approach the category as sui generis and irreducible to other, including empirical, phenomena. Latino Muslims themselves often refer to Latino Catholicism in the "religion as culture" tradition and

8

to Islam as irreducible. Increasingly, "religion," like "race" and "ethnicity" is also approached as a discursive formation whose meanings and usages are determined by academic, popular, and mediated discourses.

If the categories of race and religion and ensuing racial and religious identities are all approached as discursive formations, then it becomes particularly important to examine the media technologies through which such discursive formations are articulated. That is, we should pay close attention to the complex and fluid relationships between the mediums and content of our discourses. Do technologies like writing, newspaper, radio, television, and the amalgamation of these within internet technologies determine the range of possible human expression and the ways in which social relations are organized?[20] Will the proliferation of information technologies improve or be detrimental to human cognition, moral values, and democratic societies? Are "society" and "technology" different labels or approaches to the same phenomenon and is the question of media determination therefore based on a fictitious and erroneous division between technology and society?[21] The role of media has been the subject of much scholarly and popular inquiry particularly as internet technologies increasingly come to dominate cultural, religious, political, and economic spheres. In religious studies and ethnic studies, scholars have begun to ask whether internet technologies will allow for more egalitarian access to public discourse and representation; and whether these technologies will prompt new, digital ways of being religious and racialized.[22]

In the case of so-called minorities like Latino Muslims and the formation of their identity groups, we are ever more compelled to approach the categories of race, religion, and media as inextricably intertwined. Latinos embrace and experience Islam from a particular perspective that they and others understand as "ethnic." The conversion of Latinos out of the Catholic Church follows broader patterns in the American religious landscape as does their digitization of religion. Like many other Latinos who leave the church, Latino Muslims cite a desire for a more direct experience of God as a central motive for conversion along with finding the tenets and practices of Islam more appealing, the Islamic critique of class- and race-based inequality compelling, and

9

their familial and intermarriage connections as significant. Importantly, many also cite popular and news media representations of Islam as prompting their initial interest in the religion and having researched its beliefs and practices through internet technologies as important factors in their decision to embrace Islam.

The Islamic mandate to propagate the religion's teachings to non-Muslims has encouraged many Latino Muslim groups to organize around the production of English and Spanish language books, flyers, and websites directed at Latino audiences. Finding that their intersectional identity often alienates them from broader Latino and Muslim communities, Latino Muslims have also organized as support groups that celebrate their dual identity in their daily lives and in their mediated representations. Latino Muslims often describe their path toward Islam to journalists who produce news articles that are often remediated onto Latino Muslim websites. Corporate media is often bypassed altogether by Latino Muslims who publish original content on websites, blogs, and social media.

Attempts to describe Latino Muslims and their identity groups must take into account not only narratives published in news articles and new media, nor simply rely on cursory interviews in which predictable and relatively uniform scripts are recited by interviewees, but must include a critical analysis of these mediated narratives in relation to in-depth ethnographic fieldwork and historical research.

Through a multidisciplinary approach, this book documents and analyzes the formation of diverse Latino Muslim groups. From the 1970s to the present, I follow the lives of several Latino Muslim leaders and their efforts to organize and unify nationally in order to solidify the new identity group's place within the public sphere. In the 1970s, Khadijah Rivera moved from Puerto Rico to the mainland where she became involved in several socialist and feminist movements and began to study Islam academically before becoming a Muslim herself and starting the woman's organization PIEDAD. Juan Galvan was born and raised in Texas, studied management information systems in college, first learned about Islam through another Latino, and now runs the largest Internet-based network, the Latino American Dawah

Organization. Marta Galedary was born in Mexico, first learned about Islam while studying abroad in England, works as a registered nurse, practices Islam, and is president of the Los Angeles Latino Muslim Association.

My descriptions and analysis of these and other individuals, their communities, and the mediation of their identity narratives are based on more than four years of ethnography, media analysis, and historical research. The research was informed primarily by questions regarding the interplay between lived experiences and the mediation of these experiences and by work in the fields of lived religions and media studies.[23] Ethnographic fieldwork included over two years of participant observation at the Los Angeles Latino Muslim Association, which meets weekly for Sunday meetings at Masjid Omar ibn al Khattab in South Central Los Angeles. In addition to attending these weekly meetings, I attended dozens of other community events throughout the United States, including *shahadahs* (the Islamic proclamation of faith and initiation ritual), birthdays, picnics, baby showers, and weddings. I also attended *mawlid* celebrations of the Prophet's birthday, Sufi *zikr* meditations, the annual Hispanic Muslim day in New Jersey, several interfaith talks, college and university presentations, religious conferences, and organizational meetings. I attended *dawah* (the propagation of Islam) at the Fiesta Broadway celebration of *Cinco de Mayo* in Los Angeles, at book festivals, and at other venues. I conducted formal interviews with Latino Muslims in California, Texas, Georgia, Florida, New York, and New Jersey. Internet research included over four years of ongoing review, archiving, cataloging, and analyzing of key content on websites, blogs, and social media. Research also draws on organizational archives and newspaper articles ranging from 1999 to 2016.

Drawing from this research, chapter 1 introduces the history of Islamic Spain and the remembrance of it by the first Latino Muslim group in the United States, la Alianza Islámica, the Islamic Alliance. Although there have been several recorded instances of individual Latinos embracing Islam since the 1920s, no direct historical link exists between Muslims in Spain and Latino Muslims in the United States. Instead, the memory of Islamic Spain has been used to frame Latinos as historically connected to Islam rather than completely foreign to it. Additionally, the Alianza drew from other civil rights organizational models to develop several centers in New York where they worked to propagate Islam, provide social services, and engage in political activism. The Alianza also experienced marginalization from broader Muslim organizations and sought to develop autonomously from them. Through its unique origin histories and various activities, the Alianza helped to crystalize a first wave of Latino Muslims that inspired subsequent communities throughout the United States.

Chapter 2 examines a second Latino Muslim wave consisting of the prominent organizations PIEDAD, the Latino American Dawah Organization (LADO), and the Los Angeles Latino Muslim Association (LALMA). PIEDAD (a Piety women's group) was founded in 1988 as a support group by and for women in Florida. LADO was founded in 1997 as a network for the dissemination of Islamic information to Latino audiences via internet technologies. LALMA was founded in 1999 as a Qur'anic study group in Los Angeles. All three organizations had been inspired by the work and stories developed by the Alianza Islámica but also moved away from the first Latino Muslim paradigm in unique ways. The new organizations concentrated almost exclusively on the production and study of information, they worked within rather than autonomously from broader American Muslim groups, and they developed within a distinct historical context. By the 1990s, the civil rights era had come to an end, religious diversity had increased exponentially, and internet technologies were beginning to radically transform religious authority and concepts of space.

Chapter 3 examines the form, content, and discursive relevance of Latino Muslim reversion stories published through organizational websites. The term "reversion" is in this genre preferred over "conversion" because it frames Latinos as returning to something previous and familiar rather than new and foreign. Reversion stories are short autobiographies about how an individual Latino came to embrace Islam. The chapter includes three complete and unedited reversion stories by Khadijah Rivera (president of PIEDAD), by Marta Galedary (president of LALMA), and by Juan Galvan (director of LADO). The chapter also provides an analysis of the genre's form, content, and discursive relevance. In particular, I argue that rather than explain why some Latinos are converting to Islam, reversion stories: (1) are a form of *dawah* or outreach;[24] (2) creatively respond to critiques that Latino and Islamic identities are incompatible or foreign to one another; and (3) help to form and shape the contours of Latino Muslim communities.

In contrast to self-produced media like reversion stories, chapter 4 documents and assesses journalistic representations of Latino Muslims. In a post-9/11 media context, Latino Muslims received increased attention from journalists. I argue that these news stories have however reductively focused on "conversion" at the expense of more complex and diverse representations. Although much of this coverage has been reductive, it has generally not been overtly negative. An exception to this pattern is Spanish language news media, which has represented Latino Muslims in negative ways that echo the form but not the function of broader sets of orientalist images. Latino Muslims have responded by calling for boycotts and writing petitions to end the defamation of their identity group. I argue that some of their responses are more reasonable than others and that they will require much broader support if these are to make any positive contributions to our public discourse.

Chapter 5 is a critical appraisal of media practices that assume conflict rather than peaceful coexistence. It engages the Clash of Civilizations thesis articulated by both Samuel Huntington and the Mujahedeen Team, a Latino Muslim hip-hop group. The assumed media war, I argue, contributes to both the reduction of Latino Muslims into simplistic binaries, between so-called good and bad Muslims, but also links a so-called Latino nature to radical religiosity. News coverage of Antonio Martinez's arrest on charges of terrorism placed this problematic practice on full display. Responses by Latino Muslim leaders and organizations, however, often assumed a media war themselves. I recommend that a better approach to "clashes of civilizations" or "cosmic wars" is to deny their very existence or overshadow their discursive relevance with much more complex, diverse, and fluid visions of American diversity.

Chapter 6 examines a third Latino Muslim wave characterized by a distinct historical context, attempted consolidations of Latino Muslim groups under a single umbrella organization, and the emergence and prominence of the Islam-in-Spanish group. The latest wave of Latino Muslims is being shaped by political discourses around ISIS, immigration, and the 2016 election cycle. Increasingly negative coverage of Latinos, Muslims, and Latino Muslims within this context has prompted renewed attempts to consolidate the resources of disparate Latino Muslim groups across the nation in order to unite and collectively counter hateful characterizations of their identity groups in public discourse. The latest attempts at such consolidation include the founding of the Islam-in-Spanish group in 2003 by Mujahid Fletcher and the reformulation of LALMA to the pan-Latino Muslim moniker: La Asociación Latino Musulmana de América (the Latino Muslim Association of America). In 2016, the Islam-in-Spanish group held a grand opening for a new 5,000 square-foot facility in Houston, Texas, where they operate a new media production studio, community center, museum, and Spanish-speaking mosque. Also in 2016, LALMA echoed a call to civic action by leaders of the Alianza Islámica and began several campaigns to increase their political activism and provide social services to their communities. Although the social, political, and media impact of Latino Muslims as a so-called new minority in America is yet to be fully realized in this third wave, it is clear that the identity group will continue to play a significant role in national discourses even as they continue to struggle for their very existence.

. . . "*lā ilāha illallāh, muḥammadur-rasūlu-llāh. No hay más dios que Alá y Muhammad es su profeta. There is no god but God, and Muhammad is the messenger of God.*" Mariela looked at the group of women and men who had lined up to welcome and greet her as a fellow Muslim for the first time. She had been taught that this was a new beginning, a clean slate in which previous mistakes had been forgiven. Others had described their experience after taking *shahadah* as if an unbearable burden had been lifted and as now having a clear sense of purpose and direction. Some included the presence of angels in the retelling of their initiation rite. Like so many before her, tears of joy and of hope for a brighter future began to run down Mariela's face.

Among those who greeted Mariela after the *shahadah*, one person told her that he had been given a Spanish language translation of the Qur'an several years ago and that he would happily bring it to her as soon as he could. He was neither Latino nor did he understand Spanish; the Spanish Qur'an was for her. The conversation between the two was in English, so he must have been aware that Mariela did not necessarily need a Spanish language translation of the Qur'an when so many English ones were available. But it might be nice to have Mariela's Latina identity reaffirmed at this critical juncture in her religious life. As soon as the man with the Spanish Qur'an left, a member of the Latino Muslim community quickly intervened and informed Mariela that she would be given a beautiful four-volume copy of the Muhammad Asad Spanish language translation of the Qur'an. This translation, Mariela was told without much explanation, was better. Still wiping the tears from her eyes, Mariela smiled and warmly embraced her religious mentor. The *shahadah* had been performed, Mariela's new religious identity was celebrated in the mosque's upper room, and her initiation into Islam was completed. Mariela's life as a Latina Muslim and her interaction with Latino, Muslim, and Latino Muslim communities and institutions, however, was far from over.

CHAPTER ONE

THE FIRST WAVE

FROM ISLAM IN SPAIN TO THE ALIANZA IN NEW YORK

Occupied Palestine, Occupied Vieques. Is there some kind of connection here?
Puerto Ricans, Palestinians. Our flags even have a similar design . . .
This connection I'm talking about.
Can it possibly explain why a Puerto Rican can consciously embrace Islam,
consciously embrace Andalusia, turns towards Mecca for the Hajj . . .
We know what time it is.

—*Ibrahim Gonzales, co-founder of the Alianza Islámica*

In Union City, New Jersey, over one hundred Latino Muslims gathered to celebrate the annual Hispanic Muslim Day on October 7, 2012. The event was held at the North Hudson Islamic center's reception hall with tables adorned by small flags from various Latin American countries. It was a festive atmosphere where old friends greeted each other and new ones met for the first time. Formal presentations and speeches were given after dinner, including one by Ibrahim who was introduced as one of the first Latinos to embrace Islam back in the early 1970s. Ibrahim recounted his conversion, or as he would call it, his "reversion story." He talked about the struggle for civil rights that he had both witnessed and been a part of. Frustrated with all the different groups and organizations fighting for social justice and by what seemed to him to be a lack of progress, Ibrahim finally came across the teachings of Islam. As submission to one God, the message seemed straightforward and compelling and was embraced like a wellspring in the desert.

The more he learned about Islam, however, the more it seemed to Ibrahim that he was not converting to something entirely new. Having been raised as a Christian, there was so much that seemed familiar. There was a cosmos created by an all-knowing and all-powerful deity, a universe inhabited by angels, and a world with people who received messages from God through prophets. Among these prophets, *Isa* or Jesus held a special place in Islam. In both Christianity and in Islam, Jesus was born of the virgin *Mariam* or Mary who covered her hair as a sign of modesty. Both traditions maintain that *Isa* or Jesus brought a message from God and both traditions await his return at the end of times. But it was not just the structure of the universe, the scriptural narratives, and religious practices that seemed familiar, there were similar cultural elements as well. Family organization, art and architecture, and even certain words and phrases appeared to be connected to his Latino ethnicity somehow. The Arabic phrase *insha Allah*, uttered daily by Muslims means "God willing," and uncannily sounded similar to the popular Spanish phrase *ojalla*, which means "hopefully." What Ibrahim and many others would come to find is that these were no coincidental similarities, there was in fact a historical connection. "If you want to tell the history of Latino Muslims," Ibrahim's step-brother later explained, "you will need to start in Al-Andalus, before it was re-conquered and re-named as Spain."

This chapter draws a connection between Islamic Spain, memories of it, and the first Latino Muslim group in the United States, La Alianza Islámica, the Islamic Alliance. For nearly eight hundred years—up to the fifteenth century, Muslims in the Iberian Peninsula made significant contributions to the language, philosophy, and culture of Spain and the colonizers it sent to "Nueva España." Latin Americans and Latinos in the United States have inherited many of these contributions as well. Although there have been many recorded instances of individual Latinos embracing Islam since the 1920s, no recorded biological link exists between Muslims in Spain and Latino Muslims in the United States. Instead, it is the memory or history of Islamic Spain that has been integral to the development of a uniquely Latino way of being Muslim in the United States. Influenced by this memory as well as a revolutionary spirit of the civil rights era and the increasing diversity in

America's metropolitan environments, the Alianza emerged within and helped to crystalize a first wave of Latino Muslims in the United States.

AL-ANDALUS: ISLAMIC SPAIN

In 1491, Spanish monarchs seized Granada, the last Muslim strong-hold in the Iberian Peninsula. Previously, it had been a tributary province of the Roman Empire and the Kingdom of the Visigoths.[1] By the early eighth century, however, the first Muslim Empire, the Umayyad Caliphate, had expanded its western territories into Iberia. A mere century after the Prophet Muhamad had accomplished the revolutionary feat of uniting the familial tribes of Arabia under Islam, the Umayyad dynasty seized control and grew at an astounding rate. Within twenty years of Umayyad military campaigns and governance, the lands under Islamic rule included regions in Asia and Africa and eventually stretched from modern-day India in the east to modern-day Spain in the west.[2] Under the Umayyads, Arabic became the official imperial language, the Great Mosque of Damascus was built as well as the Dome of the Rock in Jerusalem where the Prophet is said to have ascended into heaven and received instructions regarding daily prayers.[3]

Despite its vast achievements, the legitimacy of the Umayyad family had been challenged from the start. Increased corruption, ineptitude, and discrimination fueled the flames of a revolutionary coalition of religious clergy, military leaders, and non-Arab converts who felt they were being treated as a lesser class of Muslims.[4] And in 750 C.E., the Umayyad family was all but extinguished in a bloody coup save for the solitary heir Abd al-Rahman. The young Abd al-Rahman, the sole survivor of the Umayyads, fled to the western edges of his family's faltering empire in the Iberian Peninsula. It was a long and perilous journey in which the young refugee barely managed to escape mercenaries seeking to end his life and the Umayyad lineage. For his incredible ability to endure the long and treacherous flight, Abd al-Rahman was given the honorable title of "the Falcon of the Umayyad" by his greatest enemies. And it was for this reason that the historian Thomas Ballantine Irving, who played a significant role in the development of Latino Muslim narratives, titled his book *Falcon of Spain.*[5]

By the time of the yearly Hispanic Muslim Day gatherings that began in the 2000s, Dr. Irving had helped develop a symbolic and moral link between Islamic Spain and Latino Muslim identity. Irving was born in Cambridge, Ontario, Canada, in 1914. He studied modern languages as an undergraduate and received a PhD in Near Eastern studies from Princeton University. He is perhaps most widely known for his modern English translation of the Qur'an, which featured a photograph of the Great Umayyad Mosque of Cordoba on its cover.[6] It is his historical work on Islam in Spain, however, that has been of much more significance to the development of a Latino Muslim identity. After many travels and teaching positions, Dr. Irving eventually set down roots in La Universidad de San Carlos in Guatemala. And it was while he was in Central America that Irving first published his book *Halcon de España, Falcon of Spain: A Study of Eighth Century Spain, with Special Emphasis upon the Life of the Umayyad Ruler Abdurrahman I (756–788).*[7] The monograph was first published in 1951 by Universidad de San Carlos de Guatemala, Facultad de Humanidades. This first edition was written in Spanish, totaled roughly 200 pages in length, and revealed Irving's flare for romance and dramatic storytelling. From Pakistan, English translations were subsequently published and distributed to English-speaking audiences by Lahore: Orientalia Company in 1954 and by Sh. M. Ashraf in 1962. Both the Spanish and English editions along with various other booklets written by Dr. Irving have been important to Latino Muslim communities whose members are sometimes bilingual but who also consist of some who are fluent in only one or the other language.[8] Although not a Latino himself, Dr. Irving became an advocate for a distinct Latino Muslim identity in the 1970s. In particular, he believed that the story of Abd al-Rahman, the Falcon of Spain, contained both symbolic and moral lessons for Latino Muslims.

Far from his homeland and the influence of his enemies, Abd al-Rahman, the young refugee immigrant sought to recreate the house of his family, the Umayyad Empire. He imported date trees, mosque and domestic architectural styles, arts, and learning. The trees eventually took root as did the religious culture. In his old age, having accomplished much, including many physical reminders and uprooted continuations of a previous civilization, Abd al-Rahman nevertheless lamented his loss. Far from the homeland he longed for and wished to remember, Abd al-Rahman wrote:

> *A palm tree stands in the middle of Rusafa,*
> *Born in the West, far from the land of palms.*
> *I said to it: How like me you are, far away and in exile,*
> *In long separation from family and friends.*
> *You have sprung from soil in which you are a stranger,*
> *And I, like you, am far from home.*[9]

In this poem, the palm tree becomes a metaphor for the author's own life. For Irving, the story of Abd al-Rahman is itself a kind of historical metaphor for understanding the story of Latino Muslims. Like Abd al-Rahman, many Latinos wrestle with a sense of loss and attempt to recover this loss in different ways. In the 1960s, Chicanos in the western regions of the United States and Nuyoricans in the East began telling new kinds of origin stories about themselves that celebrated Aztec, Mexican, Taíno, and Puerto Rican history and culture in new and innovative ways. These were in part a response to a sense of loss: a loss of history, culture, and identity resulting from devastating military and spiritual conquests by Spanish and American colonizers.[10] Abd al-Rahman was both conqueror and conquered. He carried with him the memory of an illustrious family history and the ever-present reminder of his violent separation from it and his homeland.

And so, Abd al-Rahman attempted to recreate what he had lost in Damascus now in the Iberian Peninsula, the westernmost frontier of what had been the Umayyad Empire. The result was not a duplication but a new kind of Islamic society in a new land that nevertheless celebrated the history and culture of the Umayyad. This land was variously dubbed the neo-Umayyad Caliphate, Al-Andalus, the Jewel of Islam for its social accomplishments and religious tolerance and later the Caliphate of Cordoba before finally settling on the title of Spain.

For almost 800 years, Muslims greatly influenced how the space was named, understood, and inhabited. Before the land became a launching ground for Columbus's expeditions and Cortez's conquests, it was Al-Andalus.[11] Latino Muslims remind us today that the religions, cultures, and societies that emerged through contact between Spain and the so-called New World, between the Spanish colonizers and the Aztecs, Mayas, Incas, Taínos, and others, cannot be fully understood without taking into account the contact that first occurred between Muslims and Christians in Al-Andalus.[12]

Following the reign of Abd al-Rahman's neo-Umayyad dynasty, many internal factions challenged the authority of the Andalusian Empire. Nevertheless, smaller Islamic states emerged and flourished economically and culturally for a time. "Arab Spain," writes Dr. Irving,

> was the epitome of refinement and courtesy. While the rest Europe lived in stables and slept on straw, the Andalusian had all the delicious luxuries known to Syria, Persia, and Byzantium: patios and fountains; balconies carved in wood and stone; arabesques traced on stucco and metal . . . marble baths with hot and cold running water; libraries and schools.[13]

Irving points out that while Europe was experiencing what is popularly referred to as a "dark age," Islamic societies were experiencing a period of economic, cultural, and scholastic prosperity. Al-Andalus was situated at the westernmost periphery of this Islamic prosperity, close enough for the rest of Europe to learn about and be envious of. Relatively open travel between the eastern Abbasid and western Andalusian territories facilitated the exchange and flourishing of commerce, practices, and ideas. It was Abd-Al Rahman who commissioned the construction of the Great Mosque of Cordoba that features horseshoe arches and other aspects from Roman, Visigoth, Byzantine, and Persian styles.[14] The great mosques, grand viziers, majestic cities, and elaborate gardens, distinctive musical forms, arts, and philosophy developed within Islamic Spain continue to be source of inspiration for many. It was in this place and time that the great philosophers Maimonides, Ibn Rushd or Averroës, and Ibn Arabi developed their work.[15] It was through a cultural intermingling cultivated in Al-Andalus that new marvelously contradictory forms of poetry developed within the various ethnic and religious groups of the region.[16] It was all of this and more that signaled a sense of sovereignty and success to both the Abbasids and the Europeans and also served as a nostalgic reminder of the glory of the Umayyad Empire.

Whether understood as a new and splendid flourishing or as a nostalgic memory of a greater but lost empire, many admirers of the Andalusian accomplishments attribute its prosperity in part to a *convivencia*, a state of coexistence with ethnic and religious difference. Proponents of this theory, including María Rosa Menocal, maintain that institutionalized forms of ethnic pluralism, religious tolerance, and collaboration between Muslims, Christians, and Jews made possible the *convivencia* and prosperity.[17] These practices were ideally rooted in Qur'anic passages: "[But] they are not all alike: among the followers of earlier revelation [e.g., Jews and Christians] there are upright people, who recite God's messages throughout the night, and prostrate themselves [before Him]" (Qur'an 3:113—English translation by M. Asad). Based on several Qur'anic references to the people of the book, *ahl al-kitāb*, Islamic law extended religious tolerance rights and protection from foreign invasion to the *dhimmi*, including Christians and Jews. Although non-Muslim *dhimmi* were not treated as complete equals, marital, linguistic, and cultural intermingling made possible many remarkable collaborations. Like mosques decorated with Arabesque designs in order to avoid the Islamic prohibition against images, many churches and synagogues in Al-Andalus also flaunted Arabic in their aesthetic designs, sometimes even including direct quotes from the Qur'an.[18] It was not just Islamic tolerance for Jews and Christians, but regular collaboration, exchange, and intermingling that made possible the Andalusian Golden Age.

Despite its many accomplishments, the people of Al-Andalus increasingly fragmented into ever smaller regions and city-states. The golden age of prosperity and tolerance eventually came to a complete end. By the time Isabella I of Castile formed a union with Ferdinand

II of Aragon, Muslims in Iberia no longer maintained a united military force. One by one, the great cities of Cordoba in 1236, Valencia in 1238, and Seville in 1248 fell to Catholic Spain. La Reconquista, the military campaigns envisioned as a "re-conquest" of Muslim-held territories by the Catholic-Spanish crown, ended in 1492 when, after a ten-year war, the last Muslim-held territory of Granada fell.[19]

Unlike the Great Mosque of Cordoba whose architectural design was inspired by Umayyad and Persian aesthetics, the Alhambra, "The Red Fort," in Granada was designed and built with military fortification in mind.[20] However, before its daunting walls could be put to the test by Spanish military forces, the 1491 Treaty of Granada was signed outlining the terms of the last Spanish Muslim state's surrender. The document included provisions meant to guarantee religious tolerance rights similar to those that had been given to the *dhimmi* under Muslim rule. Many of these rights were however revoked shortly after by the Spanish crown. The same year that Granada fell and that Columbus exposed a route to the Americas, Jews were given the choice to convert to Christianity, be expelled from Spain, or be killed. The same choice was then extended to Muslims in 1501 prompting a massive number of conversions, migration, and killing of Muslims.[21]

Jews and Muslims who chose to convert, the *conversos*, were allowed to stay in Spain and retain their land and possessions. But when the Spanish Inquisition began its institutionalized terrorism, the wealth of *conversos* accused of being "false converts" was systematically appropriated by the Spanish crown. Converts to Christianity who desperately wanted to hold on to some aspect of their Muslim past but who also feared the penalties of the Inquisition began hiding the last vestiges of their old culture and religion. In an atmosphere of fear and mistrust, *Aljamiado* documents were produced using an Arabic script to record Castilliano words.

In 2001, Mariam Saada completed her PhD dissertation at UCLA, which analyzed Aljamiado manuscripts that survive today in the Biblioteca Nacional de Madrid, Spain.[22] During and after her research, Dr. Saada has, like Dr. Irving in the 1970s, worked with Latino Muslims to help them learn more about the link between Islamic Spain and Latino culture. "It's very easy," she once encouraged a small group of Latino Muslims listening to her lecture, "once you know the sounds of the Arabic letters, you can translate the Aljamiado writings." For Dr. Saada, translating the Aljamiado manuscripts produced by Muslims under duress after the Reconquista was not merely about past events. Instead, she believed that these documents held both memories of a forgotten and connected past and also moral lessons for understanding bigotry, persecution, and loss in the United States today.

The history of Islamic Spain is forgotten, Dr. Saada teaches, because it is systematically covered up by European institutions including Spanish academics that persistently hold negative attitudes toward their Islamic heritage. The terms "Moorish," "Mudéjar," and "Morisco" used today to categorize and describe art and literature from the al-Andalusian periods are themselves derogatory labels. The historical and moral lessons contained in the Aljamiado writings are ones that Dr. Saada believes present-day Latino Muslims could greatly benefit from as they seek to make connections to their Islamic heritage.

Like Dr. Saada, Dr. Irving personally worked with Latino Muslims to help solidify the history of Islamic Spain as integral to the emerging story of Latino Muslims. *Falcon of Spain* and various other pamphlets written by Dr. Irving were produced for a popular audience and were especially accessible to early Latino Muslim communities. The story of Abd al-Rahman I, an immigrant in a strange land seeking to regain his lost dignity, was a compelling story to the Latino Muslims Dr. Irving encountered. In addition to the compelling moral lessons, the history of Al-Andalus, of Muslim Spain, reinforced the narrative that Latinos were not converting to something new. Latino Muslims understood themselves instead as returning to something culturally familiar, since, after all, Latino identity could be shown to be rooted in an Islamic past.

ISLAM IN THE AMERICAS

Despite the many cultural contributions that Islamic Spain bestowed onto Latino identity, there exists a gap in the historical link between the two groups. Some scholars have argued that Muslims had been sailing to the Americas from present-day Spain long before 1492 and had also been part of Christopher Columbus's crew. There is also evidence of some Muslim migration from Spain to the Caribbean islands and the United States as a direct result of the Reconquista when Jews and Muslims were given the choice to convert to Christianity, leave Spain, or be executed.[23] We know that many Spanish words, arts, and sciences rooted in Andalusian culture also traveled to and made an indelible mark throughout Latin America during this and also subsequent waves of immigration into the region.[24] Although there is not enough evidence to produce concrete estimates or a consensus among scholars, it is estimated that between 40,000 to 1 million of the people forcibly brought as slaves to the United States from West Africa through the transatlantic slave trade were Muslim.[25] Although Muslims had indeed migrated to the Americas during the colonial era, some by choice and most by force, the Islam that made it across the Atlantic was fated to a brief existence in the region.

In addition to military and economic conquests, European colonizers fiercely attempted to eradicate the non-Christian religions they encountered. This led to many misunderstandings, mistrust, and violence among various religious groups and actors. "We went there [the New World or Americas] to serve God, and also to get rich," wrote Bernal Díaz del Castillo in his *Historia verdadera de la conquista de la Nueva España* (The true history of the conquest of New Spain).[26] Díaz del Castillo was a conquistador who participated in Hernan Cortez's 1519–1521 military conquest of the Aztecs. His firsthand account of the people, objects, and practices he encountered reflects the military, economic, and spiritual goals of the Spanish conquistadores. In the following, Díaz del Castillo describes Cortez's encounter with the religious practices of Moctezuma, the last ruler of the Aztec Empire:

"I do not understand how such a great Prince and wise man as you are has not come to the conclusion, in your mind, that these idols of yours are not gods, but evil things that are called devils, and so that you may know it and all your priests may see it clearly, do me the favor to approve of my placing a cross here on the top of this tower." . . . Montezuma replied half angrily, (and the two priests who were with him showed great annoyance,) and said: "Señor Malinche, if I had known that you would have said such defamatory things I would not have shown you my gods, we consider them to be very good, for they give us health and rains and good seed times and seasons and as many victories as we desire, and we are obliged to worship them and make sacrifices, and I pray you not to say another word to their dishonor."

Díaz del Castillo's account provides a glimpse into the colonialists misunderstanding or negative bias against the non-Christian religions they encountered.

Díaz del Castillo's account was written as a response to Friar Bartolomé de Las Casas's, which was severely critical of how cruel the conquest and colonization of the New World had been. "Within these twelve years," wrote Bartolomé de Las Casas in his *Brevísima relación de la destrucción de las Indias* (A short account of the destruction of the Indies), "the Spaniards have destroyed in the said continent, by spears, fire and sword . . . over four million people in these their victories or conquests (for under that word they mask their cruel actions) . . . contrary to and condemned by Divine as well as Human Laws."[27] Although Bartolomé de Las Casas did not condone the manner in which the people of the New World had been treated, he nevertheless advocated for more "humane" ways of succeeding in what proved to be the impossible task of a complete and total spiritual conquest.

As an academic attempt to critique or respond to the devastating effects that colonialism has had on the production of knowledge, postcolonial and subaltern studies have added unique inflections to the stories told about the New World. Rather than as a story of how Catholicism triumphed over the religions practiced throughout the Aztec Empire, veneration of La Virgin de Guadalupe may be understood as a story of how New World religiosity survived or even triumphed over European ways of being religious. After all, it was at the hill of Tepeyac—where the honored Mother goddess of Aztec religions was venerated—that La Virgin appeared, not to Spanish clergy, but to the indigenous neophyte Juan Diego.[28]

In *Latina/o y Musulmán: The Construction of Latina/o Identity among Latina/o Muslims in the United States*, Hjamil A. Martinez-Vazquez has himself underscored the importance of the postcolonial lens for understanding contemporary Latino Muslim engagement with the history of Islamic Spain. Martinez-Vazquez points out that Latino Muslims celebrate the survival of Islam in their Latino culture rather than simply accepting the attempted erasure of their Islamic histories by European scholars.[29] Despite the important work being produced by postcolonial and subaltern studies and by Latino Muslims who celebrate the survival of Islam in their cultural identity, there remains a gap in the link between Muslims in Spain and Latino Muslims in the United States.

Although the spiritual conquest, the attempt to forcibly and completely replace one religion with another, was never as ubiquitous as the military and economic conquests, the impact of colonial violence to religion in the Americas cannot be underestimated. Muslims have been an integral part of the United States since its inception. Muslims who were forcibly brought to the Americas and enslaved against their will were not able to freely practice their religion or form Islamic communities; nor were they able to pass on a recognizably Islamic religion to subsequent generations.[30] Instead, under American slavery Islam was discouraged from being practiced. Most Muslims in the United States today do not trace their ancestry directly to the Muslims of West Africa that arrived during the colonial era; and neither do Latino Muslims trace their ancestry directly to the Muslims of Islamic Spain. Instead, Muslims in the United States trace their lineage to much more contemporary waves of community development, conversion, and immigration processes that occurred during the twentieth-century.[31] Distinctly American forms of Islam, referred to by some as proto-Islamic movements, developed in the early twentieth century, including the Moorish Science Temple of America and the Lost Found Nation of Islam. A limited number of Muslims also immigrated to the United States prior to the 1960s as laborers and refugees. The Immigration and Nationality Act of 1965 then lifted the country of origin quotas and made possible much larger waves of immigration from diverse national, ethnic, and religious backgrounds.[32] Interactions between immigrant and specifically American forms of Islam led to new developments in the American religious landscape that Latinos would encounter during the twentieth century.

In his article "Early U.S. Latina/o—African-American Muslim Connections: Paths to Conversion," Patrick Bowen traces the possibility of Latino members joining various US Muslim communities prior to the 1970s. The groups Bowen cites as possibilities include the Moorish Science Temple of America, the Ahmadiyya, the Nation of Islam, and the Five Percenters. The Moorish Science Temple of America was founded in 1913 by Noble Drew Ali. By 1930 there were Moorish Science communities in Newark, Chicago, Pittsburg, and Detroit. Its members identified themselves as racially Asiatic (though most others in the United States would identify them as racially black), as nationally Moroccan and religiously Muslim. Their religion had little resemblance to other forms of Islam however. Instead of reading the Qur'an, for example, the group drew from texts such as the *Aquarian Gospel of Jesus*, Marcus Garvey's pan-African movement, and Noble Drew Ali's own version of the *Holy Koran* (also known as the Circle Seven Koran) in order to "develop their doctrines concerning the divinity of individual members, including Ali's, the characterization of heaven and hell as states of mind, the establishment of Moorish-American businesses and communities, and a revisionist history that framed its members as neither 'Blacks' nor 'Negroes,' but as 'Moors.'"[33]

In the *Moorish Guide*, a bi-monthly periodical, Bowen identifies a "Juanita Richardson-Bey, who is listed as the managing editor and was also the secretary-treasurer of the Young People's Moorish League."[34] Bowen admits that her seemingly Latina name, "Juanita," the possibly Spanish title of her published poem "Dio de mio," and Drew Ali's eulogy in English, Arabic, and Spanish offer only circumstantial evidence of Latino converts to Moorish Science. Nonetheless, he concludes that given the Moorish Science's "openness to all races, and the continuing rise of Latino immigration, and taking into account numerous online anecdotes, it is highly probable that Latinos have been members since the 1920's."[35]

A few known Latinos also embraced Islam through the Ahmadiyya during the 1920s. The Ahmadiyya first emerged in India during the late nineteenth century as followers of Ghulam Ahmad. A faction of this community proclaimed that their leader had been a *Mujaddid* (divine reformer), a prophet, and the returned Messiah awaited by Christians and *Mahdi* awaited by Muslims at the end of times. Ahmadis followed a form of Islam that more closely resembled that of Sunni Islam than did that of the Moorish Science. They practice the five pillars of Islam and recite from the same Qur'an as Sunni and Shi'a Muslims. In 1913, Ahmadi *dawah* (missionary) workers began arriving in North America. These *dawah* workers concluded that African Americans had not only been largely ignored by other Muslim proselytizers, but that they were in many ways more receptive to Islam than white Americans.

Through its vehement condemnation of racism in the United States, Ahmadis became an important ideological precursor to the civil rights movement. In an early twentieth-century Ahmadi *Moslem Sunrise* periodical, Muhammad Sadiq presented Islam as a moral corrective to racial inequality:

> There are people fairer than North Europeans living friendly and amiably with those of the darkest skin in India, Arabia, and other Asiatic and African countries. . . . In Islam no church has ever had seats reserved for anybody and if a Negro enters first and takes the front seat even the Sultan if he happens to come after him never thinks of removing him from the seat.[36]

To some African Americans and Latinos living in early twentieth-century Jim Crow America, who encountered the doctrine of Christian love for all humanity alongside hypocritical, deep, and unjust racial divides, the Ahmadiyya message of tolerance, equality, and dignity was an attractive alternative that many chose to embrace. In 1920, Mufti Muhammad Sadiq was detained by customs officials in Philadelphia when entering the United States for the first time. Sadiq had been accused of breaking polygamy laws simply because the officials processing his case had incorrectly assumed that all Muslim men had multiple wives. While in the detention hall, Sadiq began teaching fellow detainees about Islam and according to a *Moslem Sunrise* publication, "a Spaniard, a Portuguese, two men from the Azores, and one Honduran" converted to Islam.[37]

In addition to the Ahmadiyya, the Nation of Islam (NOI) brought yet more attention to the role of Muslims in the struggle for civil rights in America. The NOI was led by Elijah Muhammad who was also considered a prophet by his followers. Elijah Muhammad and the NOI taught that all humans had originated from the black race and tribe of *Shabazz*. They taught that a cunning and devious scientist by the name of *Yakub* had created the white race who eventually took control over the black race in a historical period roughly coinciding with the colonial era. NOI members characterized white people as devils and black people as divine. Like the Moorish Science Temple, the NOI taught that heaven and hell were states of mind, rather than "pie in the sky" fairytale lands, and accordingly taught that social improvement through segregation from white America was of paramount importance for achieving salvation.[38]

Bowen identifies Tynetta Deanar Muhammad (mother of several of Elijah Muhammad's children) as a Latina. Bowen points out that she accompanied Elijah Muhammad on all his trips to Mexico and "can likely speak Spanish."[39] In 1998, she established Temple #15 in New York as the first NOI temple for Spanish speakers. Her son, Minister Ishmael R. Muhammad, "lived and studied Islam in Cuernavaca for seventeen years before being requested by Louis Farrakhan to assist the group at the Chicago headquarters."[40] Beyond the leadership of Tynetta and Ishmael R. Muhammad, less visible Latino NOI members continue to join the NOI, which currently maintains a Spanish language website at LaNacionDelIslam.org.

Although the NOI had a significant presence in several large cities across the United States, it was the media presence of Malcolm X that introduced the majority of Americans to the group. While in prison, Malcolm Little began corresponding with Elijah Muhammad, converted to the NOI, and changed his name to Malcolm X. The X signaled an unknown variable, a critique of American slavery, white supremacy, the erasure of African family names and histories, and its pervasive and persistent affects. Drawing from Harlem life and music and from his self-education and debate practice while incarcerated, Malcolm X emerged from Norfolk Prison Colony, Massachusetts, in 1949 with a fiery message from Elijah Muhammad and a rhetorical voice of his own.[41] He had a gift for addressing the masses in a compelling manner, for understanding the political complexities of his time, and for using mass media to his advantage. Malcolm X quickly ascended the NOI ranks to become Elijah Muhammad's prime minister. He successfully founded several temples and drew in tens of thousands of new members before being alienated from the NOI, going on Hajj, embracing a Sunni form of Islam, and being brutally assassinated in 1965.[42]

Although Latino members of the NOI had and continue to have a presence in the American religious landscape, albeit a muted one, early and still dominant Latino Muslim communities gravitated toward a more racially inclusive Sunni form of Islam espoused by Malcolm X (who later changed his name to el-Hajj Malik el-Shabazz) and Elijah Muhammad's son and successor Warith Deen Muhammad. The Sunni strands of Islam among black communities in the United States have been much more significant to the development of Latino Muslim groups. This is partly manifested in both Latino members of The Mosque of Islamic Brotherhood (an outgrowth of the Muslim Mosque Inc., Malcolm X's post-NOI mosque) and in Latino Muslim references to Malcolm X as an important influence on their understanding and practice of Islam as social reform. Under the leadership of Shaykh Tawfiq's, who identifies as both Native American and African American, the Mosque of Islamic Brotherhood aligned with Sunni teachings presently boasts a roughly 20 percent Latino Muslim membership.[43] In the film and trailer to *New Muslim Cool*, which follows the life and trials of Hamza Perez, a Puerto Rican Muslim hip-hop artist, Perez is depicted walking down Malcolm X Boulevard in New York and into the Mosque of Islamic Brotherhood. In other scenes, Perez wears T-shirts with iconic prints of Malcolm X and describes his social work within "the projects" as being in the spirit of Malcolm X. "We have to deliver in the strongest form possible our message," Hamza narrates, "it is the way of Malcolm X." For many Latino Muslims, including ex-NOI member and a pioneer in Latino Muslim communities—Benjamin Perez, Malcolm X continues to inspire a vision for a nationally united Latino Muslim front against social injustice in America.[44]

Latinos also joined the Five Percenters, the Dar ul-Islam, and the Islamic Party of North America. The Five Percenters, also known as the Nation of Gods and Earths, broke away from the NOI in the early 1960s. They taught that black people are the "Mothers and Fathers of Civilization" and "that the Blackman is God and his proper name is Allah (Arm Leg Leg Arm Head)." They also taught the Science of Supreme Mathematics, that 85 percent of humanity is kept ignorant, 10 percent are wicked and use knowledge to exploit the 85 percent, and that only 5 percent (hence Five Percenters) have self-knowledge and use it to creatively unleash the "under-utilized powers of the black man."[45] While incarcerated in 1965, founder Clarence 13X (also known as Clarence Edward Smith) gained new disciples. Among these, Bowen tells us, was Armando X, a Puerto Rican who had previously been a member of Harlem's NOI Temple No. 7. As part of the Five Percenter practice, Armando X underwent a series of name changes. For some time the initials of his Puerto Rican identity, P.R., became code for Power Rules. Later, P.R.'s name was changed to god Sha Sha for being the first to bring the Five Percenter teachings to Puerto Rico. Other notable individuals possibly connected to Five Percenter and Latino identities include rappers Big Daddy Kane, AZ/Anthony Cruz, and the graffiti artist Lee Quinones featured in the *Illmatic* album-*Wild Style* documentary.[46]

Despite their advancements in the American religious landscape, the Five Percenters, the NOI, the Ahmadiyya, and the Moorish Science Temple in America were in different ways understood as engaging in *bid'ah* or unacceptable innovations by most Sunni Muslims. The latter were exponentially growing in number and influence after the immigration act of 1965. The State Street Mosque in New York for example actively sought to direct black Muslims in the United States away from groups perceived to be deviations from orthodox Islam. The mosque was established in the late 1920s by Sheikh Al-Haj Daoud

Ahmed Faisal from the Caribbean island of Grenada. Interpreting the Qur'an as promoting a struggle toward justice through non-militant means, Ahmed Faisal's community engaged in various social programs such as education, feeding the hungry, and prison visits. However, by the early 1960s, a schism occurred over accusations that Ahmed Faisal was not "doing enough to help the material conditions of African Americans."[47] Influenced by the Tabligh Jamaat, a group of State Street Mosque members eventually broke away to form the Dar ul-Islam organization in the United States. In her book *Islam in America*, Jane I. Smith reports that the Alianza Islámica, considered to be one of the first Latino Muslim organizations in the United States, emerged as an "outgrowth" of the Dar ul-Islam.[48] A fuller description would characterize the Alianza Islámica as also being influenced by the Islamic Party of North America (IPNA), which like Dar ul-Islam, had also broken away from the State Street Mosque.

THE ALIANZA ISLÁMICA IN NEW YORK

In 1898, the United States annexed the island of Puerto Rico. Previously, it had been a colony of Spain. Christopher Columbus himself claimed it for the crown in 1493. Prior to colonization, the land had been called *Boriquén* by the indigenous Taíno population. As a US territory in the twentieth century, the land was used almost exclusively to supply American consumption.[49] During the Great Depression, however, purchase of Puerto Rican crops dropped dramatically. Many of the island's inhabitants sought to relieve their poverty by relocating to the US mainland where the Second World War had created a need for workers. This was possible in part because of a 1904 Supreme Court ruling concluding that Puerto Ricans were not aliens and the 1917 congressional Jones Act declaring that all Puerto Ricans are citizens of the United States.[50]

Although the people of Puerto Rico now had legal mobility throughout the United States, slow and costly transportation continued to limit their ability to move to the mainland. Then in 1936, in a development that underscores the relation between technology and social movements, the Boeing Aircraft Company began producing the 314 Clipper, considered to be the apex of flying boat design.[51] The new aircraft technology revolutionized concepts of space. Distances that once took twelve days by boat could now be regularly bridged in about half a day and at a much more affordable rate. In 1946, Pan American Airlines became the first to commercially offer fares between Puerto Rico and New York along with hope for a better future.[52] The annexation of Puerto Rico by the United States, the havoc wreaked by the Great Depression on the island's economy, the legalization of immigration to the mainland, the need for domestic laborers during the Second World War and technological developments in air travel converged to make possible a massive movement of people now termed *la gran migración*, "the great migration."[53]

By 1960, there were over 600,000 Puerto Ricans living in New York. Because neither the economic nor the political situation in Puerto Rico showed signs of improvement, much of the migrant population stayed and raised their children on the mainland. Here, a rift emerged between island-born and New York–born Puerto Ricans. Although used broadly to signal pride in their precolonial Taíno ethnicity, the term "Boricua" was now being used on the mainland to distinguish between those raised on the island and those raised in New York. The latter were increasingly called "Nuyoricans" as a way to signal what was perceived to be a negative identity. Nuyoricans were stereotyped as rejecting Boricua language and culture for ones highly influenced by those of New York. Not only was their Spanish different, as Puerto Ricans made spaces for themselves in the "barrios" of the South Bronx, Spanish Harlem, Manhattan's Lower East Side, and in Brooklyn, many reacted negatively to drug, crime, gang violence, and race problems in the metropolis. Although initially used to mark a negative difference, Nuyorican identity was later embraced and reframed as a positive, cosmopolitan, and creative outcome of intercultural contact.[54] Various artists, musicians, poets, writers, and activists began the Nuyorican cultural movement and celebrated their mixed language and cultural location between the worlds of the Boricua and of New York.

Piri Thomas was a pioneer of this movement. He was born to Puerto Rican-Cuban parents, was raised in New York, and called its *barrios* home. In his highly influential autobiography, *Down These Mean Streets,* Thomas narrates his experiences living between the two worlds that were often at odds with one another. Here, Thomas poetically struggles with issues regarding identity, freewill, and responsibility. He tries to make sense of what it means to be "born in a foreign land and to be a foreigner to his homeland," to be a black Nuyorican in the United States and identified as "a Negro without really trying," to experience poverty, drug and gang violence, and finally, Thomas tries to make sense of what it is like to wake up "in a prison hospital while not remembering why."[55]

While incarcerated, Thomas encountered a Muslim chaplain who taught him about Islam. "We are a united people, and only Allah, through his beloved prophet Elijah Muhammad, could have brought this about. . . . We have learned that our heritage is a great one. We are of a mighty race of people," the chaplain told Thomas. In recounting his acceptance of the chaplain's teachings, Thomas writes:

I was invited to join the brothers as a follower of the true religion of Islam. I accepted . . . I learned to pray in Arabic. I learned respect for the Holy Quran . . . I learned many things, because it involved me. I became curious about everything human. Though I didn't remain a Muslim after my eventual release from the big jail, I never forgot one thing that Muhammad said, for I believed it too: "No matter what a man's color or race he has a need of dignity and he'll go anywhere, become anything, or do anything to get it—anything.[56]

Piri Thomas's encounter with Islam took place within a Latino context in New York, one in which Puerto Ricans increasingly came into contact with Muslims. In Thomas's narrative, the chaplain's reference to the prophet Elijah Muhammad reveals that he was a member of or at the very least a sympathizer with the Nation of Islam (NOI) and its belief that social improvement was central to achieving salvation. For Thomas and other Puerto Ricans in New York whose dignity was consistently trampled on by both people from the mainland and from the island, Islam provided a much-needed sense of purpose and dignity in the here and now of their place and time.

There are several other instances of individual Latinos like Piri Thomas embracing various forms of Islam including the NOI, the Five Percenters, the Moorish Science Temple of America, the Ahmadiyya, and various other forms of Sunni and Shi'a Islam from the 1920s to the 1970s. But it was not until the 1980s in New York that enough Latino Muslims emerged to start forming communities, coalitions, and organizations. One of the earliest Latino Muslim groups to emerge was the Alianza Islámica. And like Thomas, this early Latino Muslim community was situated between the two worlds of the New York and Puerto Rican experience.

The founders of the Alianza, Yahya Figueroa, Rahim Ocasio, and Ibrahim González, had been school friends. They had grown up in a revolutionary center of political activism and the struggle for civil rights. Figueroa, Ocasio, and González were young, but socially conscious. At a 2016 event in Houston, Texas, Yahya told me about how he grew up in New York's *barrios*, how "gangs" like the Five Percenters were everywhere, ran the corners and educated the people in various "street philosophies." "I was a part of it since I was a kid, you had no choice, know what I mean." As a young teenager, Yahya joined the Young Lords just as the Puerto Rican street gang was expanding and transforming itself into a civil, human rights and Puerto Rican independence movement under the leadership of Jose Cha Cha Jimenez. It was in the 1970s when Figueroa, Ocasio, and González together searched for different ways to join the fight against civil and human rights violations. "We sought other outlets," recounted Ocasio, "and came upon Islam. We became serious young men seeking to elevate ourselves within our society. We got this from Islam."[57] They entered the 125th Street mosque in Harlem and took shahada, proclaiming "there is no god but God." "Islam," added González, "introduced spiritual practices that were different from the Catholic upbringing of many Latinos, such as five daily prayers, fasting and a more direct connection with God. . . . Prayer was the first thing that brought me closer to being a Muslim. It became a source of strength and peace."[58] For Figueroa, Ocasio, and González, Islam provided a means to engage in both an inner spiritual struggle and an outer activist one.

Although often misrepresented as "holy war," *jihad* is referred to in the Qur'an as the struggle to be a good Muslim, to follow the scriptural laws, and to draw nearer to God. A second and lesser form of *jihad* is referred to in the Qur'an as an external struggle to bring about just social conditions.[59] Only when the Prophet of Arabia and his followers were persecuted and tortured in Mecca and their very existence threatened in Medina was it deemed appropriate to engage in military battle: "and drive them away from wherever they drove you away—for oppression is even worse than killing" (Qur'an 2:191, English translation by M. Asad). Many Muslims throughout the world also engage in external struggle through political activism and social service. In fact, the Qur'an is believed to have been revealed as a reminder or corrective to social injustices that had resulted from moral ignorance. The quest or struggle to bring about a just society through equity and charity is a core and reoccurring theme of the Qur'an: "Hence, O my people, [always] give full measure and weight, with equity, and do not deprive people of what is rightfully theirs, and do not act wickedly on earth by spreading corruption" (Qur'an 11:85, English translation by M. Asad).

"We didn't want to give up the struggle," said Ocasio in regard to their social activism, "so we looked to different places. Islam represented a place for us to be part of a larger community. When we realized that within Islam there was every spectrum of people, regardless of class, regardless of race, we were attracted to that universal principle of human interaction and communion with the divine."[60] Like others who felt trapped and outcast in the margins between two worlds, Figueroa, Ocasio, and González searched for guidance and a community to belong to. Through Islamic spirituality and its promotion of universal inclusion and its severe critique of American racism, they found a way to cultivate their inner sense of purpose and to struggle for their outer social dignity. Islam was for them a *jihad*, that is, it was an internal moral struggle and an external social activism.

Despite their enthusiastic embrace of Islam, Figueroa, Ocasio, and González encountered unforeseen challenges. The three became increasingly aware of anti-Latino sentiments within the Muslim communities they wanted to become a part of. Spanish was both important to their sense of identity and pride but was also a source of problems among many Muslims who were not Latinos. "It seemed Latinos believed it was essential to obliterate all vestiges of their ancestral heritage," writes Khalid Fattah Griggs of the early Puerto Rican Muslims, "Dressed in turbans and robes, they would even refrain from speaking Spanish in the masjid [mosque]."[61] In addition to the alienation of their Spanish language, the extent of attire-based alienation led many Latinos to adopt foreign styles of dress as markers of their Islamic identity. Rahim Ocasio and other Latinos who joined the IPNA "even wore Pakistani style dress including a long green shirt, black pants, and black kufis or skullcaps," writes Yossuf J. Carter.[62] The young Muslim Nuyoricans now faced a new form of possible assimilation and loss of Latino language and culture. This time, they worried their Spanish would be displaced by Arabic and their culture by one from a Muslim majority society.

While Ocasio was a member of the IPNA, the organization's leadership decided to dissolve its individual chapters and called for all members to move to Washington, DC. The move was likened to the *Hijra* or migration performed by the Prophet and his followers who fled from persecution in Mecca in order to establish a Muslim community in Medina.[63] Along with other members of the IPNA, Ocasio, his wife Fiaza, and their six children joined the *Hijra* to DC. There, Ocasio found what he described as a fertile ground for teaching Islam to Latinos. Despite the large population of Spanish speakers in DC, his non-Latino brethren discouraged him from propagating Islam in Spanish. "Mostly," remembers Ocasio, "we sort of just tried to blend in with everyone else."[64]

Ocasio and his family left the IPNA and made their way back to New York. After returning, Ocasio and his old friends visited a mosque in Newark where a group known as the Bani Sakr met.[65] This community was composed of mostly Puerto Rican members, emerged in the mid 1970's and held Hajj Hisham Jaber, who led Malcolm X's funeral prayer, as their spiritual guide.[66] Inspired by this community, Figueroa, Ocasio, González, and others began a group of their own. In 1987, they founded La Alianza Islámica, the Islamic Alliance.[67] "It drew our hearts together," González said of the Alianza.[68] Not only could they now speak Spanish freely, together they learned how to be Muslims as Latinos. They shared a similar ethnic and religious identity, they shared a similar struggle for peace and justice and they shared a similar cosmopolitan space in the United States.

After about eleven years of impromptu meetings at various locations, the Alianza was able to lease a meeting space of their own on Lexington Avenue and 107th Street. It was the Spanish Harlem of New York, a Latino enclave where most people spoke Spanish. By the 1960s, the area was also densely populated, poverty-stricken, and plagued by drug abuse, gang violence, and race riots. This was the home of the famed Young Lords who began as a street gang then became involved in both political activism and social service programs. Like the Young Lords in the Spanish Harlem and other civil rights groups across large US cities, the Alianza took a grassroots approach to the poor social conditions they inhabited. Members trained in martial arts to deter gang violence and promote neighborhood security. They also brokered truces between gangs like the notorious Puerto Rican street gang the Latin Kings. The group organized drug, prostitution, and AIDS prevention programs, provided safe spaces and services for victims of domestic violence and helped neighborhood residents study for General Education Degrees.[69]

The Alianza was unique during the civil rights era, however, in the way they linked their social service programs to their propagation of Islam with a distinctively Latino inflection. *Dawah*, the propagation of Islam, is a religious mandate for Muslims. The Qur'an instructs Muslims to invite "[all mankind] unto thy Sustainer's path with wisdom and goodly exhortation" (Qur'an 16:125, English translation by M. Asad). People who received help from the Alianza were also invited to learn about Islamic beliefs, practices, and history. The history lessons were therefore a form of *dawah* that celebrated the link between Islamic Spain and Latino culture. The goal was to help Latinos understand

Islam as familiar and positive rather than as something strange and foreign.

The historian of Islamic Spain introduced earlier in this chapter, T. B. Irving, became an important partner in the Alianza's unique *dawah* efforts. It is likely that a direct connection was developed between the two through an intermediary. Carl Askia El-Amin founded an organization by the name of the Bism Rabbik Foundation. Askia El-Amin was involved in various projects including collecting and disseminating information on Islam to a Latino audience. As part of a list of suggested readings, Askia El-Amin posted several titles written by Dr. Irving on the Bism Rabbik Foundation's website. On a separate blog post, Askia El-Amin published a farewell note after Dr. Irving passed away on September 25, 2002:

> As a personal friend of Dr. Irving, I feel a great loss and sadness, and will miss him. We have worked together over the years to establish Islam in the Spanish-speaking community. He has written other books not mentioned above, primarily text books, which he has placed in our possession for translation into Spanish. Over time, inshallah, we will translate and publish those books. . . . Carl Askia El-Amin [Bism Rabbik], Executive Director.[70]

In addition to the connection between Dr. Irving and the Foundation, Askia El-Amin's organizational website also alluded to a deep relationship between himself and members of the Alianza. Several essays including "Malcolm X = Malik Shabazz: Why Did He Change?" and "Islam: The Religion of the Future" were written by Ocasio and other Alianza members and were published on Askia El-Amin's website.[71] It is possible and likely that Askia El-Amin helped connect the Alianza to Irving and his work.

With the help of partners like Askia El-Amin and Dr. Irving, the Alianza and its religiously infused social services and unique identity narratives flourished in Spanish Harlem. It was therefore particularly disheartening when they were forced to relocate in 1997. Their landlord used the group to help mediate problems with other tenants, then raised the rent while refusing to make vital repairs to the property. The Alianza's leadership had not expected such treatment from their landlord who was a fellow Muslim especially since the group was using the space to pray and to propagate Islam. The encounter was taken by Alianza members as further evidence of anti-Latino discrimination by Muslims who were not of Latino descent. Encounters like these solidified the Alianza's resolve to have a group and space of its own, a physical place where Latino Muslims could feel welcomed and dignified.

"There's a whole story about how the name came about," Ocasio told me in 2016, "the name Alianza was itself a form of resistance." The group had originally taken the name La Mezquita del Barrio, the Barrio's mosque, where they produced Spanish language *dawah* content. González tried to get ISNA (Islamic Society of North America) to publish their content. "We took it to them and said here, you don't have to do anything [any work], just publish it. They turned us down flat!" With no institutional support from broader Muslim organizations in the United States, the young Latino Muslim group began publishing their own two-sided magazine using printing plates, one side in English the other in Spanish. The magazine was called Alianza, and when the group incorporated in 1987 they did so under the name *Alianza Islámica*, the Islamic Alliance. From its inception, the Alianza dealt with critiques from Latinos who argued they were abandoning their culture and from Muslims who critically argued that they were inauthentic Muslims, were fostering ethnic schisms, or both. The name Alianza was a form of resistance against these critiques and against the pressure to assimilate into something that they had little say or control over. The group banded together to develop a Latino way of doing Islam, first in the Spanish Harlem, and when that was no longer tenable, in the Bronx.

The group moved from Lexington to Alexander Avenue in the Bronx. Members and leaders came and went. New conflicts emerged, including with other religious groups in their new setting. The grassroots approach, however, continued to be an integral part of the Alianza. Figueroa, who like Ocasio, had been a member of the IPNA, continued to organize programs that combined Islamic spirituality and social service. In the Bronx, the Alianza held classes on physical and spiritual health, provided community assistance and information on AIDS, and communed weekly for prayer, sermons, and meals.[72] When no other Islamic leaders would bury Muslims who died from AIDS for fear of the stigma, Figueroa did. The Alianza celebrated weddings, shared *halal* Puerto Rican food with each other, and held music and poetry gatherings. Through creative interactions, the Alianza had developed a distinctive way of being Latino and a unique way of being Muslim. Development through contact with diversity, a *convivencia*, was understood by the Alianza as yet another characteristic they had inherited from Al-Andalus, Islamic Spain.

The Alianza's members drew from various sources for their inspiration, including the IPNA, Malcolm X's embrace of Sunni Islam, and Dr. Irving's history of Islam in Spain. It emerged alongside and within the civil rights era. It was an activist group struggling against injustices and inequities through grassroots programs. It was also a religious group, struggling for a sense of peace and self-dignity through Islamic spirituality. It was an identity group whose central narratives were forged in response to the Latino communities that rejected their Islamic religion and to the Muslim communities that rejected their Latino ethnicity. It was a community, a space for celebrating Latino ways of being Muslim and Islamic ways of being Latino. However, in spite of its many accomplishments and its momentum during the twentieth century, the Alianza was not able to maintain its physical space and by 2005 all of its organizational activities came to an end. "But we didn't stop," Figueroa told me, "we all grew from our experience in the Alianza and went on to do other things, important work, still doing it today!" The Alianza slowly faded away but its legacy continues to be echoed in more recent narratives told by new Latino Muslim communities throughout the United States. At the yearly Hispanic Muslim day held in the North Hudson Islamic Center in Union City, New Jersey, several children of the Alianza sat at the dinner tables in the reception hall.[73] Each table carefully adorned with small flags celebrating their Latin American roots, the diversity of its many countries and many religious traditions.

CONCLUSION

As the 2012 Hispanic Muslim Day in Union City drew to a close, those who had gathered made their way from the downstairs reception hall to the main floor. Without instruction, they each took off their shoes and found a place in the main prayer hall, forming well organized rows that faced Mecca. They stood, recited the opening of the Qur'an, and remembered their maker. They invoked God's mercy and compassion, meditated on the Day of Judgment and pleaded for help and guidance on their journey—asking that they may remain firm on the straight path throughout their brief stay here on earth. They bowed, stood, and then prostrated their bodies touching the floor with their forehead as a sign of submission to God before returning to a kneeling position. After repeating the recitations and prostrations, each sat and concluded their *salat*, their prayer, by turning their heads and saying *salams* to one another, "peace be upon you."

After prayer, the community of Latino Muslims slowly began to exit the center. A table had been placed outside with English and Spanish language pamphlets on Islam, free copies of the Qur'an, and coloring books for children. The coloring books were designed for a new generation of Latinos raised as Muslims who speak English, Arabic, and Spanish. This generation will grow up hearing the stories of how their parents embraced, converted, or reverted to Islam and of the hardships they endured for doing so. They will hear these stories at the annual Hispanic Muslim Day in Union City, New Jersey, at storefront mosques in the *barrios* of New York, and in borrowed spaces within Islamic centers in Los Angeles and throughout the United States. They will read the stories about Latino Muslims, their translations of Islamic materials into Spanish, and about their social outreach and political activism. The new generation will read about the historical and cultural links between Latino ethnicity and Islamic religion from websites and social media and from journalists and scholars. They will be a new kind of Latino Muslim, one whose central narrative will lie beyond the scope of conversion. Nevertheless, for the Latino Muslim communities of the past and present, the theme of conversion has been vital for understanding themselves and for the stories they tell about themselves.

CHAPTER TWO

THE SECOND WAVE

SPANISH *DAWAH* FOR WOMEN, ONLINE, AND IN LOS ANGELES

Call thou [all mankind] unto thy Sustainer's path with wisdom and goodly exhortation, and argue with them in the most kindly manner for, behold, thy Sustainer knows best as to who strays from His path, and best knows He as to who are the right-guided.

—*Qur'an 16:125, English translation by M. Asad*

Often overlooked by those who perform dawah, Latino Muslims face a lack of literature about Islam in Spanish and Portuguese, making the work of groups like LALMA and LADO all the more important.

—*Amel S. Abdullah in "Latino Reverts Add to Mosaic of Islam"*

Khadijah Rivera was born on the island of Puerto Rico. Her short autobiography, "My Hispanic Muslim Legacy," provides some details regarding her background. As a child, it seems Rivera dreamed of becoming a Catholic nun. On numerous occasions, she told others about how much she loved the church, Jesus, Mary, and all the saints. But she also feared the bloodied image of Christ as a child. "When I used to put the host in my mouth," she once said in an interview, "I never bit it. I let it melt because I was afraid to bite the body and blood of Christ."[1]

As she grew older, Rivera became increasingly disenchanted with not just the image of Christ but also with several other Christian doctrines: "I believed that there were three gods of equal weight in the heavens, and that upon birth we inherited a mortal sin."[2] After Rivera gave birth to her first child, an idea she describes as beautiful yet frightening began to develop. She gazed deeply into the eyes of her infant and asked herself whether she was looking at an innocent newborn or at a consequence of original sin? "As a parent," wrote Rivera, "it was hard not to question if the smile of innocence behind an infant could hide a deadly sin. What if the infant died before performing the Catholic rite of Baptism? Did that mean he/she would go to hell? And if Jesus Christ had not died [on] the cross for the sins of man, did that mean that we would all have fire as our ultimate destiny?"[3]

After leaving Puerto Rico for the "mainland," Rivera began studying psychology and also comparative religions while in New York. She was a student activist who also participated in political marches, dialectical materialist, Maoist, and socialist group discussions, and enjoyed attending academic lectures on feminism. While studying foreign policy, Rivera became interested in the 1979 Islamic revolution in which Iran replaced a puppet regime supported by the United States with an Islamic republic led by a Grand Ayatollah (an authoritative religious leader in Shi'a Islam). Already critical of US foreign policy, Rivera viewed the Islamic revolution as a positive form of liberation and began participating in pro-Iranian rallies in the United States and also began doing research on Islam.[4]

Compelled by her findings, and especially the teachings of the Qur'an, Rivera took her *shahadah* as a Sunni Muslim on October 22, 1983. Recollecting her first encounters with the Qur'an, Rivera wrote: "Here's a book that explained to me in a logical matter why we're on earth. . . . What we're supposed to do and where we go afterward. All the questions you could ask are answered in the Koran."[5] Soon after embracing Islam, Rivera married a Muslim who had migrated to the United States from Egypt. She noticed that several of his Muslim friends and co-workers were, like him, married to Latina women who were also embracing Islam after marriage. Rivera became convinced that they would all benefit from a support group for Latinas that were new to Islam.

Following the Alianza Islámica, which had emerged in the 1980s as one of the first Latino Muslim communities in America, three new organizations were founded before the end of the century. PIEDAD (a piety group) was founded in 1988 as a support group by and for women in Florida. Latino American Dawah Organization (LADO) was founded in 1997 as a network for the dissemination of Islamic information to Latino audiences via internet technologies. Los Angeles Latino Muslim Association (LALMA) was founded in 1999 as a Qur'anic study group in Los Angeles. All three organizations had been inspired by the work and stories developed by the Alianza Islámica. Like the Alianza, PIEDAD, LADO, and LALMA promoted Islam to Latino audiences. They looked to the Alianza's *dawah* programs and sought to replicate the ways they had succeeded in promoting Islam in metropolitan areas inhabited by Latino populations. In particular, the Alianza's promotion of Islam as a deep and lasting influence on Latino culture made its way into the identity narratives that sustained the new organizations.

Despite the Alianza's influence on the new organizations, important differences developed between PIEDAD, LADO, and LALMA and their pioneering predecessor. First, the new organizations concentrated almost exclusively on the production and analysis of information while failing to participate in other forms of social service. Second, the new organizations worked within, rather than autonomously from, broader American Muslim groups. These first two differences should be understood in light of significant changes to the historical context in which the second wave of Latino Muslims developed. By the 1990s, the civil rights era had given way to color blind politics in public discourse, religious diversity had increased exponentially, and internet technologies were beginning to radically transform our concepts of space.

During the first Latino Muslim wave, Islam had been connected in large measure to the struggle for civil rights and the creation of a more just civil society in the United States. Along with the political and social activist fervor of the civil rights era, Latino Muslim participation in social service faded into the background if practiced at all. Instead of promoting street safety, providing G.E.D. training, and participating in drug rehabilitation and AIDS awareness programs and political activism, the new organizations practiced *dawah* primarily as the dissemination of information. Further, public representations of Islam during the civil rights era were dominated by groups like the NOI. Under Warith Deen Muhammad, Elijah Muhamad's son and successor, however, the NOI underwent a process of *Sunnification* that began in the late 1970s and abandoned a vision of racially exclusivity for an inclusive one.[6] The NOI's movement toward racial inclusivity coincided with the emergence of cultural formulation of race and color-blind politics as dominant paradigms competing with biologistic and nationalist formations of race in American public discourse.[7] America's religious landscape had also been exponentially diversified by the Immigration and Naturalization Act of 1965, which lifted country of origin quotas.[8] The result of the NOI's *Sunnification*, the Immigration and Naturalization Act of 1965, and the emergence of color-blind politics was that the second wave of Latino Muslims emerged within a context where public representations of Muslims in the United States were increasingly reduced almost exclusively to immigrant communities from Muslim majority societies—mostly from Asia. Within this context, the racial and ethnic diversity of Muslims in the United States was reduced to a Muslim-therefore-Arab stereotype in public discourse.

Internet technologies also radically transformed the spaces that Latino Muslims occupied. By the 1990s, the United States had popularized and colonized the internet. The early stages of digital networking were developed by the Advanced Research Projects Agency, a branch of the US Department of Defense. It was designed as a communications network that could both survive various kinds of disasters and also connect academic researchers remotely and thereby expand access to the few powerful computers that existed at the time.[9] As research funding shifted from government to private sources, the technology was increasingly commercialized and popularized. The development of smaller and more affordable personal computers, landline networking, and the Netscape graphical browser led to a first wave of the internet's popularization in the 1990s.[10] Then came the AOL (America Online) revolution, which at its peak put more than 30 million Americans "online." One of the most prominent Latino Muslim organizations today has no physical address, is embodied in cyberspace, and began on AOL bulletin boards.

The proliferation of various internet technologies has provided more egalitarian access to information and mass communication broadcasting. The technologies amplify, amalgamate, and speed up the rate of previous forms of communication. They facilitate transparency, activism, and representation to individuals and groups with few resources. On the other side of the spectrum, however, internet technologies have also amplified economic, social, and political inequality. They have created a digital divide between those who do and do not have access to internet technologies and also between those who are and are not adept with the skills necessary to operate them toward their socioeconomic advantage.[11] They facilitate government and corporate surveillance as well as economic and ideological domination by the wealthy. Internet technologies have both aided and impeded the growth and development of small and large identity groups. They have the potential to provide otherwise marginalized communities with representation in the public sphere and thereby gain access to social capital and vital resources.

Despite their potential to radically transform the practice of religion and to produce new forms of virtual rituals, religious groups have instead used internet technologies mostly for networking and to disseminate information.[12] Nevertheless, religious authority, fragmentation processes, and the size and influence of faith-based groups and their narratives have indeed been greatly influenced by new media technologies.[13] The end of the civil rights era, increased diversification, and the proliferation of internet technologies have been integral to the historically specific manner in which the second Latino Muslim wave has developed. This chapter provides an account of the second Latino Muslim wave and critically engages the ways in which PIEDAD, LADO, and LALMA have all been shaped by but have also contributed to our changing American religious landscape.

PIEDAD IN NEW YORK AND BEYOND

Khadijah Rivera led the formation of PIEDAD in 1988 as a support group for new Latina Muslimahs (Muslim women) in Florida. *Piedad* is the Spanish word for piety and also serves as an acronym for: La Propagación Islamica para la Educación de Ala el Divino (Islamic propagation for education on and devotion to Allah the Divine).[14] The women's group connects Islamic piety to *dawah* (the propagation of Islam) in its educational activities, support for women who are new to Islam, and social service.[15] It is self-described as "a national network of Muslim women coming together for the common good: spiritual development, community building, sisterhood, and educational outreach, with a focus on the Latina/Hispanic community."

PIEDAD's organizational model envisioned a four-step *dawah* process that includes (1) friendship, (2) teaching, (3) inclusivity, and (4) a continued life of learning. PIEDAD's mission statement describes the first step as the formation of "sincere and deep friendships that allow mistakes and are non-judgmental." Instead of calling out every mistake or missed opportunity to enacted piety, an especially daunting task for new Muslims, PIEDAD members focus on cultivating friendships rather than hierarchical relationships between the Islamically adept and the ritually inept. Although many are attracted to the simplicity of the *shahadah*, the belief in one God, new Muslims quickly find out from fellow Muslims that there is so much more to their new religion than just proclaiming a brief statement of faith. New Muslims struggle with trying to memorize, recite, and understand the Qur'an and also with trying to learn what might seem to some like an excessively difficult task of having to master numerous rituals and consider moral pronouncements on all human actions as either: required, encouraged, neutral, discouraged, or forbidden. PIEDAD teaches that piety is a practice that requires practice, it is not an overnight experience or transformation. Ritual, doctrinal, and moral errors will be made along the way and the best response to such mistakes is patient friendship. Because the group is made up of people who know firsthand what it is like to struggle through the newness of Islam, the group considers itself to be well positioned to address the specific needs of new Muslim women.

PIEDAD's second *dawah* step is "to teach only what we are sure is correct and for deeper questions always have a sheikh or imam available for advice." In this manner, PIEDAD is dependent on broader

Islamic institutions that can connect them to Muslim scholars (i.e., a "sheikh or imam"). Traditionally, religious authority in Sunni Islam is concentrated in the *ulema*, Islamic scholars who specialize in Islamic jurisprudence. They study the Qur'an and Hadith (the recorded sayings and deeds of the Prophet) in order to judge whether an action is required, encouraged, permissible, discouraged, or forbidden by God. Although these Islamic scholars are not universally accepted as authoritative religious leaders, they are nevertheless generally regarded as being more knowledgeable than lay Muslims. Although the Alianza had produced its own religious leaders, PIEDAD did not. Because traditionally and generally the *ulema* are male and because PIEDAD's membership is comprised of women, it is less likely that Islamic scholars would emerge from within its membership. The group therefore relies entirely on the sponsorship and teachings of an outside, male, and usually non-Latino Islamic scholar. The Islamic scholar provides religious guidance but also symbolically authenticates the group to broader Muslim communities who might be concerned about new Muslims teaching new Muslims about Islam—a concern, or rather critique, that was not only hurled at groups like the Moorish Science Temple and the NOI but also at the Alianza Islámica, which emerged during the first wave of Latino Muslims.

PIEDAD's third *dawah* step is to "assure the new Muslimah that Islam is for everyone." The history of Islam in America includes groups who formulated Islam as racially exclusive. Broader Muslim groups assessed such racial exclusivity to be guilty of *bid'ah*, a deviation from Islamic teachings. "True" Islam, they argued, promotes racial inclusivity and equality instead, even if this is not always the case in practice. Commentators from broader Muslim groups hypothesized that one reason for the deviation was that groups like the NOI developed without the guidance of *ulema*, Islamic scholars trained in one of the legal traditions. Groups like the NOI thus informed broader Muslim concerns that groups like the Alianza and PIEDAD may also be promoting ethnically exclusive forms of Islam in ways that deviated from the "True" teachings of Islam. Although there is no consensus as to which individuals or groups should have the authority to define the boundaries between so-called True Islam and innovations, the critique remains a popular concern among various Muslim communities. Although originally formed as a Latina women's group, in light of such critiques PIEDAD later expanded its focus to include any and all women new to Islam regardless of their race or ethnicity. According to PIEDAD's leadership, the change occurred partly due to concerns expressed by both members and by non-Latino Muslims. Both groups worried that focusing on Latino ethnicity created unnecessary divisions in the *ummah*, the Muslim community, which should be united rather than divided. Perhaps as important, many of PIEDAD's members were not of Latino descent, and so the organization's decision to expand its mission statement may have also been inspired by a desire to more accurately reflect its ethnically diverse membership.

In the 1970s and 1980s, the Alianza Islámica had leased property in Spanish Harlem then in the Bronx, which they used as a prayer room, community hall, and office. They had procured a space of their own because they had opted out of the Latino Christian spaces they had been raised in and because they wished to avoid criticisms and the rejection of Latino culture and Spanish language by broader Muslim groups. Every space available to the first wave of Latino Muslims discouraged the pairing of Latino and Muslim identities. Unlike the Alianza, however, PIEDAD never leased a space of its own. In fact, no other Latino Muslim group since the Alianza had procured a physical space of its own until 2016. Instead, PIEDAD, like most other Latino Muslim groups since the Alianza, met in homes, Islamic centers, and mosques. Rather than working autonomously from broader American Muslim groups as the Alianza had sought to do, PIEDAD worked with and within American Islamic institutions. By doing so, PIEDAD began a practice that would be replicated by most other Latino Muslim groups to follow. In the changed American religious landscape, one in which the NOI's racially exclusive Islam faded from public discourse and was replaced with a reductive Muslim-therefore-Arab stereotype and which increasingly brought diverse Latino and Muslim groups into contact with one another, it seemed morally, financially, and politically prudent to work with and within broader Muslim groups rather than apart from them.

Despite the changed landscape and challenges to developing spaces of their own, PIEDAD did manage to purchase and maintain a toll-free telephone number, 1-800-44-ALLAH. The financial costs of the telephone services were supplied through a collaborative effort by the five PIEDAD chapters in Georgia, New York, Florida, Illinois, and New Jersey. The goal of the phone number was to create a channel through which anyone in the nation could access PIEDAD's support services. The Alianza's audience had been regional, with its toll-free 1-800-44-ALLAH number, PIEDAD's audience became national. Interested individuals or individuals new to Islam could phone in and talk to and learn about Islam from a PIEDAD member and even schedule or attend regularly scheduled in-person meetings. This was another innovation instituted by PIEDAD that would greatly influence subsequent Latino Muslim organizations. PIEDAD was using communication technologies to connect individuals to others who shared their identity narratives. In the past, most Latino Muslims had lived out their unique ethno-religious identity in isolation.

PIEDAD's phone service was eventually replaced with a much more cost-effective yet simple website that provided basic information on Islam to Latino audiences. In its first design, the website was a replacement of the telephone technology and was used mostly for connecting people through email communication rather than branding. PIEDAD also published content on a blogspot site, including a February 9, 2007, post dedicated to the life of the historian of Islamic Spain, Dr. T. B. Irving. The page included a letter originally published by Carl Askia El-Amin, who was himself affiliated with the Alianza. In the letter, El-Amin reminded PIEDAD's audience of Dr. Irving's contributions and grieved his death.[16] Additionally, PIEDAD founder Khadijah Rivera published the following statement on the historian of Islamic Spain:

> Dr. Irving was once a fixture at Muslim conventions. I met him and was sincerely moved by his professional presentation at one of our PIEDAD lectures on Mudejar Art in Latino America. He was inspiring when chatting about Andalusia and how my roots were Hispanic even before birth. He pushed me to lecture and socialize among Latinos and other Muslims.

He gave me his braveheart to do outreach in spite of what my Id told me [*sic*]. Al hamdulilah he was my teacher and I am forever grateful of the times I met him or read his books. Allah grant him paradise. . . . We need to remember our scholars. We need to be there for them with our concern, our Dua's and our good wishes, especially in the last moments of their lives. Warmly, Khadijah Rivera.[17]

Like the Alianza, PIEDAD also developed a relationship with Dr. Irving who helped promote Latino identity as rooted in Islam. In turn, Rivera and the PIEDAD group made it a point to promote and amplify the message of a historical link between Islam in Spain and Latino identity and also to recognize Dr. Irving's work in this respect through the media technologies available to them. Like its toll-free number, PIEDAD eventually outgrew the simple website and the blog it had maintained.

In the late 2000s, the original website was replaced with one that was professionally designed and that allowed for massive amounts of information to be uploaded by PIEDAD members without much training in web design or coding. The new site's visual aesthetic included a matted yellow background with Andalusian inspired red and grey geometric patterns fading into transparency and a crimson red color pallet. The website's header featured a black and white photograph of an out of focus and veiled woman in the background with the organization's logo superimposed on to the foreground. The logo combined the letters "PIEDAD" in a stylized font with a red rose (fig. 2.1). The site and its graphics were produced by the incorporated design company, Iman Studios (*Iman* is the Arabic word for "faith"). The Los Angeles centered web design firm was established in 2001 and has a portfolio that appears to cater mostly to Muslim individuals and organizations, including musician and producer Akon, professional basketball player Gilbert Arenas, the UmmaClinic.org, DawaCorps.com, UmmahFilms.com, and TheDeanShow.com.

Although professional companies like Iman Studios provide valuable branding services, small identity groups like PIEDAD are often left to their own devices when producing, organizing, or uploading content. Digital content managed by PIEDAD focuses primarily on examples of

FIGURE 2.1.

Screenshot of PIEDAD's website. The organization had previously used a Blogspot site then had a static website designed by LADO president Juan Galvan. This third website was professionally produced by Iman Studios. PIEDAD's logo was also professionally produced and combines an image of red rose with the Spanish world for piety as an association between beauty, womanhood, and religious piety. http://www.piedadislam.org.

pious women, discussions on veiling, lists of women's rights in Islam, and advice for victims of domestic violence. A "Wise Women" page on PiedadIslam.org lists several hyperlinks to stories of the "Mothers of the Believers and *Sahaabiyat* [the female companions of the Prophet]." Along with Hājar (Abraham's wife and Ishmael's mother), Mariam (virgin mother of Isa or Jesus), and Khadijah (Muhammad's first wife), Fatima (the daughter of Muhammad and Khadijah, wife of Ali and mother of Hasan and Husain), the wise and strong willed Aisha (wife of the Prophet), and other members of the Ahl al-Bayt (the family of the house of the Prophet) form core hermeneutic models for developing discursive representations of Muslimah piety, women's issues in Islam, and Muslim women leadership roles.[18]

On PiedadIslam.org, the issue of veiling is addressed through several documents and hyperlinks to outside organizations, including to a Spanish language brochure by the Islamic Circle of North America's WhyIslam titled "Revelando el misterio del jiyab" (Revealing the mystery of the *hijab*). The brochure promotes veiling as "an external manifestation of an internal commitment to worship Allah—it symbolizes a commitment to piety."[19] Additionally, the brochure and many of the other documents on veiling respond to critiques that the practice is a form of oppression and a violation of human rights. Instead, PIEDAD's digital content contends that veiling is both a form of religious piety and a form of feminist liberation—one that seeks to situate women outside of the sexual male gaze and beyond the objectification of female bodies. Although it is important to critique simplistic arguments that the veil is a sign of oppression, it is also important, as the scholar Lila Abu-Lughod argues, to avoid uncritical and simple endorsements of particular forms of veiling practices that do not take issues of colonialism, nation, identity politics and authenticity into account.[20]

PIEDAD's reactionary reliance on outside organizations like Islamic Circle of North America's (ICNA) WhyIslam for its voice on issues of veiling flatten much more nuanced, critical, and diverse understandings of veiling practices among Latina Muslim women. With regard to the way in which PIEDAD manages its digital views on veiling, women's rights, and domestic violence—there is indeed a form of agency practiced in choosing which content it will or will not republish on its site. However, in order to avoid ideological marginalization, Latino Muslims will in the future have to address the issues that are important to them in much more dynamic, proactive, and critical ways than merely endorsing media produced by others.

In addition to its use of internet technologies, PIEDAD has engaged in various activities that have led it to be recognized by larger audiences. In the early 1990s, PIEDAD hosted talks at Columbia University and other institutions, held the first Hispanic Muslim conference and sent representatives to the Islamic Society of North America, ISNA, for a conference that featured Latino Muslims.[21] PIEDAD's founder, Khadijah Rivera, was nominated by the Los Angeles Latino Muslim Association to attend the Second Annual Latino Islamic Congress in Spain, which sought to foster a global Latino Muslim community. In the winter of 2008, PIEDAD members joined the American Congress for Muslim Youth (ACMY) and sent one Latina Muslimah to study in the United Arab Emirates.[22]

By training and providing Muslim women with leadership roles within Islamic communities, PIEDAD seeks a religious path toward women's empowerment. US programs devoted to training a specifically American Muslim clergy for communities in the United States question the fit of a Muslim clergy unfamiliar with the social, cultural, and political context of the adherents they serve. Likewise, PIEDAD's call for more Muslimah training programs not only identifies women as leaders of Muslim organizations but also emphasizes women's rights. This zeal for empowering Muslimah leaders reflects PIEDAD founder Khadijah Rivera's life-long struggle for equality on various fronts, including on gender. On November 22, 2009, Rivera passed away, leaving Nylka Vargas in New Jersey in charge of the organization. In honor of Rivera's life and service, the following statement was published in the Islamic Society of North America's *Islamic Horizons* magazine:

> One friend summed up her life as a perfect example of how to be American and Muslim as well as how Muslims can be a positive social force. Another tribute said that not only did she feed empty stomachs, but she also touched the hearts of the fallen and downtrodden. Regardless of how society saw these people, she treated them with the respect and dignity she believed everyone deserves.[23]

PIEDAD began as a way to address issues specific to Latinas new to Islam. The group later expanded its *dawah* mission statement, its moral, financial, and ideological stances and activities to better reflect the racial and ethnic diversity of its membership. It continues to work with and within broader Muslim groups even as it seeks to produce information on Islam geared to Latino audiences. PIEDAD's membership is exclusive to women. The organization relies on the symbolic authority and religious guidance of a male Muslim scholar. Despite this negotiation with patriarchy, PIEDAD nevertheless seeks to discourage other forms of gender inequality, to promote women's rights in Islam, and to empower Muslim women in leadership and *dawah* capacities.

Although PIEDAD has engaged in social service in the past, including feeding hungry populations in downtown areas, it has not continued to do so in the present. The group has instead focused primarily on the reproduction and consumption of Islamic information geared toward Latino audiences, especially for Latina women who want to learn more about Islamic piety. PIEDAD does not maintain a physical space of its own and meets instead within mosques and centers managed by broader Muslim groups. However, PIEDAD does maintain its own virtual space on the web—albeit one whose graphics and content are produced by non-Latino Muslims.

LADO ON THE INTERNET

Unlike PIEDAD whose founding members first began meeting face to face, Juan Alvarado, Samantha Sanchez, and Saraji Umm Zaid first met on AOL bulletin boards. Juan Alvarado was born in the Bronx to Dominican immigrants who fled from political repression, persecution, and economic uncertainty in the 1960s. He was raised as a devout Catholic. As a teenager, however, Alvarado renounced Catholicism and began exploring other options in the American religious marketplace. When he was twenty, Alvarado came across an Ansaru Allah publication and took his *shahadah* with the group three years later. One day, a member from the Alianza Islámica met Alvarado and noticed that he wore the insignia for the Ansaru Allah. He told Alvarado that this group did not represent the teachings of Sunni Islam and that most Muslims did not even consider the group to be part of the religion of Islam. After two years of soul searching and doctrinal research Alvarado took a second *shahadah*, this time with the Alianza as a Sunni Muslim. Alvarado masterfully occupied the emerging digital spaces and used internet technologies to develop his own religious worldviews in conversation with others. While engaging in his religiosity online, Alvarado gained many valuable insights from other Muslims who were also exploring the connection between their ethnicity, religion, and new communications technologies.

Samantha Sanchez was a graduate student at a Jesuit college and it was on this campus that she had her first encounter with a Latina

Muslim. Sanchez was intrigued and wondered why a Latina would choose Islam. She decided to focus her master's thesis research on Latino Muslims and began looking for people to interview. It was during this search that she met Juan Alvarado on an AOL bulletin board, interviewed him there and continued to stay in touch through email correspondence. Sanchez's research led to profound personal insights and she eventually accepted Islam as her own creed. The same day that Sanchez took her *shahadah* at an Islamic Center in Queens, Saraji Umm Zaid, another pioneer of the online group, also made the public proclamation of faith. Although the two did not know each other at the time, they would later refer to their synchronized *shahadahs* as providence rather than as an interesting coincidence. Zaid had privately taken her *shahadah* as a teenager but was then afraid of how her family and friends would react. So she kept her new religious identity hidden from her family and friends out of fear. Now, Zaid was not alone. Accompanied by "a Latina sister from New Jersey," Zaid publically professed her Islamic identity in 1997.[24] Alvarado, Sanchez, and Zaid met each other on a digital message board and became close friends. For the three internet savvy religious pioneers, the long distances between them and the lack of resources to rent or purchase a physical space of their own could easily be overcome with a personal computer, internet service, and a little know-how. The internet became a new meeting space where Latino Muslims across the United States could proactively and communally shape their own identity narratives.

Alvarado, Sanchez, and Zaid began their first listserv newsletter and asked members and other organizations to help supply content in Spanish and English. They wanted to give a voice to the growing number of individuals who identified as Latino Muslims. "I wanted something established," reported Zaid, "so that by the time my daughter was old enough to think for herself and notice how the world works, she would see Latinos represented in the Ummah."[25] The term *ummah* refers to a community of Muslims. It is often used to refer to a universal community of all Muslims across the globe and across all time periods. It is also sometimes used to refer to regional and local communities like the American *ummah* or the *ummah* in LA. The three digitally connected companions put a lot of thought into the emerging vision of their *ummah*.

After many long discussions, they agreed to call themselves the Latino American Dawah Organization or LADO. They were Latinos, Muslims, and Americans all at the same time, and they were organized to teach others about Islam, to perform *dawah*. The LADO acronym is also the Spanish word for "side," and as such was used to produce slogans like *¡A su LADO!*, "at your side" or "we're there for you" and *Puro Latino! ¡Puro Islam! ¡A su LADO!*, "Fully Latino! Fully Islamic! At your side!" The group was developing their Muslim identity at the same time as they were developing their skills with digital information technologies. They understood that without an engaging presentation the information would get nowhere, so they put a lot of thought into their slogans, their logo, and most important, their content. "Our *dawah* efforts have attempted to address these needs in various ways," wrote Alvarado, "For example, Zaid offers practical advice for new Muslims in her article: "How Do I Tell My Parents and Family I've Become a Muslim?" In another article, Zaid recalls that the mother of one reader complained because her daughter stopped eating her pastels (pastries). "Pastels and tortillas do not necessarily have to be haram, or prohibited in Islam. We have been fortunate to address these kinds of misconceptions among Latinos."[26] For Latinos who are new to Islam, learning the various religious prohibitions around food and practices can be just as overwhelming and confusing as trying to reconcile the two identities at a conceptual level. And both have been central to LADO's mission: to help new Muslims learn about Islamic teachings and practices and to reframe their narrative not as Latinos who convert to Islam, but as Latino Muslims who are rediscovering the historical and cultural connection between their ethno-religious identity.

Stories and articles were first shared through email then through the *Latino Muslim Voice*, the longest running and most prominent periodical by and on Latino Muslims. Samantha Sanchez used her personal AOL homepage to produce the group's first website and published an archive of the newsletter. Along with her internet service subscription, Sanchez had access to website hosting through AOL's servers. The internet revolution had not only made it possible for Latino Muslims from across the United States to meet and connect with one another, it also helped the small group broadcast its message to mass audiences.

The list of readers, contributing members, and topics covered by the newsletter grew. Articles began to include Qur'anic quotes of the month, discussions of doctrinal issues, and links to news stories on Muslims and Latino Muslims. The *Latino Muslim Voice* also published announcements for upcoming events and original stories of how individuals came to embrace Islam, poems, songs, and recipes that mixed Latino cuisines with those from Muslim majority countries. "Exploring other cultures always implied a culinary exchange to me," wrote Anisa Abeytia in a *Latino Muslim Voice* article titled "Curries, Tajeens and Moles: Exploring Culture and Conversion through Food."

> Food holds our history and can reveal a story with each bite. It can take the global and exotic and turn it into the local and the intimate. We usually do not try new food alone and many times a friend from another culture introduces us to it, along with an explanation of the way a food is prepared or if it holds a special significance in the culture, like couscous on Friday in Morocco or tamales for Christmas in Mexico. This turns something novel or strange into an intimate and non-confrontational introduction. Food was one of the ways I was first introduced to Islam. The food seemed to be as foreign to me as the religion.[27]

Abeytia goes on to narrate her first encounter with Pakistani food, how the hot spices brought her discomfort and tears to her eyes, and how this was kind of like the discomfort and pain she would later feel after first embracing the religion of Islam. Her initial discomfort was managed, and Abeytia went on to make her own versions of curry mixed with elements of mole, a traditional Mexican dish similar to curry but that uses chocolate as its base. Like her unique mix of culinary exchanges, Abeytia also found her own way within Islam. "Is it exactly like a traditional curry?" Abeytia continues,

No, but it is my version. It is true that to call something a curry does not make it a curry. It has to include all the basic ingredients of a curry. The same is true for a religion. If one removes one or more of the fundamentals or pillars of Islam, say prayer for instance, one cannot really call herself a Muslim. However we all find ways to make Islam a living and breathing way of life and it is a day-to-day struggle that sometimes takes an unexpected turn and ends up on our plates.

The article concludes with five unique recipes that blend Latino cuisines with those from Muslim majority countries and asks the readers to "Enjoy the food and make Islam your own. *Bismillah* [In the name of God]!"

Using the work of Benedict Anderson, Patrick Bowen's own scholarly work interprets the *Latino Muslim Voice* and its articles as a medium for "imagining," that is, for shaping the transcript or story of who the emerging Latino Muslim community is. "LADO and the Voice have served to not only help make non-Latina/o Muslims more aware of the Latina/o Muslim presence," writes Bowen, "but also to connect disparate Latina/o Muslims, and in the process have created an 'imagined community' on a scale that might not have been possible without the internet."[28] Although LADO has been described or critiqued as a purely online group, Bowen's use of the term "imagined community" is instead a reference to the performance of agency through proactive creativity. In this way, LADO's *Latino Muslim Voice* magazine and its content produced primarily by Latino Muslims provides a contrast to uncritical remediation or the endorsement of media by non-Latino Muslims. It is an act of self-creation, a technology of the self.[29]

Like Abeytia who narrates her ethno-religious identity through cuisine, many of the newsletter's contributors creatively narrate connections between their Latino and Islamic identities. Like the *dawah* strategies shared by the Alianza and PIEDAD, the historical and cultural connection to Al-Andalus or Islamic Spain was again here featured prominently. And when Juan Galvan, a fourth LADO leader, joined the group, he helped to crystalize the prominence of the organization and the dissemination of Latino Muslim information. "Life's twists and turns are strange," wrote Alvarado recalling how he first met Galvan,

> After some time, I lost touch with Samantha and the other LADO peo-
> ple. After regaining internet service, I either forgot all of the people's e-
> mail addresses or they had been changed. Years later, while working for
> the Los Angeles Times, I came across an article in the *New York Times*
> mentioning LADO and Samantha. Alhamdulillah, [praise be to God] I
> was able to contact her and Juan to find that LADO continued. I have
> found a good "virtual" friend and brother with [Juan] Galvan.[30]

Galvan had embraced Islam after befriending a Latino Muslim who taught him about the history of Islam in Spain and meaningfully answered all of his questions about religion and life. Galvan's questions included: "How can the Father be the Son? Why can't God just forgive anyone he wants? What happens to babies who die before baptism?" and so on. After three years of questions, Galvan took his *shahadah*. While searching for other Latino Muslims to talk to, Galvan found LADO's website and joined the organization in 2001. He had earned a bachelor's degree in management information systems at the University of Texas at Austin, which proved to be extremely useful to the organi-zation's use of internet technologies.

After Galvan joined LADO the now dominant LatinoDawah.org domain name was registered, a national survey of Latino Muslims was initiated, and HispanicMuslims.com, a collection of Latino Muslim rever-sion stories was launched by Galvan and Sanchez. That same year, LADO was also officially endorsed by several US Muslim organizations including ISNA and the ICNA. LADO representatives of the organization attended the Annual Latino Muslim Conference sponsored by ISNA. The online group was featured in various news media outlets including the *Islamic Horizons* magazine produced by ISNA, it established relationships with various other Muslim organizations across the United States and began a social networking Yahoo Group with limited editorial involvement.

In January 2002, LADO overhauled its website and moved it off the AOL service to a private server. The new website's structure allowed it to maintain, add, and manage vast amounts of data. This feature would be integral to publishing original content and archiving the rapidly increasing production of articles on Latino Muslims by news media. Following the attacks of September 11, 2001, news coverage of Muslims surged as did coverage of Latino Muslims. This increased attention was recorded and made available to others as a collection of post-9/11 media productions on Latino Muslims. Also in 2002, LADO helped coordinate the first *Islamic Horizons* edition dedicated completely to Latino Muslims. In 2004, LADO members attended the second Annual Hispanic Muslim Day held in New Jersey and coordinated a Latino Muslim edition of *The Message International*, a nationally distributed Muslim magazine.

In 2005, LADO redesigned its website again through a collaborative effort, this time including a Spanish language version. In 2014, the LatinoDawah.org website was visited nearly 90,000 times per month and consistently dominated search engine queries for searches on Latino or Hispanic Muslims. Through its online presence, the organization serves as a hub and gatekeeper to information on and by Latino Muslims. LADO is today one of the most widely recognized and well connected Latino Muslim organizations in the United States. Regarding the group's organizational structure, Galvan wrote:

> LADO is a very loosely knit organization. LADO does not have physical offices, such as a headquarters. Although people may constantly move, LADO remains available online to provide a number of services. LADO understands that the internet allows information to be easily and inexpensively distributed to anywhere and accessed from anywhere. LADO also understands that the internet allows people to easily and inexpensively communicate with other people from around the world. As mentioned previously, LADO provides a way for Latino Muslims from different states to be accessible via the internet.[31]

The Alianza, Dr. Irving, El-Amin, and PIEDAD had each helped develop a set of stories that connected Latino identity to Islam and that were increasingly found both off and on the World Wide Web. LADO, which had developed within online bulletin boards, understood the potential that internet technologies presented and made good use of it. Although the message was indeed digitally amplified beyond the East Coast where the Alianza and PIEDAD had made its presence felt, it could only reach people in the West who had access to internet services. A third Latino Muslim organization would however develop and fill in the analog gaps left by the limited reach of the Alianza, PIEDAD, and LADO.

LALMA IN CALIFORNIA

In 1848, the United States annexed the state of California. After the Mexican-American war, Mexico was forced to secede much of its vast northern territories including Alta California to the United States. Residents of California received American citizenship if they decided to stay, over 90 percent did.[32] There are still many descendants of those who stayed and who remind us that it was the US border that crossed over them and not vice versa. At over 14 million, 39 percent of the state's population, California has the largest Latino population in the nation and the overwhelming majority is of Mexican descent.[33] Many Latinos in California have made a living through its immense agricultural economy. Mostly, however, these have been poverty wages earned in brutal and inhumane working conditions. It was against these civil rights abuses that Dolores Huerta, Larry Itliong, César Chávez, the United Farm Workers of America, and others fought against.[34] And it was on these same farms that migrant farmworkers from the Punjab first came into contact with Latinos of Mexican descent.

Race laws in the early twentieth century prohibited "nonwhites" from legally marrying a white spouse. From the Punjab in India, mostly men came to work the California farms. Given the race laws and an increasing realization that their stay would be permanent, many of these male Punjabi farmworkers married the Mexican women they came into contact with and were legally allowed to. The majority of the Punjabi farmworkers identified religiously as Sikh. But there were also a small number of Muslims. Some of the earliest Latino conversions to Islam in the United States occurred through marriage between Mexican and Punjabi farmworkers in 1920s California.[35] Over two decades later, in 1946, the first mosque "west of the Mississippi River" was founded by Punjabi Muslims in Sacramento with no mention of possible Latino members.[36] The first Latino Muslim community in California would develop much later, further south of the state's capitol, and with little to no connection to the Punjabi community in the region.

In 1953, a group of Near Eastern immigrants and Angelino converts formed an association known today as the Islamic Center of Southern California (ICSC). The Islamic Center of Orange County was then established in 1976 and the Omar Ibn Al Khattab Foundation in 1982.[37] It was within these three locations that one of California's oldest Latino Muslim communities emerged. The first Latino Muslim organization in California, however, met at a storefront mosque near masjid Omar and the University of Southern California. Here, Reymundo Nur and a group of Latino Muslims used the space to meet and learn about the Qur'an in Spanish. "I told my mom I didn't want to go to church anymore when I was around 8 or 9 years old," Nur recounted, "and so I stopped going right about that age." Nur was born and raised in the Panama Canal Zone where, until 1945, racial segregation was practiced and patterned after Jim Crow laws. "Because we were of dark skin," remembers Nur, "we couldn't go to the church where the white people attended, their racism was even instituted in religion . . . we couldn't even drink from the same water fountain." Nur began investing his time learning martial arts instead of spending time at the racially segregated churches in the Canal Zone. At age twelve, Nur began training with a martial arts instructor who was also from Panama, but who had traveled to the United States and embraced Islam there. "When I realized that Islam transcends all racial boundaries," continued Nur, "I said this is good. This is what mankind needs, and this is where I'd like to be." Nur was captivated by the Islamic idealization of racial equality and at age twelve he took his *shahadah* and began a lifelong dwelling within Islam.[38] Reymundo Nur went on to study the Qur'an in Saudi Arabia and also helped to found La Asociación Latina de Musulmanes en las Américas (the Latino Association of Muslims in the Americas) in 1997.[39] In 1999, the organization was renamed as the Latino-Muslim Movement (LMM). That same year, however, Nur left the United States to continue his Islamic studies abroad. With Nur gone, the LMM encountered internal disputes over doctrinal issues and ritual practices and soon after dissolved.

In 1999, the same year that Nur's group dissolved, a second community of Latino Muslims began meeting in the ICSC to study the Qur'an in Spanish. Marta Felicitas Ramirez de Galedary, Fatima Mijangos, Iris Patricia Lopez, Judith Aquino, Valerie Curtis-Diop, and Diane Fregoso made up the founding members of the Los Angeles–based community. What had begun as a study group eventually crystalized into a prominent fixture within several mosques throughout the greater Los Angeles region. The Los Angles Latino Muslim Association (LALMA) is today one of the oldest and most prominent Latino Muslim organizations on the West Coast.

At LALMA's regular weekly meetings on Sundays, participants learn Arabic, study Islamic teachings, pray, eat, and share stories with one another. The pillars and central tenants of faith are regularly reviewed at these meetings. It said that if Islam were a house, its structurally necessary pillars would include the following five practices: (1) the *shaha-dah* or proclamation of faith that "there is no god but God"; (2) *salat* or five daily prayers; (3) *zakat* or required charity; (4) *sawm* or fasting during the month of Ramadan; and (5) the *hajj* pilgrimage to Mecca required once in the life of all Muslims who are physically and financially able to. The central tenants of faith include belief in (1) *tawhīd* or the Oneness of God; (2) the existence of Angels; (3) the revealed books (including those revealed to Jews and Christians); (4) the Prophets (including Adam, Moses, Jesus, and Muhammad); and (5) resurrection on the Day of Judgment.[40]

In addition to studying the Qur'an, *Hadith* (the sayings and deeds of the Prophet), and the pillars and tenants of faith, LALMA also explores various topics and strands of Islamic teachings. One way that LALMA studies the traditions of the Prophet is through a Spanish language translation of Martin Lings's book titled *Muhammad: His Life Based on the Earliest Sources*. The book was originally written in English for a popular audience unfamiliar with the biography of the Prophet. Some critics have argued that Lings's biography draws from weak *Hadith* (sayings or deeds whose authenticity are found to be questionable or unacceptable) in key areas. The result, it is argued by these critics, is a negative portrayal of the Prophet especially with regard to the way the Prophet fails to uphold *tawhīd* (the Islamic doctrine of the Oneness of God) when reentering Mecca and the Kab'ah (the Cube). "Apart from the icon of the Virgin Mary," writes Lings, "and the child Jesus and a painting of an old man said to be Abraham, the walls inside (the Ka'bah) had been covered with pictures of pagan deities. Placing his hand protectively over the icon, the Prophet told 'Uthmaan to see that all other paintings, except that of Abraham, were effaced."[41]

"Can it be believed," responds Aboo Bilaal Mustafaa al-Kanadee, a critic of Lings, "that the Prophet (*sallallaahu 'alayhi wa sallam*) would protect such icons of Mary, Jesus and Abraham in this manner, and that he would allow these idols to be left intact inside the sacred Ka'bah, the very symbol of pure unadulterated *Tawheed*?!"[42] Despite some of its controversial aspects, Lings's text is a popular biography of the Prophet read by both non-Muslim and Muslim Americans. Spanish-speaking Muslims did not have many other materials available to them to learn about the life of the Prophet. The text has therefore been critically studied regularly at LALMA meetings because it is both stylistically and materially accessible.

LALMA has also explored more spiritually oriented strands of Islamic thought. A great deal of Islamic scholarship has been characterized as legal discourses regarding what actions are required, beneficial, neutral, permissible, and forbidden by the Qur'an, the *Hadith*, analogies drawn from these sacred texts, and by a consensus of the Muslim community. In response to the overwhelmingly legalistic character of these discourses, a more spiritually oriented interpretation of the sacred texts popularly known as Sufism developed early in the history of Islam. Many Sufis describe their experience of deeper forms of reality and consciousness or of a more direct experience of the divine through poetic metaphors that emphasize love. These experiences are both sought out and described in many ways, including through poetry, music, or dance and through ecstatic or sober meditations and *dhikr* (remembrance of God) practices.

Sufi thought and practice is very diverse and this diversity is represented in the numerous Sufi brotherhoods, sects, and teachings that exist. Some of these strands came to be interpreted as heretical and dangerous by many Muslims. Nevertheless, various bridges were formed between Sufi and more legalistic strands of Islamic thought, including those by the highly influential scholar and mystic Al-Ghazali (1058–1111). From a website produced by an Islamic group in Spain, Junta Islámica and its WebIslam.org media, LALMA obtained several study materials including Spanish language translations of Al-Ghazali's writings. The documents were downloaded through a landline internet connection. It was a slow and frustrating process, but once completed, the digital text was printed, photocopied, and distributed among LALMA members. LALMA was able to engage Al-Ghazali's writings because they had been made available to them by Spanish translators through internet technologies and because they were interested in learning more about Islamic spirituality.

Members of LALMA also study Arabic, the language of the Qur'an, at their weekly meetings. It is believed that the full meaning of the Qur'an can only be transmitted through the linguistic and tonal qualities of the original Arabic version.[43] Not only is it important to learn Arabic in order to engage the Qur'an's teachings, it is in Arabic that passages are recited during the five ritual prayers Muslims perform each day. Although poetically rewarding, Arabic is a difficult language to learn and many LALMA members struggle with it even after years of training. Instead of mastering the ability to read, write, and converse in Arabic, most LALMA members memorize Arabic pronunciations of Qur'anic passages to recite during prayers. Nevertheless, the weekly Arabic lessons demonstrate the community's level of commitment to their religious education.

This commitment to educating Latinos about Islam is also evident in the group's *dawah* efforts. In order to propagate Islam, both as a religious mandate and to help deter hate crimes against Muslims, the group meets with the Los Angeles Police Department, provides history lectures at public libraries, and participates in interfaith talks. The first time I saw Marta without a veil was at a 2011 interfaith symposium titled "Muslim Neighbors." I had never seen her without a *hijab* prior to the event and was surprised to see her without it then. I knew she did not regularly wear a veil while working as a nurse because she said it felt too cumbersome. Perhaps, I thought, this was an ecumenical gesture designed to dispel stereotypes of forced veiling. After being introduced, Marta stood up and began to describe how she came to embrace Islam. The story was situated in mid-twentieth-century Mexico, where her family's devotion to the church and their faith was intertwined with daily life. She talked about her older sister who became a nun and about her grandmother's piety. She was a good Catholic, Marta told us, morally excellent and religiously devout. And as was the tradition in Mexico, Marta recalled, her grandmother practiced her religious piety as a woman through the cultural optics of modesty. And as the audience imagined Marta's grandmother veiled in early twentieth-century Mexican pueblos, churches and homes, Marta brought us back to the twenty-first-century interfaith dialogue being held at the Catholic University in Los Angeles, California. Her grandmother's veil, Marta explained, was a piece of cloth much like the scarf she was now wearing. She then pulled the scarf over her head. Marta had performed, at the same time and with the same veil, both her grandmother's Catholic piety and her own Islamic one. La Virgin Maria de Guadalupe, Marta went on to say, has been a central and traditional model of women's piety for those of Mexican descent.

LALMA members also share their stories and distribute informational pamphlets at colleges and universities, at prisons and at festivals like the yearly Fiesta Broadway celebration in LA. The Cinco de Mayo fiesta on Broadway celebrates the May 5, 1862, victory of a smaller and poorly equipped Mexican military force at Puebla over the premier French military, which sought to control the region after the Mexican-American War. The fiesta in LA was originally organized and sponsored by patriotic clubs for Mexican migrants in the 1920s but has increasingly come under commercial control.[44] Today it is sponsored by corporations like Telemundo (a Spanish-language broadcasting corporation that televises and provides funds for a large stage and for performing artists) as well as Home Depot, Kmart, Coca-Cola, and others who all rent booths at the annual celebration.

LALMA does not have the resources to rent their own booth at the fiesta, instead the funds are provided by a broader Muslim organization, Why-Islam? In 2011, a *dawah* booth was nestled between corporate giants at the fiesta, it was filled with professionally produced Spanish and English language pamphlets on Islamic teachings, and it was staffed by Latino Muslim volunteer workers. Most of the volunteers were happy with the positive attention their booth received from people who were surprised to learn that there were fellow Latinos who had embraced Islam. One Latino Muslim, however, reported that someone pointed at him and yelled "Osama bin Laden." "I guess it's because of my beard," he said, "I'm used to it, I figure it's because of all the TV they watch." The fiesta had taken place just a few days after bin Laden was killed by US military forces—a news story that generated an inordinate amount of public discourse at the time. The spaces that Latino Muslims occupy are very much influenced by media—and it is LALMA's hope that education will deter the hate speech and crimes that many of its members experience on a regular basis.

LALMA does not have the financial resources to obtain its own space at celebrations like Fiesta Broadway nor for its own regular meetings. Instead, the small group relies on broader Muslim groups for such spaces. There are both positive and negative aspects to being perpetual guests in spaces that "belong" to someone else. LALMA's regular presence at prominent mosques in Los Angeles provides the group with more opportunities to interact, learn from, and cooperate with broader Muslim groups. By networking in this way, the small community of Latino Muslims is able to gain more local visibility and recognition. At a banquet held by the Islamic Shura Council of Southern California in 2012, LALMA was officially recognized and given an award for its *dawah* work within the Latino community in LA. This kind of recognition helps LALMA connect to other intellectual and economic resources from broader Muslim groups, such as access to

Islamic scholars and study materials and the funding of *dawah* events like the Fiesta Broadway booth.

Meeting at borrowed spaces, however, also means that LALMA experiences limited access to their meeting rooms. Further, it has become apparent to LALMA members that the group is sometimes perceived as unnecessarily fracturing the Muslim community, that some Muslims have negative stereotypes of Latinos, and that many worry that Latinos might create a distinct and unacceptable form of Islam. Latino Muslims have been dealing with these issues since the Alianza. Because the majority of LALMA's members and leaders are women, however, the group carefully navigates patriarchal structures within broader Muslim communities regarding these and other concerns.[45]

For example, LALMA protects itself from the critique of possibly deviating from acceptable forms of Islam by having an Islamic scholar sponsor the group as PIEDAD does. It is the sponsor's role to provide teaching and guidance and to make sure the group does not engage in *bid'ah*, religious innovation. The sponsor has been almost invariably male, as most Islamic clergy are, and invariably non-Latino.[46] The sponsor's identity as a religious scholar, as a non-Latino, and as a male provides LALMA with a symbolic counterargument to possible critics within broader Muslim communities. LALMA is thus able to retain a great deal of autonomy by accepting the patriarchal practice of requiring a male scholar of Islam to be responsible for its religious education. An important part of this autonomy is the very act of choosing which male scholar the group will invite to be its sponsor and which offers it will reject. Up until his death in 2010, Dr. Fathi Osman served as LALMA's sponsor. The group felt confident with Dr. Osman, his scholarship and promotion of women's rights—had it not, LALMA would have sought out sponsorship from someone else. For example, when asked by LALMA members during a Q&A session if Muslims can assist family celebrations of non-Muslim events like baptisms, weddings, Christmas, and so on, Dr. Osman responded:

> In my opinion, Islam should not be the cause of division or separation of families. . . . We are happy that Jesus was born. Let's not [waste] time

arguing whether or not Jesus is the son of god or not, if he resurrected or not. Muslims believe that Jesus was a prophet, that his birth was a miracle, that he was born without a father. But family reunions are not the place for serious discussions . . . we do not hide our convictions, but neither do we go out of our way to express them during inappropriate times.[47]

LALMA respected the work of Dr. Osman and understood that he was highly regarded by broader Muslim groups. But even more important, they found his answers to their questions to be both rooted in Islamic texts and reasonable for their particular situation. Limitations regarding meeting spaces thus have important effects on the kind of religious education that Latino Muslims have access to and choose to engage with. These limitations are not, however, perceived as altogether negative, they are always negotiated and are often welcomed by communities with little resources.

Like the Alianza, PIEDAD, and LADO, LALMA has made the historical link between Al-Andalus Islamic Spain and Latino identity central to their work. The group holds month-long seminars, conferences, and lectures led by themselves or invited scholars on various topics on the history and culture of Al-Andalus. The Muslim Empire's golden age and its periods of stagnation and decline are rigorously studied as are the Spanish Reconquista and the persecution of Muslims and Jews during the Spanish Inquisition. LALMA members learn and teach about the tolerance and prejudices that existed within Al-Andalus and also about the disparaging ways its people have been portrayed in Spanish scholarship and culture, in specific history books and in paintings. "Notice how Queen Isabella is on a white horse," explained one LALMA member in reference to a painting by Francisco Pradilla Ortiz titled *La Rendición de Granada* (The surrender of Granada), "and see how the Christian army is brightly illuminated while there is gray cloud over the darkly painted group of Muslims." For many of the Latinos listening to the impromptu art history lesson, specific examples such as these help bring the issue to life: Latino Muslims are connected to a historical and contemporary public relations battle with the reputation of their ethno-religious identity at stake. For all of their differences, Latino Muslims across the United States share an interest in the historical connection between Latinos and Islam. This interest also extends beyond the geographical boundaries that define US territories and into the harder to define frontiers of our digital networks.

Conclusion

The end of the civil rights era, increased diversity, and the proliferation of internet technologies have been integral to the second Latino Muslims wave. PIEDAD, LADO, and LALMA have been shaped by these changes to the American religious landscape; they have provided a bridge between the first and second Latino Muslim wave; and they have themselves also contributed to our changing American religious landscape. PIEDAD, LADO, and LALMA extended the legacy of the Alianza Islámica. Like the Alianza, the second wave of Latino Muslim organizations promoted Islam to Latino audiences in various ways, but especially by linking Latino identity to Islam. In the late 1980s, PIEDAD began meeting in New York and partnered up with Dr. Irving and El-Amin who had also worked with the Alianza. PIEDAD extended its reach to Florida and throughout the East Coast and also amplified its message through internet technologies. Also on the web, a group of tech savvy Latino Muslims from diverse backgrounds began meeting in digital bulletin boards and formed LADO as an online community and network in the mid-1990s. In Los Angeles, a community of mostly Mexican American Muslims borrowed spaces in various mosques to meet and study the Qur'an in Spanish during the late 1990s. Through digital networks, the Los Angeles community obtained Islamic literature translated to Spanish from a group in Spain and together they also promoted the history of Islamic Spain.

The second wave differed from the first in important ways however. PIEDAD, LADO, and LALMA focused almost exclusively on the production, dissemination, and consumption (i.e., studying and discussing) of information. PIEDAD introduced a unique emphasis and engagement with gender and women's issues. With the exception of PIEDAD's

73

Project Downtown, the second wave of Latino Muslim organizations made little effort to develop and participate in social service work. The second wave's willingness to work within rather than separate from broader American Muslim groups was also an important and formative difference. The info-based approach to *dawah*, the reliance on broader Muslim groups, and a changing American religious landscape have been formative differences between the first two waves of Latino Muslims.

It is important to keep in mind that there are no exhaustive explanations of why PIEDAD, LADO, and LALMA developed in the manner that they did. The remaining chapters of this book, for example, deal with other formative aspects of this second wave, including the development and proliferation of reversion stories and the 9/11 factor on media representations of Islam. Reversion stories are popular short autobiographies that describe why individual Latino Muslims embrace Islam. Although many Latino Muslim reversion stories have been written within and influenced by a post-9/11 context, the genre pre-dates the events of 2001 and offers a set of self-produced representations in contrast to news coverage of the group.

CHAPTER THREE

REVERSION STORIES

THE FORM, CONTENT, AND DISSEMINATION OF
A LOGIC OF RETURN

So direct your face toward the religion, inclining to truth.
[Adhere to] the fitrah of Allah upon which He has
created [all] people.
No change should there be in the creation of Allah.
That is the correct religion, but most of the people do not know.

—*Qur'an 30:30 (translation by Sahih International)*

If anyone were to ask me when I became Muslim, I guess the only
feasible answer would be that I was born Muslim, but just wasn't
aware of it. We are all born into a state of Islam.

—*Themise Cruz in "Becoming a Muslim"*

The production and dissemination of reversion stories, short autobiographies about how an individual Latino came to embrace Islam, have played a pivotal role in the development of Latino Muslim identity. They are titled "reversion" in opposition to the term "conversion." They are framed as a return to something previous and familiar rather than as a turning to something new and foreign. Stories help to shape and make sense of our experiences. Some leave us with lasting impressions that become a lens for how we see the world and ourselves. Others provide us with a momentary sight, a brief glimpse of how the world may appear to others. Stories give us guidelines as to what is and is not possible. They inform us with great detail or mystify us with profound silence. They help us to think about difficult decisions and they help us try to make sense of painful and dangerous situations.

Whatever else stories might be, it is clear to the authors of the stories presented in this chapter that they can be exceptionally powerful and should be nurtured and shaped rather than abandoned or forgotten. These stories build communities. They help forge new visions for navigating the challenges encountered in America cityscapes. The stories are also a form of social capital. They prompt a sense of dignity. They produce a social commodity traded for material goods in the information economy. And they engender public conversations about so-called minority groups in America. Stories are potent, but so too are the gatekeepers of such stories.

This chapter explores a particular narrative genre that has emerged within Latino Muslim communities in the United States—the reversion story, an individual's retelling of how they came to embrace Islam. The narrative structure of these stories is partly rooted within an American tradition that places individuals and their free will at the center. The content, however, is filled with historical specificities that reveal a growing and rich diversity in the United States. They are also infused with broad themes regarding alienation and how it should be engaged. Reversion stories reframe the spiritual nature of Latinos and pull a forgotten past into a present in order to help shape a new identity, a new way of being Latino, Muslim, and American.

Although there are many studies that try to answer the question of why people convert to different religions, I focus instead on the mediation of Latinos embracing Islam, the strategic act of translating experiences into stories. The first book-length study of Latino Muslims focused almost exclusively on reversion stories as a form of postcolonial identity formation. It was written by Hjamil Martinez-Vazquez in 2010 and was titled *Latina/o y Musulmán: The Construction of Latina/o Identity among Latina/o Muslims in the United States*. In it, Martinez-Vazquez engages Latino Muslim stories through a postcolonial analysis of identity and through Rambo and Farhadian's social-psychological stages of religious change (the seven stages are: context, crisis, quest, encounter, interaction, committing, and consequences). Rather than approach reversion stories as data for understanding psychological, metaphysical, or social processes, as Martinez-Vazquez does, I approach reversion stories as discursive techniques for the construction of the self.[1] They are publicly shared identity narratives that creatively constitute subjects as members of a developing community.

This is therefore an examination not of the motives for conversation or of the direct experience of conversion per se, but rather of the narrative retelling of those motives and experiences. A discursive analysis allows for a more appropriate approach to the kind of data that is available for understanding Latino Muslim conversion (i.e., stories published on the web and in newspapers). "Given the infinite possibilities of motive, or combination of motives," writes Yasin Dutton in *Conversion to Islam: The Qur'anic Paradigm*, "it is, ultimately, impossible to explain why people become Muslims."[2] Further, Lewis Rambo, a prominent theorist of religious conversion, writes: "All conversions (even Saul's on the road to Damascus) are mediated through people, institutions, communities and groups."[3]

In addition to examining the form and content of reversion stories, it is important to shed light on their discursive functions as well. Some hope that the stories will explain the causes of a transition and thus help predict future trends or shed light on broader demographic shifts that take place in America's religious landscape. Others hope the stories will provide inspirational and instructional models to help others achieve a similar transition. Still others hope the stories will help unite a group of people to one another, to foster and cement a communal identify and life.

The first section of this chapter includes three complete and unedited reversion stories by Khadijah Rivera (president of PIEDAD), Marta Galedary (president of LALMA), and Juan Galvan (director of LADO). These stories are then followed with an analysis of the genre's form, content, and discursive relevance. In particular, I argue that rather than explain why some Latinos are converting to Islam, reversion stories: (1) are a form *dawah* outreach; (2) creatively respond to critiques that Latino and Islamic identities are incompatible or foreign to one another; and (3) help to form and shape the contours of Latino Muslim communities.

My Hispanic Muslim Legacy

By Khadijah RiveraWhat Islam Means to Me: To Be Qualified Is to Know GOD?

I was raised as a Roman Catholic from a very strict and practicing Hispanic family. To even think of leaving the aristocratic Catholics was considered a sin. Actually having been raised by nuns in private schools taught me that one did not have the luxury of questioning the Bible or even the Catechism that was engraved in our memory banks as children. I once had the audacity to ask my teacher why we did not study the Bible; her answer was a blunt, You might misinterpret it. As an adult I once asked the very same question of priest, and once again I received a similar response. In other words, they had led me to believe that only qualified officials of the church teach and understand God's Word. How sad, I thought; soon after I began to search for an answer.

The strongest component of Catholicism was the belief in the Trinity. It believed that there were three gods of equal weight in the heavens, and that upon birth we inherited a mortal sin. So, right from the start we were sinners and needed repentance or a sacrament to clear away this sin. As a parent it was hard not to question if the smile of innocence behind an infant could hide a deadly sin. What if the infant died before performing the Catholic rite of Baptism? Did that mean he/she would go to hell? And if Jesus Christ had not died in the cross for the sins of man, did that mean that we would all have fire as our ultimate destiny?

Reverting to Islam would be complicated by my childhood training that Jesus Christ was my savior and salvation. To pray to anyone but him would be blasphemy. I therefore studied several religions when I left my church and its rigid teachings. But they were all Christian and not much different from the original one. Of course they all believed that the papal aristocracy was nonsense and I praised them for that. But they could not justify Jesus Christ in a sensible nor logical manner. Point in fact: ask three Christians of different denominations to explain the Trinity or better yet, ask them if Jesus is the son of GOD. Ask them what version of the Bible they read, and you will also find astonishing variations. I actually turned away from religion completely for many years and became a leftist. I left the religious dogma and found a replacement.

A REPLACEMENT TO RELIGIOUS DOGMA?

In my college years I opened up to a radical way of saving the world. I believed that if we could promote change in the political realm, then we could bring equality and economics that would ultimately change and save the physical world. I was an American activist going from marches to study groups of Dialectical Materialism, Maoism and Socialism. All this journey proved was that I was still empty for it left a gap in my very existence. I had one thing in common with the Christians and one thing opposite the ones I was attempting to emulate: I loved God! I just needed a vehicle to surrender.

For years I watched closely the events in Iran and yet the student movement that I was following could not afford me a way to make change in that country. I joined student marches and met with like-minded idealists. While we sat in brainstorm sessions planning our next poster spread in Manhattan, an old man sitting on a rug in Paris dictated a revolution. He told the dictator Shah of Iran to leave because he was coming back to Iran and guess what, he left! I began to study this man's political assessment, but the more I read about what he proposed to resolve in Iran the more I understood the religion of Islam. At no time was I looking for a new religion as I was a diehard Christian who was not even practicing. But this became a turning point in my life. I had to evolve as a human, in order to evolve as a Muslim.

SURRENDER TO GOD

On October 22, 1983, I took my vows of submission as a Sunni Muslim with sincerity to ONE GOD. Allahu Akbar (God is great). I have been a practicing Muslim for over twenty-two years and have never regretted it. In fact, in the face of tyranny and prejudice I have become stronger and more resolved to not only raise a family of Muslims but also to become a Daiee and spread the good word [of Islam] among Hispanics. After the tragedy of 9/11, many Muslims removed their veils for fear of assaults. I was destined to die as a Muslim if need be, for my only defense was faith! Alhamdulilah (all praise be to God), neither did I remove the veil nor hide. I stood up and went on live television to speak to Hispanics on Telemundo on the noted Christina Show from Miami. I had become a modest but resonant Muslimah. Rather than rollover, I made an uproar about the injustices done to Muslims.

The faith of Islam has brought me strength in the face of adversity and an inner peace which I never had. It was not difficult for my extended family to accept my new found faith. But for my immediate family it was very difficult. I lost all my non-Muslim friends that I had grown up with, but found an extended family in Islam. I no longer pray to a saint in order to request intervention with Jesus Christ. I now understand that if I follow the true teachings of all the prophets and the Ten Commandments that there can only be ONE GOD. Thou shalt not bear false gods before me. Therefore, my destiny with Islam is fulfilled. I worship Allah directly, as it should be.[4]

How Allah Found Me in Texas
by Juan Galvan

In high school, I received a jolt to my long-held belief when a Christian friend told me that the Holy Trinity was not true and that Jesus was not God. "He was wrong" I told myself. Jesus had to be God. God and humanity were disconnected by the sin committed by Adam and Eve. God sent his only 'begotten' son to die because He loved us so much. Because only God forgives, Jesus had to be God. I even had the Bible quotes to prove it! Indeed, being a devout Roman Catholic Christian, I have read almost the entire Bible. In high school, I was a lecturer, usher, Eucharistic minister, and CCD [The Confraternity of Christian Doctrine] teacher. I am the godfather for a nephew and a niece. The idea that Jesus was God made much sense.

I am a Mexican-American who comes from a modest background. I spent my adolescent and teenage years in such small Texas Panhandle towns as Quitaque, Turkey, Lakeview, and Memphis. None of them has a mall, a movie theater, or a McDonald's. Memphis, Texas, population 2,300, proudly proclaims itself "The Cotton Capital of the World." In Memphis, if you hear a fire truck or police car, either your neighbor's house is on fire or your neighbor is being arrested. Growing up in small communities gave me much appreciation for the simplicity in God's creations.

I graduated from Memphis High School in Memphis, Texas in 1994. I did well in high school and would attend Texas Tech University in Lubbock. In 1998 I began attending the University of Texas at Austin. I graduated with a bachelor's degree in MIS [Management Information Systems] in December 2001. Not bad for a kid who had to hoe cotton most of his junior high and high school summers to pay for his clothes and school supplies! My dad was a cotton ginner. Now, he is a custodian at a junior high school in Pampa, Texas. I had eight siblings, but in 2000 my 17-year old sister died in a car wreck.

I have always had respect for other religions. I would often attend other Christian churches and join interfaith Bible study groups. While in one such group, I told my friend Chris that I was a Catholic. Chris blatantly told me that the Catholic Church was "a false doctrine." As you can imagine, I defended my religion. Chris accused me of worshipping Mary, Saints, and the Pope. I argued that we only revere them. Around this time, I happened to see a man praying. His knees, hands, and forehead were touching the ground, and he was barefoot. After he finished praying, I introduced myself to him. He said his name was Armando, and that he was a Muslim. I thought to myself: "Ok, freaky, you're Muslim. You can't be Muslim. What's this Hispanic guy doing praying to Allah?" He later told me that Spain was Muslim for over 700 years and that thousands of Spanish words have Arabic roots. The ruins of mosques with Qur'anic writings have been found in Cuba, Mexico, Texas, and Nevada.

Most importantly, Armando spoke to me about Islam. I began to realize that my reverence for Mary and Saints was much more than mere reverence. Chris was right. However, we were both worshipping Jesus! Armando said that Jesus was only a prophet and that nothing and no one is worthy of worship but Allah. Allah literally means "The God" in English and "El Dios" in Spanish. Muhammad (pbuh) perfected religion. Islam is the true, universal religion of God.

Many of my questions were answered! What is the purpose of life? How can the Father be the Son? Why can't God just forgive anyone He wants? What happens to babies who die before baptism? In Qur'an 5:83, Allah states: "And when they (who call themselves Christian) listen to what has been sent down to the Messenger, you see their eyes overflowing with tears because of the truth they have recognized. They say: 'Our Lord! We believe; so write us down among the witnesses.'"

Indeed, my eyes overflowed with tears as I read that verse. Yet I did not embrace Islam until three years after meeting Armando, because I did not want to change. A struggle occurs within everyone, everyday, and everywhere. We struggle to attain what is most important for us. By embracing Islam, we tell Allah (swt) that He is most important and that we are prepared to struggle to do what is right and to avoid what is wrong. I am a Mexican-American Muslim.[5]

KHADIJA'S REVERT STORY
BY MARTA FELICITAS KHADIJA GALEDARY

I embraced Islam in December 1983. Mexican born; became U.S. Citizen in 1987.

During my college years in Mexico City, I was influenced by Marxism, existentialism, feminism, and leftist friends. These relationships and books took me away completely from my strong Catholic beliefs to the point that I stopped believing in God. I thought I could survive with no God and no rituals. I found myself lost, confused, and living an extremely conflictive and painful life. I could not find the reason for my existence nor mission in this world. I was influenced by extreme feminist ideas against motherhood.

In the summer of 1981 while living in Mexico City, I travelled to England to practice my English. At this point God had reserved for me the opportunity to meet the most important people in my life: Hassan, Ismael, and Kitar Muslim students from Brunei (in Malaysia).

These three students never talked to me about Islam. The most important factor that attracted my attention was the way I was treated as a woman, with respect, kindness, and a clean attitude. I had the feeling of being safe with them. The only conversation we had on one occasion was about God. Since I told them that I believe in God, they adopted me as a Muslim, without me knowing anything about Islam.

As I returned to Mexico, I kept in touch with my Muslim friends. I received a copy of *Islam in Focus* and I started reading. I memorized the Shahada and I always sought refuge from Allah in dangerous situation. I was amazed to experience the solution of my problems after I recited the *Shahada*, at this point I still did not understand Islam nor the meaning of the *Shahada*.

Later on, I decided to travel to the United States on a summer vacation in 1983. I enrolled in a public adult school to continue practicing my English. I met more Muslims from Turkey and Bulgaria. Also, I became friendly with a Muslima teacher of Jewish background who was married to Senegalese Muslim. I asked to be taken to a mosque, since I was reading a book on Islam. The first time I stepped in a mosque was very emotional; with mixed feelings of peace and fear, my heart started beating faster.

I attended introduction to Islam classes for non-Muslims and new Muslims for several months.

In December 1983, close to Christmas time, I gave my testimony of faith by saying "I bear witness that there is only one God and Muhammad is His last messenger." My English teacher was my witness. I was in tears during my prayers. Finally, I had found peace in my heart; I knew that Allah was with me, I knew what my role in this world was and the reason for my existence. I have returned to the One God and I will never be lost again.

Islam has given me a new life and has enlightened my way of life and thinking. The more that I learn about Islam the more I strengthen my faith in the One God and Muhammad as the last messenger. I have embraced the duty of sharing my experience to the large population of non-Muslim Latinos by providing them with information on Islam and making them aware that the history of religion does not stop with Christianity.

I also enlighten them to the fact that many Latinos have Muslim ancestors and the proof is that many Latinos have Middle Eastern and North African features. The time has come for Latinos to find out the truth about their Muslim origins, a truth that has been denied to Latinos for over five hundred years. With these emotions and newborn ideas, four Latino Muslims and I started forming LALMA in 1999.[6]

CONVERSION AND/OR REVERSION STORIES

Conversion stories have served a formative role in the discursive creation of America. Eighteenth-century conversion stories by New England Puritans have been identified as perhaps the first distinctively American literary form.[7] These were short autobiographies that captured the difficulty of the voyage to and life in early America. Most were produced to authenticate the author's spiritual nature and to gain acceptance into the religious and political life of the New England colony.[8] The stories thus shared a similar form, content, and fulfilled similar discursive roles to one another. They have also, however, provided historically specific data or mediated experiences unique to each author. Verbal, written, audibly, and visually recorded testimonies of religious change, like those by New England Puritans, have been central to the stories we tell about America. They are part of our ongoing struggle for civil and religious liberty and equality. They have described and shaped the ways in which we live out our individuality and our communal lives. Nevertheless, historians and other scholars are increasingly weary of identifying a single American story, identity, or character. This cautious approach is a prudent one. Instead, we are much more prepared now to describe the identity narratives of specific groups rather than of the entire nation. Latino Muslim reversion stories, like the eighteenth-century Puritan conversion stories, serve a formative role in the ongoing creation, a discursive creation, of a much more diverse America.

Reversion stories are shaped by broader testimonial narrative forms. They are short autobiographies usually less than 1,000 words in length. They are written from a close first-person perspective. Most begin with an invocation and all provide a brief description of the author's background. The place and relationship through which the protagonist encounters Islam is then described. This encounter is followed by a crisis of meaning that prompts a serious consideration of Islam. Ultimately, however, the protagonist is responsible for their culminating decision to take *shahadah*, the proclamation of faith which initiates the individual into the abode of Islam. Despite the influence of broad narrative forms found in religious and American testimonials, Latino Muslim reversion stories also articulate historical specificities. Additionally, reversion stories have been used to accomplish distinctive religious, discursive, and communal tasks in the development of Latino Muslim identity.

INVOCATION

"In The Name of Allah, The Most Gracious, The Most Merciful," begins Ali's reversion story *A Chicano's Story of Becoming a Muslim*. Not all reversion stories include the *basmala*, invocation, like Ali's. Those that do, however, follow a common Muslim practice. Reciting the *basmala* and other common Arabic phrases are both religious acts of piety and performative acts of belonging. *As-salamu alaykum* (peace be upon you) and the response *wa alaykumu s-salam* (may peace be upon you as well!) is a common greeting and parting expression used between Muslims. Many also follow up their use of the prophet's name with a form of *alayhi as-salām* (peace be upon him) and in English writing will often add PBUH as an abbreviation. In Latino Muslim circles, the Spanish phrase "que la paz sea con el" has also gained some traction. "Just as that pattern [i.e., the *basmala*] is woven into the pattern of simple activities as a form of reminder," writes Michael Sells in *Approaching the Qur'an*, "so 'Praise be to God' (al-ḥamdu lillāh) has become part of everyday speech. It is used after any good news or any praise, and as a response to the greeting 'How are you?' "[9] The *basmala* is found at the beginning of all but one of the chapters in the Qur'an. It is a request for God to bless an act, journey, or event. Many Muslims recite it before beginning their daily tasks, taking a drive, preparing or eating a meal, making a speech, taking an exam, and so on.

85

The *basmala* is also itself an act of worship. It is an oral and public proclamation that God alone is capable of insuring a good outcome and that it is therefore God who should be acknowledged for any good that may come from the act, journey, or event being blessed by the invocation. In this way, the *basmala* is similar to a common Christian invocation: *en el nombre de Cristo Jesus*, in the name of Jesus Christ. For many Latinos, the audible invocation of Jesus can have a powerful effect. Charismatic Christians will often use the words to conjure a miracle, ward off evil spirits, or cast out demons. For Latinos who transition from Christianity to Islam, the *basmala* offers a bridge that facilitates the move.

Galedary often describes the *basmala* as her little (or brief) "magical words." The words are powerful for her because they conjure up God's intervention and are spiritually and psychologically transformative. Galedary will often recommend and teach others to recite "b-ismi-llāhi r-raḥmāni r-raḥīmi," "In The Name of God, The Most Gracious, The Most Merciful," before boarding a plane, being interviewed for a job, and before beginning any other important or dangerous endeavor. She often recounts how these words have helped her by providing additional emotional and physical support. The *basmala* helps many Latino Muslims in their transition from Christianity to Islam. It is a familiar way of requesting divine aid and of worshiping God, even if the Islamic invocation has distinct aspects to it.

The *basmala* differs from the Christian invocation in the characteristics or attributes of God that it emphasizes. It is Allah/God who is called upon rather than the name of *Cristo Jesus*. Additionally, the Islamic invocation includes two of the names or attributes of God from an Islamic tradition which holds that there are ninety-nine. At one of the LALMA's Qur'anic study sessions, the group dedicated over an hour to learning about the difference between the two names, *Ar Rahman*, the Most Gracious, and *Ar Rahim*, the Most Merciful. These are the two names or attributes of God invoked in the *basmala*. Both Grace (sometimes translated as Compassion) and Mercy are capitalized in Ali's reversion story because he understands each not as simply adjectives, but as proper nouns, they are two of the ninety-nine names of God in Islam.[10]

These attributes or names of God, should not, however, be understood as composing different parts of God. Instead, the exceedingly important doctrine of *Tawhīd*, the Oneness of God, renders God not only as unique and as having no counterparts, but also as indivisible. One of God's names or attributes cannot be considered apart from another, they are one and the same and together the collection is meant to help believers better understand and describe the Oneness of God.[11] The modern poet and philosopher Muhammad Iqbal interpreted the doctrine of *Tawhīd* as a critique of the separation between the secular and sacred.[12] The doctrine of the oneness of God and the correlated view that Islam is not simply a private religion but a way of life inspired the Alianza Islámica's critique of separating spirituality from social service and political activism.

From the outset, the *basmala* frames the reversion story as an Islamic, religious, and public performance. Ali is performing a prayer of supplication; he is requesting God to bless the act of writing. He is also disseminating his reversion story as an act of pious obedience to inform others about Islam; it is a form of *dawah* work. The *basmala* is also an act of worship, requesting that any good that may come from the story be attributed to God. Lastly, Ali's *basmala* frames the story as an Islamic one by calling on and worshiping God the Most Gracious, the Most Merciful, and not on *Cristo Jesus*.

THE ROLE OF BACKGROUND

After the invocation, reversion stories almost always begin by establishing how the author self identifies:

"Mexican born," writes Marta Galedary in her reversion story, "I became [a] U.S. Citizen in 1987."

"My background," writes Juan Galvan, "I am a Mexican-American who comes from a modest background."

"I'm a 31 year old Mexican born in America," writes Ali, "or as some would say a Chicano."

"My story begins at my birthplace, El Salvado," Walter 'Abdul-Walee' Gomez.

"To begin with, I am of Latin American descent," Juan Alverado.

"I was born in . . . Ecuador," Monica.

First and foremost, the background information provided in reversion stories establishes the genre as Latino stories both written by and about individuals who claim descent from Latin America, Central America, Mexico, and Caribbean Islands where Spanish is spoken and for whom the United States is home. Further, the authors often link their place of descent to their religious background:

> "I was born in a Catholic family in Ecuador," writes Monica, "they [her family] sent me to a Catholic high school."

> "Typically, like other Latinos," writes Alverado, "I was born into the Catholic faith."

> "Catholic and Protestantism are the leading religions in Latin America," writes Abdul-Wallee Gomez, "so these are reasonable religions for any Latin American to convert to."

A close relationship between place and spirituality and between national and religious identity are implied but not critically examined in the narratives. Instead, the author's background, placed at the beginning of the story, brings uncritical attention to a connection between race and religion.[13] This places the story in terrain that most readers can experience as familiar and intelligible. The connection between race and religion is thus presented as a natural linkage. The importance of the story's inclusion of background information is further underscored by what is absent. Most stories are silent on issues regarding the author's age, city of residence, vocation, social and economic class, and so on. They say nothing about the author's interests and characteristics. Instead, the background information is focused on establishing the author as Latino and therefore also as Christian prior to their embrace of Islam. This widely accepted view, that race and religion are somehow causally connected, is brought into focus early on in the narrative only to later have the "Latino therefore Christian" narrative shattered into more diverse fragments.

SPATIAL MODES OF CONTACT

Reversion stories offer a narrative bridge for readers to move beyond the dominant "Latino therefore Christian" paradigm. Often, the stories are presented or interpreted as causal explanations of the protagonist's transition from Christianity to Islam. As such, they are mined for critical narrative moments such as the resolution of a crisis in order to translate these moments as causal explanations.

When approached as causal explanations, it is easy to conclude that the only significance of the reversion story is its answer to the question: Why are Latinos converting to Islam? Such a reading would yield a wide variety of conclusions, including that Latinos convert to Islam because of the increasing ethnic, racial, and religious diversity in America's metropolitan areas; because Latinas are increasingly marrying Muslim men; and because Latinos are increasingly dissatisfied with Catholicism. In as much as the authors provide such explanations, they express more of a fuzzy logic, that is, they describe one event that may have not come about without a previous one. These descriptions, however, fail to sufficiently explain all of or perhaps even the main causes of the sequence.[14] Rather than mining reversion stories for causal explanations of why Latinos convert to Islam, I propose these same narrative moments be approached as necessary modes of contact and not as sufficient explanations of why Latinos choose to embrace Islam. When approached in this manner, reversion stories include: (1) spatial, (2) relational, and (3) emotional modes of contact with Islam.

In Ali's *A Chicano's Story of Becoming a Muslim*, contact with Islam is initiated within an apartment while sampling marijuana from a stranger. "One day a friend of mine told me that he knew where to get some good marijuana," writes Ali,

> I agreed to check it out. We arrived and went inside this apartment there were a couple of people inside, we sat around and talked for a while and sampled the weed. My friend and I bought some and were getting ready to leave when my friend said one of the guys there invited us to his apartment to give him a book. We left for this guy's apartment when we got there, he

89

gave my friend a book and asked him to read it, and said that it might help him out with his problems in life. On the way home I asked my friend to show me the book that the guy gave him, it was the Qur'an.[15]

Although Ali did not know it at the time, one of the individuals in the first apartment house was a Muslim. It is likely that Latinos come into contact with Muslims on many occasions without even realizing it. It is also significant that Ali came into contact with a Muslim while engaging in an activity prohibited by US federal law. And though there are some Muslims who maintain that it is *halal* or Islamically permissible to smoke marijuana even if it is discouraged, most would agree that it should not be used as a means for propagating Islam. Ali expresses his experience and belief that even in the unlikeliest of places, like an apartment where he was "sampling some weed," your life can be reoriented in dramatic ways.

Reversion stories like Ali's reveal that Latinos come into contact with Muslims in residential spaces, in schools and universities, in malls, on street corners, and even within digital spaces. They help us understand not only where contact first occurred for the author, but where it can occur for others yet unfamiliar with Islam. These spatial modes of contact indeed reveal historically specific instances of America's growing diversity and the resulting exchanges between such diversity. This diversity, however, is not a sufficient or exhaustive explanation of why some Latinos who dwell in the same spaces as Muslims and come into contact with one another choose to embrace Islam while others do not.

RELATIONAL MODES OF CONTACT

Relationships constitute another important mode of contact between Latinos and Muslims. Ali first encountered the Qur'an through someone he had only met once, while buying marijuana. In contrast to Ali's casual encounter, 'Abdul-Walee' Gomez describes contact through a close friend he had made in high school. "The football team was not interested in freshmen only but in Latinos in general. We were terrorized so bad that we used to hide in bathrooms. . . . In the middle of

the year we formed a Gang to protect ourselves."[16] The gang stayed
together even after high school. Then, three members of the gang were
stabbed at a club and Gomez and his old high school friend started
looking for revenge. They eventually found the rival gang members,
"We started to get ready and I said to my buddies to run, because several of them pointed guns at us, so we ran and I was too drunk to run
so I got caught by six of them. They beat me severely, kicked me with
their boots and hit me with theirs fists all over my face and body."[17]
After their dramatic and violent experience, his good high school buddy
started searching for a different way of life.

> That same friend who was with me at the train shooting and the night-
> club started to become more aware of life. After this incident, he started
> learning about different doctrines. His philosopher was Carl Marx [sic],
> his sociology was communism, and his theology was Islam. To me, he
> was becoming aware of life, and I myself started to search but in the
> Protestant church. . . . My friend started preaching about his thoughts
> and beliefs and I told him that my love for the Protestant church was
> growing more so he could leave me alone. I told him Jesus is my teacher;
> not a black man named Elijah Muhammad or Farrakhan.[18]

Several important elements stand out from the relational mode of contact described in Gomez's story. First, it reveals a complex and hidden
web of interconnectivity. His friend, it seems only starts to "preach
about" Islam after his near death experience. And the references to
Elijah Muhammad and Farrakhan also reveal that it was a particular
form of Islam, the NOI, that Gomez was being introduced to. However,
because we are never told how Gomez's friend himself first came into
contact with the NOI, we can only speculate. Perhaps he was raised
as a Muslim, or had learned about Islam from another close friend, a
relative, a coworker, maybe from a casual or infrequent acquaintance,
or from someone he had met on just one occasion. Was it before or
after the near death experience? Did he first learn about Islam in the
school they went to, in their hometown, or while traveling elsewhere?
It is their friendship that connects the two to Islam in the narrative.

However, much of the interconnectivity to other groups and networks of Muslims and Muslim communities beyond this friendship is absent from the story, though it is certainly implied.

Second, unlike an encounter with a stranger, most will read the friendship described in 'Abdul-Walee' Gomez's story as a mode of contact that is more likely to have a profound and potentially life-changing impact. The friendship had been forged while working together to survive what Gomez describes as race-based terrorism while in high school. The friendship had endured beyond the public school and for many readers could be interpreted as exerting a strong influence over Gomez's decision to embrace Islam. Indeed, it this kind of reasoning (i.e., that certain kinds of relationships will compel Latinos to convert) that has led many commentators to conclude that Latinas are converting to Islam because they are marrying Muslim men.

Even though there is to be no compulsion in matters of religion according to the Qur'an (2:256), Latinas who marry Muslim men encounter Islam through a relational mode that may seem to exert a profound influence over their decision to embrace Islam. However, through this kind or reasoning couldn't we consider Latinas who convert because of marriage de facto converts the moment they agree to marry a Muslim man? Even if this was sound reasoning, which it is not, we would be left with several questions that are not addressed, questions having to do with why Latinas are marrying Muslim men in the first place. I suspect answers to these kinds of questions will be as complex and varied as the answers given to the question of why are Latinos in general converting to Islam. Both questions are similarly misguided, distracting, and problematic. Because there are many Latinas who choose not to embrace Islam after marrying a Muslim, because the Qur'an mandates that no one be forced to accept Islam, because there is a lack of empirical evidence, and because the overwhelming majority of Latina Muslimahs I have talked to find this explanation of their experience highly reductive and offensive, it is more appropriate to conclude that close friendships and marriage constitute important modes of contact rather than sufficient explanations of conversion.

EMOTIONAL MODES OF CONTACT

Although spatial and relational modes of contact play important roles in reversion stories, it is the emotional or existential modes of contact that the authors themselves underscore as essential. The state in question is that of dissatisfaction. Almost all of the authors describe feeling increasingly dissatisfied with Christianity prior to their embrace of Islam. Often, the authors describe this state of mind as being prompted by critical questions regarding Christian doctrines and practices that are for them either left unanswered, insufficiently addressed, or are explained in unacceptable terms. In a series of scathing questions, Juan Galvan asks "How can the Father be the Son? Why can't God just forgive anyone He wants? What happens to babies who die before baptism?" The questions are presented as critiques of Christianity and its inability to answer them. The only acceptable alternative, for the reversion story authors, is Islam.

Another set of questions express the author's experience with a more general form of existential angst. Rather than critique specific Christian doctrines or practices, these questions express feelings of hopelessness and of meaninglessness. In most reversion stories, these kinds of feelings are presented as being prompted by a life-changing or life-threatening event. Recall that in Gomez's story it is his fight with rival gang members, his experience of running away from assailants who had pointed guns at him and his friends, and who had physically assaulted him and left him for dead that prompted a dissatisfaction with his life. Feeling forced to re-evaluate their previous worldviews, the protagonists either fall into a state of crushing bewilderment or begin to search for more satisfying answers. Although Gomez had initially turned toward Protestant Christianity in his search for meaning, his close friend had turned toward Islam. And because Gomez was still seeking, and because his friend meant so much to him, the narrative implies that he was nevertheless open to his friend's "preaching" of Islam.

Wrestling with death, like Gomez had, is a prominent feature of many reversion stories. "As I was driving one Saturday morning," writes Juan Galvan, "a red truck moved into my lane. I had no time to react; I found myself hitting it. I could have died. My left lung collapsed and I needed a chest tube to survive. I had broken ribs and a broken arm." The near death experience prompted Galvan to reevaluate his life. "Under these circumstances, my priorities shifted from the worldly to the spiritual." Galvan describes this reevaluation as "an intense desire to embrace truth."[19]

Themise Cruz also includes an encounter with death, though not of her own but of a loved one. Like Galvan, Cruz describes the experience as prompting a similar desire for truth:

> My mother died when I was 23, and all the money, my home, my education, the cars, jewelry, they all meant nothing. I tried to go on with life as though her death was just another event. But it was at this point that I could no long ignore Allah. If I went on my current state of mind, then my mother's life had been in vain. What purpose did she serve here on this earth? To what greater significance did her life have in this world? I could not believe that she meant so little. It was at this point that I began to hunger for this knowledge, and I opened all of myself to Allah.[20]

Cruz's and Galvan's experiences with death led them to desire or hunger for knowledge and truth. They were searching for knowledge that would satisfy an absence, what Cruz describes as a "vast hole that was in my heart." The crisis of dissatisfaction adds symbolic significance or interpretive connections to the other two modes of contact and vice versa.[21] The places and relationships through which the authors encounter Islam foreshadow the religion as an important part of the sequence of events leading up to the crisis and resolution. Some stories directly describe the spatial and emotional modes of contact as providence, as a form of God's mercy, as an attempt to remind the protagonist of their purpose in life. It is dissatisfaction, however, that is presented as a crisis. Like a dissonant tone, we are thrust into a situation that is not just a reminder but is a demand for a resolution.

The crisis is an interruption, a wakeup call, it is an imperative realization that failure to reorient the direction their life has taken will have disastrous consequences. In *Islam: The Straight Path*, John L. Esposito writes: "For Muhammad, Islam was not a new faith but the restoration of the true faith (*iman*), a process that required the reformation of an ignorant, deviant society. Repentance, or the heeding of God's warning, required turning away from the path of unbelief and turning toward or returning to the straight path (*sharia*) or law of God."[22] The crisis thus serves as a reminder, it is a call to the individual to reorient themselves onto the straight path. In the form of a crisis, the interruption in reversion stories puts a tremendous of weight on the narrative by symbolically connecting the crisis to both internal narrative elements (e.g., spatial and relational modes of contact) and to Qur'anic metaphors (e.g., restoration and the straight path).

Dissatisfaction stemming from critical and existential questions not only does the work of making the rejection of Christianity and embrace of Islam more intelligible, it drives the narrative forward. In a state of dissatisfaction, the protagonist is either rendered as hopelessly lost or as lost but seeking. Whether they are in need of a jump start or direction, contact with Islam provides a resolution to the crisis made necessary by the narrative form. Although the authors will often present this kind of conflict resolution as the principle explanation for their embrace of Islam, during more thorough conversations with several authors, including Juan Galvan and Marta Galedary, it became clear that their own understanding of the process was much more complex than what was captured in their own reversion stories. Nevertheless, when friends, family, acquaintances, researchers, and journalists ask why they "converted," a question that is problematic in that the request for a reductive answer is implied, it is the emotional mode of contact, the narrative crisis, that is most often offered by Latino Muslims as the principle reason for why they embraced Islam. However, whether understood as a necessary or sufficient explanation of conversion, it is clear that dissatisfaction creates a narrative moment of crisis, one that sets the stage for the ritual enactment of the *shahadah*.

THE MOMENT OF EMBRACE

"In December 1983, close to Christmas time," writes Galedary,

I gave my testimony of faith by saying "I bear witness that there is only one God and Muhammad is His last messenger." My English teacher was

95

my witness. I was in tears during my prayers. Finally, I had found peace in my heart; I knew that Allah was with me, I knew what my role in this world was and the reason for my existence.[23]

The *shahadah* is a public proclamation that "there is no god but God." It is whispered into the ears of infants and should be the last words spoken before death. It is also an initiation ritual. It marks a redirection, a fresh start, a wiping away of all previous sins. Muslims do not believe that human nature is predisposed toward sin. There is no doctrine of original sin in Islam. Instead, it is believed that humans sin because they are forgetful by nature.[24] People are said to be easily distracted by material goods, careers, and relationships and therefore constantly forget what is most important: God. To stay on the straight path, people need constant reminders. Like the crisis in reversion stories that serves as a reminder, and like the Pillars of Islam (the proclamation of faith, prayer, charity, fasting, and pilgrimage), the *shahadah* is also a form of *zikr* or remembrance. It is a publically witnessed testimony of an individual's commitment to a morally disciplined life.

After taking *shahadah*, an individual is required to pray five times a day. These prayers will themselves include a recitation of the Qur'an's opening chapter, Al-Fatiha (The Opening):

> In the name of God, the Merciful and Compassionate: praise belongs to God, the Lord of the Worlds, the Merciful, the Compassionate; Master of the Day of Judgment, You do we worship and You do we call on for help; guide us on the Straight Path, the path of those whom You have blessed, not of those who earn your anger nor those who go astray.[25]

Prescribed by the Qur'an and exemplified by the Prophet, the prayers are a remedy to a sort of moral amnesia. Their recitation will conjure up a remembrance of what is most important and thereby guide the individual on to "the Straight Path." The community who witnessed the *shahadah* will support each other, invite each other to prayer, meditate on the teachings of the Qur'an and help each other to live a good life.

For Muslims who proclaim the *shahadah* as an initiation ritual, it is a public reclamation of an essential truth that had been forgotten or ignored. It is also a testimony of how the author has recovered their purpose in life and evidence that the narrative crisis has reached a resolution. Finally, the *shahadah* also marks a kind of inclusion into a family of believers. It is an embrace of and into the *ummah* or community of Muslims and the beginning of a new narrative not contained within the reversion story. "I could smell the mercy and the sweetness of heaven, felt the presence of God in my torn, sick heart," writes Gomez, "I felt a clean brightness in my new way of life. My life was ready for the next journey on earth, the journey to Paradise."[26] Equipped with a sense of moral direction, hope, and joy, the authors conclude their reversion stories by foregrounding a new narrative yet to be written. It will be about a new earthly journey or quest, one that—if all goes well, *insha Allah*, "God Willing" they would say—will end in Paradise.

Reversion stories follow narrative patterns similar to other American testimonials. They also, however, provide unique details about specific individuals, places, and time periods. Through invocations, they request help from and worship God using two of the ninety-nine names of God in Islam—thereby introducing the story as an Islamic one. Background information is used to introduce the Latino-therefore-Christian thesis. Spatial, relational, and emotional modes of contact foreshadow and describe a sequence of events that led up to the resolution of a crisis in the taking of *shahadah* as an initiation into Islam. Reversion stories problematize the Latino-therefore-Christian thesis by describing diversity. They also, however, conform to dominant media structures even as they flow through unique channels and accomplish unique functions.

THE DISSEMINATION AND LOGICS OF REVERSION

The preference for the term "reversion" over "conversion" is manifested in several forms. Reversion may refer to a historical-cultural return (i.e., a reclamation of lost or forgotten histories and the cultural practices that emerge from them), an ontological return (i.e., a return to an original nature or disposition) or both. "Reversion" talk is most prominent on the internet and in journalistic articles. The Latina Muslimah organizational website, PiedadIslam.org, published a webpage titled "Muslim Reverts/Our Stories" which contained four reversion stories including one by its founder Khadijah Rivera. Additionally, the page contained links to three news articles that referenced several other reversion stories. The LALMA website, LALMA.org, featured a sidebar on its home page titled "Latino Muslims Revert Stories," with links to six reversion stories, including one featured at the beginning of this chapter written by Marta Galedary, co-founder and president of LALMA. The website HispanicMuslims.com was designed by Juan Galvan, president of LADO, to collect and publish reversion stories, including his own.

Stories about how individual Latinos came to embrace Islam are diverse in content, media form, and framing. This diversity, however, does not figure prominently in online search engine queries for "Latino Muslims" and "Hispanic Muslims." Although internet technologies allow for a diversity of media formats and content and also allow for greater access to representation in public discourse, these possibilities have not been achieved in practice by Latino Muslim communities. By 2012, less than a dozen Latino Muslim websites came to dominate search engine queries for "Latino Muslims" and "Hispanic Muslims." These sites and their gatekeepers exert a great deal of influence over public representations of the group. And it is the dominance of media practices like these that shape the message (i.e., the stories told by and about who Latino Muslims are and who they are not).

On digital spaces or in internet communications and the news, reversion is defined in contrast to conversion. The term "conversion" has multiple and contested meanings and connotations. It is rooted in Christian theology and many religions, including Islam, have no analogues to it. The closest term to conversion in Arabic comes from verb *aslama*, which literally means to submit and is the root from which the terms Islam (submission) and Muslim (one who submits) come from.[27] *Aslama* is better understood as a becoming rather than as converting.[28] In a 2002 interview, historian of Islamic Spain and friend of the Alianza Islámica and PIEDAD, Dr. T. B. Irving described his embrace of Islam through the language of "becoming" while critiquing the term conversion and change:

> I became a Muslim (never changed, never was anything else, just as the Prophet says) in the 1930's at Toronto. Please don't call me a convert because that implies change and what did I change from? I became a Muslim only in the sense that at a point in time I realized that was what I was.[29]

Dr. Irving rejected the term "conversion" on the grounds that it is foreign to Islamic language and Islamic formulations of human nature.

One of the most widely circulated conversion narratives, Saul's in the Christian New Testament book of Acts 9:1–19, is often described as a drastic 180 degree turn, a change toward the opposite direction that his life had previously followed. The dramatic transformation is from Saul, persecutor of Christians, to Paul, disciple of Christ; and perhaps more important, from sinner to saint. Conversion is here a kind of death (to an old sinful nature) and rebirth (to a new nature).[30] As mentioned previously, rather than formulate human nature as sinful and in need of a radical transformation, human nature is instead understood as forgetful in Islam (Qur'an 20:115). Dr. Irving rejected the term "conversion" because he rejected the suggestion that humans have a sinful nature that can be transformed for a godlier one. Such a concept would be foreign to Islam. His nature, Dr. Irving believed, had not changed. He was born a Muslim, was raised as a Christian, then realized or remembered that his essence or ontology had always, from the start, been Muslim. It was a remembrance and return to the straight path rather than a conversion to a new one.

In Latino Muslim reversion stories, Islam is both an original ontology and a familiar historical past whose traces reverberate throughout present-day Latino spirituality and culture. "You are probably wondering what reversion means," writes Galvan as an introduction to the "Reversion Stories" webpage on HispanicMuslims.com:

> Well, we Muslims believe people are born Muslims. Our parents and society are what make us choose other religions. We believe people are

born in a state of fitrah. Fitrah is our natural tendency to believe in one God. Consequently, by embracing Islam, you return to your natural disposition.[31]

The ontological framework of the reversion stories is drawn from the Islamic theological concept of *fitrah*: the innate disposition to believe in the Oneness of God.[32] A Hadith, a recorded saying of the Prophet Muhamad, states that: "There is not a newborn child who is not born in the state of *fitrah*. His parents then make him a Jew, a Christian or a Magian, just as an animal is born intact. Do you observe any among them that are maimed (at birth)."[33] Using a literal translation of the term "Muslim" as one who submits to God, many Latino Muslims further conclude that all humans are born Muslim and only stray away from their *fitrah* nature through various cultural forces. The Latino-therefore-Christian paradigm, for example, is accused of causing Latinos to stray away from their "original Muslim nature" and toward devotion to Jesus, the Virgin Mary, and other Catholic saints. For Marta Galedary, Juan Galvan, and other Latinos who embrace Islam, reversion narratives frame the process as a remembering and *re-embracing* of who they believe they have always been rather than as an abandoning of their Latino identity.

The discursive relevance of reversion logics rests in its ability to address accusations that Latino and Muslim identities are incompatible or foreign to one another. Reversion stories have emerged at a time when Latino and Muslim identities dominate public discourse and continue to be represented through essentialized and problematic formulations. Latinos who consume racialized mediations of Muslims as Arab often accuse Latino Muslims of rejecting their Latino ethnicity. Muslims who consume essentialized mediations of Latinos as beer drinking, pork eating, and licentious have conversely accused Latinos of being incapable of being good Muslims. Perhaps the "convert" can never shed the suspicion of not being a real Muslim and a real Latino at the same time. And perhaps this suspicion is tied up with questions regarding Latino and Muslim natures, a perceived incompatibility between the two and a perceived inability to change nature.

If it is granted that race-religion is a type of nature that cannot be changed and that Latinos who embrace Islam are attempting to change their Latino-therefore-Christian nature, then Latino Muslims are susceptible to accusations of being inauthentic.[34] Although such accusations are rooted in problematic and morally dubious logics that echo those that were imposed on to *conversos* during the Spanish Inquisition and to nonwhite Americans when biological formulations of race dominated our identity politics, they are accusations that Latino Muslims nevertheless experience and narrate. In response to this accusation, one Latino Muslim reported: "They ask why I want to change my culture. I tell them I'm changing religion, not culture. I still eat tortillas."[35] Although this response relies on a categorical separation between religion and culture rather than on the logics of reversion, it nevertheless narrates the Latino Muslim experience of being critiqued as either inauthentic Latinos, inauthentic Muslims, or both. The logics of reversion maintain that Latino Muslims can be both authentic Latinos and authentic Muslims at the same time based on a universal human ontology or nature. Compatibility between the two identities is rendered possible because Latinos who embrace Islam are formulated as remembering and re-embracing/celebrating their original ontology, rather than as converting or changing to a different race-religion.

Despite its unique and responsive characteristics, there are several concerning aspects to the logics of reversion. Many Latino Muslims use the term "reversion" only when addressing public audiences, while using the term "conversion" in their everyday language. Others are unaware of the term, choose not to use it, or find it problematic. The latter of these worry that suggesting that all humans are born Muslim may inspire greater hostility toward Muslims. They also point out that tradition characterizes a Muslim through specific elaborations of how one is required to express their submission to God (e.g., publically proclaiming that there is no god but God and Muhamad is the final messenger of God).

Additionally, I myself find it troubling that the logics of reversion fail to directly criticize the general practice of essentializing identities. In its ontological formulation, the logics of reversion actively participates in promoting the existence of an immutable human nature or a core, an unchangeable essence, and also condemns deviation from this essence as unnatural and immoral. Its historical and cultural formulation is less problematic in that it relies on contextually contingent events rather than on a priori and contested propositional definitions of humanity. If, however, this form of reversion claims that Islamic Spain is a more appropriate origin narrative for Latino identity than Catholic Spain, then it is also guilty of essentialization. Why not instead identify Visigoth or Aztec religio-culture as more appropriate origin narratives for Latino identity and for remembering, celebrating, and practicing in contemporary life? If Catholic Spain is rejected on the grounds that it was a foreign culture imposed on to their New World ancestors by force, then why not make the same claim regarding the conquest of Iberia by Muslim forces? The problem with identifying the origin of Latino identity with Catholic Spain, Muslim Spain, Visigoth Spain, pre-colonial Aztecs, Taínos, or some other group, is that that it flattens a much more complex story that can and should be told about Latino identity.

Rather than deny any historical influence, we should instead celebrate Latino roots as complex, diverse, and fluid, in order to also celebrate contemporary Latino identity as complex, diverse, and fluid (i.e., non-essentialized). To their credit, Latino Muslim reversion stories help, on the one hand, to debunk Latino-therefore-Christian and Muslim-therefore-Arab essentializations. On the other hand, however, if reversion as an ontological return promotes Latino and Muslim identities as compatible with one another only by formulating Latino identity as essentially Islamic, then this is to the genre's detriment. Latino Muslim stories could make a much clearer contribution to pluralism, to the celebration of diversity as a democratic strength, by promoting Latino and Muslim identities as compatible by formulating both Muslim and Latino identities as complex, diverse, and fluid.

CONCLUSION

Reversion stories provide a bridge between being Latino as a Christian and being Latino as a Muslim. They respond to the question of why Latinos are converting to Islam, even as they provide much more than simple explanations of why conversion occurs. Proximity to Muslims and Muslim communities, new and long-term relationships with acquaintances and trusted individuals, dissatisfaction with Christian doctrines and practices, near death experiences, or the death of loved ones each add layers of complexity to the stories about Latinos embracing Islam. They provide a more nuanced and personal understanding of the threat of chaos or the absence of meaning. On this edge, between purpose and insignificance, the authors bring us in close, open up, and reveal to us an extremely personal experience, describing their crisis as "an intense desire to embrace truth" and as a "hunger for knowledge." The crisis is presented through an Islamic prism, as a reminder of an important truth that has been forgotten. Like much of the Qur'an's content and tonal character, it reveals a state of loss.[36] It is a realization that an essential piece of knowledge was surrendered somewhere along the way and must now be recovered.

Reversion stories invoke God's blessings, they both ask for help and recognize God's ability to help. They introduce individuals as Latinos and as therefore linked to Christianity even if only to remind us that counter-narratives proliferate, including their own. They provide first-hand accounts of where and through whom the author first encountered Islam. They detail a crisis of meaning and the resolution of this crisis through the embrace of Islam. Reversion stories follow a similar narrative and mediation patterns to American testimonials and conversion stories within other religious traditions. But they also add historically specific content regarding the unique experiences of individuals. Their dissemination and function also constitute historical specificities. They are uniquely framed through the logic of reversion as both an ontological and historical return. The logics of reversion, both in reversion stories (and in the news, as shall be explored in the next chapter) challenge accusations that Latino and Muslim identities are incompatible.

Further, reversion stories promote pluralism in America by helping to debunk Latino-therefore-Christian and Muslim-therefore-Arab misrepresentations. Unfortunately, they also work against pluralism by promoting Latino ontology as essentially Islamic. Finally, Latino Muslim reversion stories conclude by suggesting a sequel, a story yet to be lived out about a journey yet to be completed: "the next journey on earth," wrote Gomez, "the journey to Paradise."[37]

CHAPTER FOUR

THE 9/11 FACTOR

LATINO MUSLIMS IN THE NEWS

On Monday, December 17, 2001, the *New York Times* published "A New Minority Makes Itself Known: Hispanic Muslims" by Evelyn Nieves.[1] Just a few months after the tragic events of September 11, 2001, the Latino Muslim story was published as part of national mobilization of journalists assigned to "the Muslim" beat. For a new generation of reporters who had not experienced the round-the-clock coverage of the Iranian hostage crisis in the 1980s or the live bomb coverage of the Gulf War in the 1990s, 9/11 ushered in a new era of American media and its coverage of Islam. After the 2001 attacks by al-Qaeda, US media generally increased its coverage of all things related to Islam. This news industry phenomenon was referred to by many as the 9/11 effect or the 9/11 factor (i.e., the increased quantity and negativity of Islam-related coverage).[2] Negative stereotypes of Muslims in US media both reflected and contributed to an increase of what is often termed "Islamophobia," an irrational fear of Muslims. Despite the negative bias, the increased coverage has also reportedly contributed to what has been termed "the other September 11 effect," an increased interest in and embrace of Islam, including by Latinos.[3]

The American media context in which the Latino Muslim beat emerged was thus shaped by both the 9/11 factor and its "other effect" but also by the advent of new media technologies and dramatic changes to readership and media economies. Contending not only with television and radio but also now, and apparently more significantly so, with industry-wide changes wrought by digital media, the 2001 *New York Times* article on Latino Muslims was nevertheless distributed to over 1.14 million readers in print form alone.[4] This wide readership, in print and in online re-mediations of the article, was no doubt part of the allure for the Latino Muslims interviewed by Nieves for the story. Nieves had spoken with Marta Galedary from LALMA, Khadijah Rivera from the women's piety organization PIEDAD, and Juan Galvan from LADO. And despite the increasingly negative coverage of Muslims in news media, Galedary, Rivera, and Galvan all agreed to be interviewed.

Despite the risks of working with journalists in a post-9/11 media context, these leaders of Latino Muslim organizations saw something advantageous in the relationship. Perhaps they hoped to increase public awareness of Latino Muslims and to help shape a more positive public perception of Muslims and Latino Muslims. Perhaps they also hoped to help increase their numbers and gain symbolic capital and access to vital resources through such media coverage. In any case, such gains could only be made through a negotiation with complex and reductive media processes in the United States. Media coverage of the group, though not overtly negative, has overwhelmingly framed Latino Muslims primarily as converts and both implicitly and sensationally ask: Why would a "minority" group freely choose to multiply their "minority" status?

The 2001 New York Times article title itself framed Latino Muslims as "A New Minority" and its content asked "Why Islam?" To the question, why do Latinos freely choose to convert to Islam, answers reported in stories like the Times's vary but usually include issues regarding doctrine, social equality, and marriage. According to these articles some Latinos convert to Islam because its doctrines or rituals made more sense to them than Catholic ones. Others, we are told, embraced Islam because it helped them to navigate racial and ethnic inequality in American society. Lastly, and most controversially, the stories report that Latina women are converting to Islam because they married Muslims.

For Latinos who are new to Islam, including those who are introduced to the religion by their spouses or future spouses, Galedary from LALMA and Rivera from PIEDAD have emphasized the importance of distinguishing Islamic religion from Latino ethnicity. "You don't leave your culture because you convert to Islam," Galedary told Nieves, the *Times*, and its readers. This distinction, between religion and ethnicity, is an important discursive maneuver by Latino Muslim leaders who must navigate puzzled reactions to their ethno-religious identity on a regular basis. Galedary, we read, "had to convince her mother that she had not joined a cult."[5] Rivera reported in the same article that she had been verbally harassed on several occasions for wearing a veil after 9/11: "I was insulted in the supermarket, on the street. I would be waiting for a bus and people would see me and just yell obscenities. I have had dirty looks from Latino people, too."[6] News media representations of Latino Muslims are the result of, among other processes, a negotiation between Latino Muslim aspirations (e.g., to reduce misunderstanding and hate speech) and corporate media goals (e.g., to share compelling stories and attract consumers).

The relationship between Latino Muslim leaders and the American news industry has shaped and amplified narratives on Latino Muslims that focus on identity-based alienation and a historical-cultural return to Islam and an ontological return (i.e., return to an original nature or disposition). It is my goal in this chapter to not only document post-9/11 coverage of Latino Muslims but also to critically engage the mediation processes that frame Latino Muslims as a new American "minority." Media coverage of Latino Muslims should be understood as part of a post-9/11 media context. Although not overtly negative, news reports on Latino Muslims have nevertheless been mostly sensational and have reduced the group to issues regarding conversion. This has not been the case in one subgenre of American news media however. Spanish language media in the United States has instead overtly represented Latino Muslims, and especially Latina Muslim women, negatively. Some Latino Muslims have responded to both sensational and outright negative media attention through an "any coverage is good coverage" approach. Others, however, have been much more critical of journalistic practices and in some instances have even refused to grant interviews and have also gathered petitions to call for an end to the defamation of their identity group. I argue that media consumers should be weary of the "minority" label because it covers up more than what it reveals.

THE LATINO MUSLIM BEAT

In a post-9/11 media context, coverage of Latino Muslims exponentially increased. Before the turn of the twenty-first century and over a decade after the founding of La Alianza Islámica, the first Latino Muslim organization in the United States, only five news stories had been produced on Latino Muslims. By 2011, a decade after the 9/11 attacks, over 140 news articles had been published on Latino Muslims. The *New York Times* alone published five articles on Latino Muslims—in 2001, 2002, 2009, and twice in 2011. Significant media attention was given to Latino Muslims in 2002 (seventeen stories), 2006 (twenty-two stories), and 2011 (twenty-five stories) and an average of about ten news articles on Latino Muslims during all other years between 2001 and 2011.

Although not overtly villainizing, most news stories on Latino Muslims are nevertheless highly reductive. Similarly to Edward Said's assessment of news media coverage of Islam in general, I argue that Latino Muslim news stories "cover up" the complex and diverse character of individuals and groups by myopically focusing on one particular narrative element.[7] In the case of Latino Muslims, "coverage" has focused on conversion. There is so much more to Latino Muslims than conversion, yet this is the dominant emphasis in news stories on Latino Muslims over and over again. The myopic focus on conversion is evident through a quick reading of headlines like: "Number of Hispanic Muslim Converts Growing," "More Hispanic Women Converting to Islam," "Growing Number of Hispanics Converting to Islam," "More Hispanic Americans Are Converting to Islam," "From Cross to Crescent—Latinos Increasingly Converting," and "Latina Converts to Islam Growing in Number," to name just a few. Although it is true that Latinos are the largest and fastest growing so-called minority group in America, that Islam is the fastest "growing" religion in America, and that Latino Muslims are indeed increasingly growing in number, the growth of Latino Muslims is not as startlingly rapid nor as sizable as what is implied by the quantity and character of these headlines. Instead, the increased coverage of Latino Muslims is better understood as part of the 9/11 factor (i.e., the general increased coverage of all things related to Islam after the Al-Qaeda attacks of September 11, 2001).

Although the majority of post-9/11 coverage of Muslims has overwhelming connected Islam to terrorism, Latino Muslims have not been overtly villainized in news media representations for the most part. Nevertheless, the decision to embrace Islam by Latinos is questioned in the news and implicitly characterized as puzzling if not senseless. One article directly asks in its title: "Hispanic Muslims: Why Are Catholic Hispanic Americans Converting to Islam?"[8] The question is often framed against the backdrop of the negative effects of converting to Islam. The stories ask why would individuals from a so-called minority group freely choose to embrace another identity that will doubly marginalize them in the United States. Why would Latinos abandon Christianity when it leads to alienation from their Latino families and friends? And why would Latinos embrace Islam if they report not being fully accepted by Muslims who are not Latino?

These questions have often been answered in the news with strikingly similar responses. Latino Muslims are "converting" to Islam, many of the articles report, because Islam provides what they perceive to be a better yet familiar alternative to Catholicism; because Islam promotes racial, ethnic, and gender equality; and because Latinas are marrying Muslims. With the exception of marriage, news reports reproduced many of the themes found in the reversion story genre discussed in the previous chapter—including that of ontological and historical-cultural reversion. The reversion framework, the description of Latinos returning to something previous rather than converting to something new, is thus not only found in media produced by Latino Muslims has also made its way into broader American news media as well. Despite the narrow focus on issues of conversion and the consequent covering up of Latino Muslim complexity and diversity, the increased news coverage provides a sense of legitimization to Latino Muslims and also allows them to amplify the reversion framework in the public sphere. These gains are made, however, by settling for simplistic and sensationalized descriptions of Latino Muslims in the news. News media representations reduce complex processes and diverse beliefs and practices to a new so-called minority who are represented as bizarre for freely choosing to multiply their marginalization from the rest of America.

On April 11, 2011, Lara N. Dotson-Renta published a news article titled "Latino Muslims in the United States after 9/11: The Triple Bind."[9] The piece was published in the Muftah.org online news magazine, whose self-described mission is to produce a more diverse alternative to conventional media coverage of the Middle East and of North Africa (MENA).[10] Dr. Dotson-Renta is herself an academic who authors various media for diverse audiences, and her "Triple Bind" article provides a nuanced synthesis of nearly a decade of regular news coverage on Latino Muslims. In it, Dotson-Renta develops a terminology for referencing the multiple forms of alienation that Latino Muslims experience. "At a time when immigrants and Muslims are under increased scrutiny," writes Dotson-Renta, "Latino Muslims are experiencing some of the most extreme forms of social alienation."[11]

In *Prophesy Deliverance: An Afro-American Revolutionary Christianity*, Cornel West expands on W. E. B. Du Bois's concept of dual consciousness: "Black Americans labored rather under the burden of a triple crisis of self-recognition"[12] Early colonialists wrestled with "being American yet feeling European," and it is in this context that African Americans additionally wrestle with "being in America but not of it, from being black natives to black aliens."[13] Latinos in the United States similarly experience a triple crises of self-recognition, albeit from a historically distinct set of experiences. In the words of mestizaje theologian, Virgilio Elizondo, Latinos are "a people twice conquered, twice colonized, and twice mestized."[14] The first conquest and colonization Elizondo is referring to is that of Mesoamericans by Spaniards, which led to the development of mestizo or hybrid identities known today as Latin American or the various nationalities comprising it. The second conquest and colonization is of Latin America by the United States, which led to the development of hybrid identities known today as Latino, Hispanic, Chicano, Nuyorican, and so on. Identity-based marginalization experienced by Latinos in the United States is multiple: it is a Latin American hybridity—both and neither Spanish and "indigenous"; it is also a Latino hybridity—both and neither Latin American and American (in or from the United States). Embracing Islam, according to news coverage of Latino Muslims, only compounds the group's "minority" status in the United States.

Dotson-Renta terms the multiple forms of alienation experienced by Latino Muslims the "triple bind," which is a reference to: (1) alienation from a broadly conceived American culture for being Muslim (Dotson-Renta should have also here included alienation for being Latino in America), (2) alienation from Latinos for embracing Islam, and (3) alienation from Muslims for being Latino.[15] Given this triple bind, journalists often implicitly or sometimes even directly ask: Why do any Latinos freely choose to embrace Islam? Before discussing mediated responses to this particularly confining question, let us first further consider the kinds of alienation referenced by the triple bind.

MULTIPLYING MARGINALITY

In an April 14, 2011, interview by Hajer Naili published in *ILLUME Magazine*, Dr. Akbar Ahmed described "a double challenge," experienced by Latino Muslims: "they face double prejudice being a Muslim and being Latino."[16] And in *The Venture*, Audris Ponce wrote that: "Latino and Muslim are two words that come charged with various sentiments in American society. Being a Latino Muslim comes with the challenge of facing both religious and ethnic ostracism."[17] Ponce then goes on to quote a Latino Muslim she had interviewed for the piece: "You feel in that weird in-between-place; you're not quite part of them," he said. "You feel tri-cultural, not bicultural: American, Hispanic and Muslim."[18] Note that rather than celebrate his tri-cultural experience, the interviewee describes it as a form of ostracization. In an article by Elisa Cordova for the *Cronkite News Service*, another interviewee is referenced as believing that: "Many Hispanics don't feel accepted in the United States because of illegal immigration and other issues. By converting to Islam, she said, they become a minority within a minority."[19] Latino Muslims thus report experiencing alienation from multiple groups for multiple reasons.

In a November 16, 2011, *Huffington Post* article titled "Islam in America . . . en Español," Wilfredo Amr Ruiz, who has become a prominent voice for Latino Muslims in the media, described the alienation experienced by Latino Muslims: "When it comes to Latino Muslim acceptance in the American landscape, they are not exempt from experiencing challenges and struggles confronted by the broader American Muslim community."[20] Although Ruiz does not represents all Latino Muslims by any stretch of the imagination, the *Huffington Post* article was unique in that rather than merely quoting Latino Muslims, it was written by someone who identifies as such. In a much more critical tone than other articles on Latino Muslims, Ruiz's piece indicts specific individuals who directly participate in the practice of alienating American Muslims, including Latino Muslims, on the basis of their religious identity.

Concluding the *ILLUME* article previously discussed, Hajer Naili asks: "Do you think Latino Muslims can change the perception of Islam in the United States?" to which Dr. Akbar Ahmed responded:

> No, it will be difficult because in America there are already some prejudices against Latinos. Lot of Americans think that among Latinos there are many illegal immigrants. Many Americans associate Latinos with drug smuggling and all sorts of chaos. So in that sense, if Americans are told Latinos are becoming Muslim; for most of them, Islam is a minus and Latinos are also a minus. So it's a minus plus a minus, if you know what I mean."[21]

If Latino Muslims agree to participate in journalistic interviews with the goal of reducing misunderstanding and hate speech or crimes, Akbar Ahmed's quote is nothing short of demoralizing. Although it is unclear why having a second negatively stereotyped identity prohibits one from reducing negative stereotypes of the first identity or both, Akbar Ahmed is nevertheless correct in that there is no shortage of negative representations of Latinos in American media.

Being a Latino and a Muslim has been represented in American news media as a triple bind, as a tri-cultural identity (and not in a good way), as a doubly prejudiced experience, as a minority within a minority, and as "a minus plus a minus." The decision to embrace Islam, news coverage tells us, comes with the negative consequence of alienating Latino Muslims from broader groups in the United States for both being Latino and for being Muslim.

In addition to alienation from broader groups, Latino Muslims also experience more intimate forms of alienation from their Latino families and friends and also from their Muslim communities. Latino Muslims are often accused of rejecting their Latino heritage. The rejection accusation stems in part from both a conflation between religion and culture and also from negative perceptions of Muslims. If a tourist were to go, for example, to Plazita Olvera in Los Angeles, California, to encounter "Latino culture," it would not be so easy to distinguish between Latino culture and Latino (or Mexican American) religiosity. Likewise, Islam is often conflated with Middle Eastern cultures if not Arab ethnicity. The conflation becomes more problematic when Islam is not only understood as a potential replacement to Latino identity, but when the replacement is viewed unfavorably altogether. In a *CT Latino News* article titled "More Latinos Turning to Islam," journalist Rod Carveth cites a Pew Hispanic Center survey concluding that "non-Muslim Latinos view Muslims rather unfavorably, with roughly a fourth of Latinos (27 percent) expressing favorable views, compared with 37 percent expressing unfavorable views."[22] Carveth then augments these statistics with reports from individual Latino Muslims interviewed for news articles. In an *Islamic Horizons* interview with the co-founder of LADO, we learn that Juan Alvarado

> used to feel lonely when he first converted 22 years ago . . . not everyone in Alvarado's family has accepted him, especially his father. "I think to this day he thinks I was brainwashed," Alvarado said. . . . Alvarado's mother was less critical than his father but worried someone might hurt him since he dresses in distinctive Islamic garb, he said. "As Hispanic people, we see ourselves as having it [as] bad as it is," he said. "To add something to it, most people wouldn't choose to do that. So that kind of worried her."[23]

Alvarado is not alone in his alienation from Latino communities and family. In "Olé to Allah: New York's Latino Muslims" by Hisham Aidi, Khadija Rivera, co-founder of PIEDAD, reported: "My father used to pull the veil off my head," she recalls. "My mother used to cook with pork tallow. It was war."[24] Especially when reporting on alienation from family, the negative experiences that women report are much more detailed and violent than those of men.[25] In addition to alienation from family, news media thus often reveals a "fourth," gender-based bind or form of alienation.

Michael J. Feeney's NY Daily News article "Hispanic Woman Who Converted to Islam Experiences Prejudice from Fellow East Harlem Residents" not only brings attention to the "fourth bind" but makes it, as the result of conversion, the center of his news story. One of the women he interviewed for the piece reported that: "Even my own Latino people feel like I betrayed them. . . . They see me veiled and they think 'she's under [her husband's] grasp' and that's not the case."[26] And in a 2006 National Public Radio (NPR) piece titled "Latinas Choosing Islam over Catholicism" by Rachel Martin, one Latina Muslim woman narrated her post "conversion" experience as follows: "My mom said, okay, you know, that's it. I've had it. You have to speak to her. I can't have her here anymore. You know, she—I feel like she's not, like, with—like us and everything. So my father took me aside and he told me—he asked me either Islam or us."[27] The "fourth bind" is a gender-based aggravation of the already multiple and multiplied forms of alienation experienced by Latino Muslims in America. Although Latino Muslim groups like PIEDAD and LALMA are trying to address gender-based discrimination, the majority of news media has failed to provide coverage of such efforts. Instead, news media has mostly used coverage of the fourth bind to further sensationalize the question of why would any Latino, especially Latina women, freely choose to "convert" to Islam when it means further multiplying their alienation in America?

And as if alienation from family were not already challenging enough on its own, Latino Muslims also report experiencing alienation from their Muslim communities. Aidi continues in "Olé to Allah":

Although the local Latino community has been largely supportive of the Alianza, some non-Latino Muslims have not. Mendez says many Arab and Pakistani Muslims seem critical of the Latinos' efforts to adopt Islam. Immigrant Muslims sometimes attend jumma (Friday) prayers at the Alianza, but they often criticize the group's command of Arabic and their understanding of Islam; one Pakistani Muslim even said that Puerto Ricans are "too promiscuous" to be "good" Muslims. And in fact, the Alianza is actually being ousted from its current location by an immigrant Muslim landlord.[28]

Although alienation from non-Latino Muslims is reported less frequently than alienation from Latino families and friends and from broader American groups, it is often described as the least expected and one of the most hurtful forms of rejection experienced by Latino Muslims. In "Even as Islam Booms, Its Many Faces Can Deter Converts," Mrinalini Reddy describes one Latina Muslimah's negative experiences among Muslims:

> Abeytia took issue with hostile attitudes from Muslim women she met when she began her conversion to Islam in Los Angeles. . . . "I really had and still have a hard time with Muslims," said Abeytia. "They have this gemstone of Islam that can really help people, yet they pile it with manure and you really have to dig through it. And the deeper you get, you see there are so many social ills that are really not coming from the religion."[29]

The challenge with alienation from Muslims is that many Latino Muslims often find Islam attractive precisely because of its promotion of equality. So when Latinos find that the ideal of equality is not always practiced within Muslim communities, it can be very troubling. For Abeytia, the Latina Muslimah in Reddy's article, the hypocrisy is a social ill likened to a pile of manure.

In contrast to some of these more negative reports, it should be noted that a few articles also describe acceptance from Latino family and friends and from Muslims.[30] These positive interactions are much less frequently reported however. Instead, news media has generally focused much more on the multiplied alienation experienced by Latinos who freely choose to embrace Islam. The focus on conversion is not only connected to descriptions of alienation however. It is also manifested in the reported answers to the question of why are Latinos "converting" to Islam. For the Latino Muslims that participate in journalistic interviews, what seems to be of much more value than satisfying the curiosity of news consumers is promoting a particular set of themes regarding who Latino Muslims are. Many of these themes, including ontological and historical-cultural reversion, are thus found in both reversion stories produced by Latino Muslims and in news coverage of Latino Muslims produced by news media institutions.

WHY LATINOS CONVERT

Latino Muslims choose to "convert," journalists report, because Islam provides what Latino Muslims perceive to be a better alternative to Catholicism, because Islam promotes social equality, and because Latinas are marrying Muslims. Latino "conversion" is not just part of the post 9/11 beat, it is also a news story about the exodus from the Catholic Church in America and the role that Latinos play in these drastic changes to the American religious landscape. Rachel Martin's "Latinas Choosing Islam over Catholicism" makes this the center of her news story. The story aired on September 24, 2006, and formed part of the 2006 spike in Latino Muslim coverage. The news story was introduced by Liane Hansen who reported that: "Over the past few decades the Catholic Church in America has seen an exodus of Latin American congregants from its pews. Experts point to growing competition from other denominations, primarily evangelical Christianity. However, an emerging segment of the Hispanic population is converting to Islam."[31]

Martin reports that in addition to searching for more gender equality, Latino Muslims "also come to Islam for something more, something they didn't get from the Catholic Church," and then continues by reporting that in 2006: "The Catholic Almanac estimates that roughly 100,000 Hispanics in the U.S. leave the Catholic Church every year." One interviewee is paraphrased as reporting that she "found the Catholic Church too bureaucratic and too impersonal. She also had a hard time with certain aspects of the faith, like the hierarchy of the church, belief in the Trinity and original sin. She remembers going to mass weekly with her grandmother and cousins, and just feeling lost."[32]

News stories like Martin's thus report that the puzzlement over why Latinos would embrace Islam should be understood as part of a broader exodus from the Catholic Church in America. In "Latino Muslims a Growing Presence in America," Lisa Viscidi adds that: "According to Juan Galvan, Vice President of the Latino American Dawah Organization, 'most Hispanic converts were Catholic. Many Hispanics had difficulty with the church, believing in original sin, and in the Holy Trinity. Islam solves the problems many Hispanics have with the Catholic Church. For example, in Islam there is no priest-pope hierarchy. Everyone who prays before God is equal. Many Latino converts feel Islam gives them a closer relationship to God.' "[33] Islam is thus reported by Latino Muslims to be a better alternative to Catholicism for theological, experiential, and organizational reasons.

Additionally, many Latino Muslims also report that the promotion of racial, ethnic, and gender equality in Islam is what made the religion attractive to them. Viscidi's story also features quotes from Dr. Fathi Osman who was a resident scholar at the Omar ibn Al-Khattab mosque where the Los Angeles Latino Muslim Association meets and who was also chosen as the group's sponsor in part because of his advocacy for women's rights. Viscidi reports that:

According to Osman, as minorities, Latinos are not understood or supported by the United States Church, which continues to side with the elite. In his view, the Catholic Church advocates equality and justice in theory, but does not implement them in practice. Osman contends, "most Latinos are poor and feel oppressed. They don't get justice in their original countries or in the U.S. They want a religion that cares about those who are oppressed."[34]

Viscidi finally concludes that "perhaps it is Islam's doctrine of racial equality and unity that appeals to minority groups."[35] Although some have offered race-based explanations of "Latino nature" as being attracted to so-called radical religions like Pentecostalism and Islam, as will be explored further in the next chapter of this book, it is a so-called minority nature that is used in this instance to explain the attraction to Islam. This kind of explanation runs the risk of idealizing "minority nature." Both the race-based and minority-based explanations are extremely reductive and problematic and are indicative of the severe methodological problems with causal explanations of conversion.

Islam also provides a "new" sense of belonging, an accessible source of social capital for those who experience constant alienation based on their Latino identity. Although Muslims also currently experience intense forms of alienation in the United States, globally, Islam is the second largest and fastest growing religion in the world.[36] For Latinos that are disenchanted with Christianity and who are searching the religious marketplace for new options, Islam is perhaps alienating in America but can be understood as advantageous at the global level. The Nation of Islam, for example, tried to capitalize on their inclusion within a global Muslim *ummah* or community. Latinos who embrace Islam also connect themselves to new networks that may provide socioeconomic benefits. Some Latinos, we read in the news, find that the truth and day-to-day value of Islam outweigh any potential disadvantages that might come from identifying as a Muslim in the United States.

A third, and much more controversial, reason that Latinos are "converting" to Islam, according to news media, is marriage. Although this controversy is described in more detail elsewhere in this book, I document a few examples here to demonstrate its prevalence in news coverage of Latino Muslims. In *The Christian Science Monitor*'s "More US Hispanics Drawn to Islam," Amy Green reports that "marriage, post-9/11 curiosity, and a shared interest in issues such as immigration are key reasons" why Latinos "convert" to Islam.[37] With few exceptions, it is the journalist or some non-Latino Muslim commentator who concludes that marriage is causing Latina women to convert to Islam rather than Latino Muslim interviewees themselves. A 2002 piece by the Associated Press reported that PIEDAD "began in 1988 to help Spanish-speaking women who married Muslim men."[38] Here, PIEDAD leader Khadijah Rivera does not necessarily conclude that Latina women are converting because they marry Muslim men. Instead she is only describing how the organization has helped women who are introduced to Islam by their non-Spanish-speaking husbands.[39]

Because coverage of Latino Muslims has been mostly sensational and reductive, several critiques of such coverage continue to emerge. Eren Arruna Cervantes's article "5 Reasons Why Media Coverage of 'Latina' Converts Does Not Represent Me" for *Muslimah Media Watch* offers one such example. In it, she questions what is meant by "Latin," rejects both the "convert" and "revert" label opting for just Muslim instead, points out that the *hijab* does not necessarily protect women from sexual harassment, and also writes:

> I Don't Need a New Identity. The idea of identity troubles me. I have multiple and intersecting identities that cannot be boxed into the idea of my conversion to Islam or my place of birth . . . the fact that we attribute women's conversion to a lack of identity or the rejection of a previous identity speaks to a notion that women cannot hold multiple identities and reconcile them; instead, they need to stick to the interpretations of men, who tell them what to do and how to think.[40]

MEDIA GOALS

Despite the reductive and sensational focus on "conversion" and also on the negative effects of "conversion" on Latino Muslims, news media coverage of Latino Muslims has provided the emerging identity group with a sense of legitimization and has also helped amplify the reversion framework in the public sphere. In an article previously referenced in this chapter, "Latino Muslims a Growing Presence in America," Lisa Viscidi reports, "Lacking an organized network and longstanding cultural background within the United States, Latino Muslims are not as visible as other U.S. minority groups, but evidence of their existence has sprouted around the country."[41] Latino Muslims, Viscidi concludes, lack representation in the American public sphere even as she diminishes this limitation with her own article. And in an *Islamic Horizons Magazine* article, Samantha Sanchez and Juan Galvan of LADO report that:

> Latino Muslims have been gaining media attention. Headlines such as "A New Minority Makes Itself Known: Hispanic Muslims" and "Hispanos musulmanes de Nueva York" are just a few that signify that America is realizing what Latino Muslims have known for quite a while . . . that we exist! While it may still seem strange for the Muslim community to hear about us, the general public in such places as New York, Chicago, Houston, Los Angeles, and Miami is becoming more aware of this fact.[42]

Sanchez and Galvan are not only aware of the increased media coverage of Latino Muslims, they also acknowledge that the increased media attention is amplifying knowledge of their existence. Latino Muslim leaders are also keenly aware that increased representation in the public sphere provides them with increased opportunities to connect with valuable resources. Media coverage thus becomes a form of legitimization, a "we exist!" and also a social form of capital that can be purchased through interviews and spent by connecting to broader groups that can help them.[43]

Media coverage not only helps Latino Muslims amplify knowledge of their existence, it also helps amplify the reversion framework in both its historical-cultural and ontological forms. The reversion framework is in part a discursive response to news media representations that reduce Latino conversion to Islam as a senseless multiplication of alienation. The reversion framework posits an alternative narrative, one in which Latino identity is historically, culturally, and ontologically linked rather than puzzling or incompatible. Latino Muslims remind news media consumers or introduce them to the fact that Muslims were in regions now known as Spain for over 800 years. They point to a historical link between Muslims in Al-Andalus, the Spanish Reconquista, and the Spanish colonization of the Americas. Latino Muslims inform reporters and their readers that this historical link has engendered a cultural link between Latinos and Muslims. Several thousand Spanish words and phrases have their etymological root in Arabic. Foods and cuisine can be attributed to cultural contact. Islamic aesthetics have in part informed artistic expressions in Spain and in the "New World." Latino Muslims also attribute similarities in family organization to the historical and cultural link between Latinos and Muslims. Based on interviews, journalists therefore report that one reason Latinos convert to Islam is to reclaim a lost historical heritage. In an ABC News piece, Sameera Iqbal writes:

> Hundreds of Spanish words have Arabic roots. Historians have concluded that "olé" is the Spanish adaptation of the Arabic word for God, Allah. Today, some Latinos feel they are reclaiming their Muslim heritage by returning to the religion. Gonzalez said, "We felt Islam, within our culture, was a hidden treasure."[44]

Gonzales here frames his identity group not as a "minority" who choose to "convert" to something that is foreign and that multiplies their alienation in America, but rather as people who are uncovering a treasure covered up by colonial histories. Not only are Latino and Islamic identities historically linked, they are described in these news reports as vibrant and dynamic connections thriving within Latino and Muslim cultures today.

In addition to the historical-cultural link, Latino Muslims describe their connection to Islam as having an ontological origin. Interviewees have reported that all humans are born Muslim and that when a Latino embraces Islam, they are returning to their original *fitrah* or ontic nature. In Marion Piekarec's 2002 article for *Le Devoir*, titled "¡Hola! or Salaam alaiykum," both the historical-cultural and ontological forms of reversion are addressed by Wilfredo Amr Ruiz, who was interviewed for the piece. "Ruiz also believes his Islamic experience is reversion rather than conversion. 'Muslim means "that which submits [to God]." We believe that everyone was born a Muslim, but that your religion changes based on what you learn.' "[45] In this way, Latino and Muslim identities are formulated not as categorically incompatible but as ontologically linked.

The media attention that Latino Muslims have received should be understood as part of a post-9/11 media context in which Islam has received increased and increasingly negative attention. Contrary to the popular linkage within this context between Islam and terrorism, Latino Muslims have not been overtly represented negatively for the most part. Coverage of the group has however myopically focused on conversion and the reasons for conversion, including doctrinal, social equality, and marriage-related issues. The conversion coverage sensationalizes the group in order to implicitly present the decision to multiply alienation as unsound. In exchange for such reductive coverage, Latino Muslims seek to amplify their call to Islam and their own narratives (e.g., of reversion), and to procure legitimization, social capital, and access to vital resources. Latino Muslims therefore willingly participate in the production of highly reductive media representations of themselves as a strategic maneuver. Such participation becomes less negotiable, however, when the coverage is not only reductive, but is also overtly negative.

LATINO MEDIA AND LATINO ORIENTALISM

Spanish language media has been generally much more overtly negative in their portrayal of Latino Muslims than its English language counterparts. Telemundo, a US-based Spanish language television network that broadcasts nationally and internationally, aired a particularly scathing news story titled *Hispanos Detras del Velo*, "Hispanics behind the Veil," in 2010. The segment's title alone echoed a long history of recycled and negative caricatures of oppressed Muslim women in European and American media. "Many ask themselves," José Díaz-Balart "reported" when introducing the series, "why in the world, in the twenty first century, are there women who choose to be part of a religion that requires them to live covered head to toe and to additionally live in submission to men?" Having provided this derisive question not as his own but as that of an unidentified "many," Díaz-Balart goes on to introduce Carmon Dominicci as the lead investigative reporter who "broke the story," a story that had been by then already presented as new news over 140 times in English language media. "Today," Díaz-Balart continued, "in the first chapter of the "Hispanics behind the Veil" series, Carmen Dominicci explores how much is myth and how much is reality, and why everyday more Hispanic women in this country," Díaz-Balart's facial expression suddenly turned to a puzzled frown, "are converting into Muslim women?" Dominicci then responded "That's right, many consider it a *machista* religion and for this reason many are surprised that thousands of women who enjoy all kinds of liberties in this country [the United States] are converting into Muslim women."

These opening lines effectively present Islam and the oppression of women as inextricably linked. They echo the sensationalist puzzlement over people who freely choose to multiply their marginalization in the United States. And as if to cement these opening lines, they are immediately followed by a torrent of orientalist images and sounds focused on veiled women. The majority of the women are in *niqabs*, a style of dress that leaves only eyes exposed. Several of them are being beaten violently by brown skinned and black bearded men in turbans. One video clip features one such woman, in an open court yard, on her knees, face turned away from the camera, and her assailant, a turbaned man who holds a high-powered rifle to her head. The video freezes suddenly just before what is suggested to be an execution.

There are important similarities and differences between English language and Spanish language coverage of Latino Muslims in US media. Like English language representations, the Spanish language news series myopically focuses on the question of why would anyone freely choose to multiply their marginalization through conversion. As we have seen, however, on the one hand, the bulk of English language news on Latino Muslims references the marginalization of all Muslims as an American phenomenon instead of overtly participating itself in the slander of Islam on theological or moral grounds. The Telemundo news series, on the other hand, begins with an attack of Islam as sexist, oppressive, and violent. At the end of the three-part series, Dominicci expresses that after all of her investigative research she has come to several surprising discoveries, including that women have rights in Islam! Nevertheless, by both starting with disturbingly negative stereotypes and by ending surprised that such stereotypes are not necessarily true, the "Hispanics behind the Veil" news series by Telemundo capitalizes on and helps perpetuate orientalism among Latino communities.

In his seminal work *Orientalism*, Edward Said critiques the discursive processes through which highly reductive and negative depictions of Muslims have come to dominate the public sphere. Orientalism, the late Edward Said proposed, is not just the academic study of "the East," it is the production of highly reductive and problematic stereotypes regarding people from the East through structures of dominance.[46] Dominant images of the orientalist repertoire include the irrational, enraged, and oppressive Muslim male terrorist as well as the oppressed and hyper-sexual Muslim woman. These images or stereotypes are found within all forms of orientalism, including in Spanish language media.

In his essay "Let Us Be Moors: Islam, Race and 'Connected Histories,'" Hisham Aidi explores two media channels through which Spanish-speaking audiences have encountered such orientalist images. In addition to pop singer Shakira's use of belly dancing and Arab musical motifs in videos and performances, the wildly popular *telenovela* (a Spanish language serial drama akin to English language soap operas) titled "El Clon," which sparked considerable curiosity among Latino audiences. The telenovela's protagonist, Jade, performs an orientalist form of Islam through the repetition of a few Arab words and phrases (including *Ay, porfavor, Allah!*—"oh please, God!"), dress (she paradoxically sometimes dawns a veil in modesty and at other times reveals her belly to dance seductively for male onlookers), and other such orientalist imagery. Jade's character, a Moroccan immigrant in Brazil, struggles to maintain her Islamic traditions in a modern world, as if the two were fundamentally opposed. The *telenovela*'s reductive and orientalist misrepresentations reportedly reached 2.8 million viewers in the United States, 85 million in Brazil, and tens of millions more across the rest of Latin America.[47] Aidi writes that "the Moroccan ambassador to Brazil, in a letter to a Sao Paolo newspaper, criticized the [*telenovela*] series for its egregious 'cultural errors,' 'gross falsification' and 'mediocre images' promoting stereotypes of Muslim women as submissive and men as polygamists leading lives of 'luxury and indolence.' "[48]

Although the repertoire of images used in Spanish language media like the "Hispanics behind the Veil" news series and the "El Clon" *telenovela* follow the pattern of European and American depictions of Muslims, it is important to keep in mind that form does not necessarily equal function.[49] In *Islam and the Blackamerican*, Sherman Jackson points out that within different contexts, the same images or forms serve different functions or have distinctive meanings.[50] So that even when the images or tropes appear to be similar if not near-exact replicas within colonial Britain, neo-imperialistic America, and black American communities, the meanings or functions are different in each historically specific form of orientalism. Similarly, Latino orientalism, as a repertoire of negative depictions of Muslims, is both similar to and distinct from other forms of orientalism in several ways.

First, unlike British and American forms and similar to black American forms, Latino orientalism lacks an imperial impetus. In other words, the stereotyping of Muslims by black Americans and Latinos is "unrelated to any desire to control or dominate [Muslim majority nation states]."[51] Second, unlike black American orientalism, which Jackson argues imagines Muslims as a precursor to European and American anti-black racism, Latino orientalism is not driven by the suspicion that Muslims have subjugated Latinos in the past. Third, like black American forms, Latino orientalism competes with narratives that frame Islamic practices not as exotic and other, but as historically and culturally familiar. Latino Muslims will, for example, frequently describe Islamic family organization as similar to that of Latino families. A second prominent example considers veiling practices to be a source of continuity between being Latino and being Muslim.

Many Latino Muslims, including Marta Gallery from LALMA, recall a past when women would were a headscarf as a form of religious piety when going to Catholic mass. They point out that nuns still wear a headscarf as does La Virgen de Guadalupe. In addition to being culturally familiar rather than exotic, Latina Muslim women like Khadija Rivera from PIEDAD argue that veiling functions to counter a "male gaze" that renders women as nothing more than sexual objects.[52] Finally, veiling practices offer a means of negotiating power and leadership roles within specific meeting spaces that Latino Muslims borrow from broader Muslim groups in the United States.[53] As a repertoire of negative depictions of Muslims, Latino orientalism is thus both similar to and distinct from broader forms of American orientalism. Deservedly so, much critical attention has been given to the 9/11 effect, to the increased quantity and increasingly negative coverage of Muslims in American media. However, very little critical attention has been given to the similarities and differences of such orientalist images in Latino media and even less to the critiques of Latino orientalism voiced by Latino Muslims and Latino Muslim organizations.

In an interview for Dr. Akbar S. Ahmed's 2009 documentary film *Journey into America*, Khadijah Rivera from PIEDAD revealed the challenges she faced for wearing a veil in post-9/11 America. "Post 9/11," Rivera told Dr. Ahmed,

> directly after it, I was working here, and it was very hard. I had to actually leave Miami. I was working for the district attorney's office, and people were spitting at me. Yes, I was on the Cristina Show because people were spitting at me. Became very vicious. And I decided to go one step further rather than hide. Some people were even told to take off their veils for safety. I refused. I said, I'm not going to take off my veil because that's sort of like a sign of defeat. I didn't do anything. None of the people that I knew had anything, knew anything about what was going on. So I felt like, sort of like a challenge.[54]

Inspired by the unjust challenges she faced for wearing a veil in post-9/11 America, Rivera decided to fight back. She would not stop wearing her veil as some had suggested, she would not let ignorance and hatred win the battle over what she should and should not wear. Instead, Rivera decided to appear on television in order to set the record straight: she had done nothing wrong and refused to accept the censorship of her veil. Instead of responding with a silent retreat, Rivera responded to the people who spat on her for wearing a veil by going on TV, on the *Show de Cristina* to be precise.

El Show de Cristina, The Cristina Show, was a popular talk show that aired on the Spanish language Univision broadcasting company from 1989 to 2010. Prior to the 1970s, Spanish language broadcasting was co-ethnic: "Mexican media entrepreneurs broadcast several hours of Mexican soap operas, movies, and variety shows to audiences in the Southwest, while Puerto Rican entrepreneurs broadcast programing from San Juan to audiences in New York."[55] By the time of Rivera's appearance on Univision's *El Show de Cristina*, Spanish language broadcasting had become pan-ethnic: its audience and content had become Hispanic or Latino and national rather than Mexican or Puerto Rican and regional. Although Rivera was herself Puerto Rican, her work with PIEDAD and with mass media like the Cristina Show was intended for a broader, pan-ethnic Latino audience.

In 1989, the Spanish International Network was renamed Univision, and *El Show de Cristina* along with the variety show *Sábado Gigante* were created as the rebranded network's new flagship programs. Cristina Saralegui's talk show dominated Latino media in the United States for over a decade. At the height of her popularity, she was referred to by Univision executives, ABC News journalists, and others as the "Spanish Oprah."[56] The show was eventually cancelled in 2010, but not before establishing a media legacy and helping to shape Latino discourse on many topics and issues, including that of Muslims and of Latino Muslims in post-9/11 America.

On December 17, 2002, Khadija Rivera appeared on television sets across the nation through Univision's broadcast waves. On this day, *The Cristina Show* brought national attention to the PIEDAD organization and to Latino Muslims more generally. Rivera's appearance was not without controversy however. Members of various Latino Muslim organizations have since then engaged in heated debates regarding the prudence or lack thereof, of granting interviews to journalists and other media personalities given the negative effect on media practices after 9/11.

The episode featuring Khadijah Rivera was not received well by Latino Muslim leaders. In a rare instance of organized unity, many Latino Muslims and organizations set aside their differences in order to come together, draft, and sign a petition against the slander of Islam by Latino media. The groups utilized PetitionOnline.com, a now defunct internet-based petition service, to disseminate their grievances and to collect support for their requests by gathering virtual signatures. The document was drafted by leaders from the three prominent organizations that developed during the second Latino Muslim wave: Kahdijah Rivera from PIEDAD, Samantha Sanchez from LADO, and Marta Galedary from LALMA. It was titled "Petition to Protest the Defamation by the Spanish Communication Media against Muslim Women and Islam" and was signed by 790 people. The articulated grievances included: the defamation of Islam and of Muslim women on Spanish Radio and Television. And the principle example of such defamation cited in the petition was the 2002 *Cristina Show* in which Rivera had appeared. Despite her intention to fight back against negative stereotyping and the mistreatment of women who choose to wear a veil, Rivera's media appearance was used to perpetuate the negative stereotype instead of diminishing it.

The petition critiqued journalistic practices that have also been criticized by Edward Said in his book *Covering Islam*. By relying on so-called experts, journalists chuck off both the work of thorough investigative research and their responsibility for the accuracy of their reporting.[57] "It is unjustifiable" the petition admonished "to judge a religion and its congregates using a so called Religion Expert as Khalid Duran. This man is an Islamaphobic due to his passionate aversion to Islam. His goal is widespread defamation of Islam."[58] Khalid Duran is a scholar of Middle Eastern languages and Islamic studies and has held visiting professor positions at various universities including Temple University and the University of California, Irvine. The use of so-called experts in journalistic reporting cannot be used to replace thorough investigative research. On the other hand, critiques of such journalistic practices should themselves be rooted in more carefully researched and thought out conclusions. Latino Muslim leaders should have clearly articulate the basis for calling Khalid Duran Islamaphobic, but failed to do so. The result is a discourse riddled with conflict and ambiguity, both sides relying on simplistic stereotypes that encourage visceral responses while discouraging deeper dialogue.

Despite the shortcomings of the petition, its requests were reasonable. Latino Muslims are not large in number however. According to the most generous reports, there are no more than 200,000 across the nation today and much less when the petition was signed. And 790 petitiononline.com signatures amounts to less than 0.5 percent of this estimated total number of Latino Muslims in the United States. Either our current projections are grossly overestimated or both leaders and internet technologies have failed to organize Latino Muslims around specific issues that affect all of its members. Even if Latino Muslims could manage to procure signatures from each and every one of its identity group's members, this would only amount to a drop in the ocean when compared to the estimated 100 million viewers of *El Show de Cristina*.[59] It is no wonder then that Univision never responded to the petitions. The document's requests included: (1) to respectfully end the undemocratic and unjust negative stereotyping of Muslims; and (2) to provide "airtime to expose the misinformation that is being broadcast. Or rebuttal time to answer the allegations."

If we agree that media, and news media in particular, are vital to our democratic processes, that they offer public forums to discuss and inform issues that are relevant to many, then we should also agree with the petition's first request that such forums be civil and not unduly slanderous of any identity group. We should, as Amy Gutmann argues in *Identity in Democracy*, demand fair treatment for all even if we do not belong to the identity group being negatively stereotyped. Although Latino Muslims should indeed be at the forefront of our collective critiques against reductive and negative stereotypes of Latino Muslims, it is the moral obligation of all, including those in privileged positions with access to social capital and other vital resources, to become more familiarized with each other and to also participate in such critical discourse.[60] Internet technologies facilitate our participation in signature collecting for social justice petitions. We can choose to support the end of unduly negative representations of identity groups like Latino Muslims in Latino media from the convenience of our smartphones, tablets, laptops, or desktop computers. However, though such support is in theory made easier through internet technologies, in practice—it remains to be seen how many outside of the group actually lend their voice to the cause or even if a larger but virtual voice will be taken into consideration by the gatekeepers of mass media.[61]

The second request, for airtime to present a rebuttal, may be less reasonable than the first. Instead, internet technologies like websites, blogs, YouTube videos, and social media present a more practical means for bypassing the neglected request for rebuttal time. Latino Muslims produce and disseminate both critiques of how they are negatively and inaccurately represented in Latino media and also offer alternative autobiographical representations of themselves online.[62] Once again, however, it remains to be seen how much and what kind of influence such self-produced digital media will have on public discourse. It is not enough for small identity groups to be able to broadcast to mass audiences. The attention of potential audiences must also be gained, a feat that in our current communications systems require vast amounts of capital.

In order to reform unjust media practices that are negatively affecting our democratic processes, all participants in the media cycle will have to radically reform their morally implicated practices. Executives and media producers should consider the moral implication of their practices and content and they should also be persuaded to do so by petitions, boycotts, lawsuits, and legal reforms. Interviewees chosen to be so-called experts should carefully choose when and to whom they speak, they should only engage topics in which they are well informed, and they should clearly articulate evidence or support for their views.

Media consumers should thoughtfully choose the content they consume and critically engage the views presented in such content. As consumers, we should also help support the end of undemocratic and unjustly negative stereotyping of identity groups by signing petitions, creating our own, writing letters, and engaging in thought out, organized, and publically expressed boycotts. Members of identity groups that lack access to social capital and the economic resources to dissuade their defamation in mass media have and should continue to screen journalists and the institutions they work for and in some instances choose not to provide interviews. They should also seek support from broader audiences for fair representation and produce and disseminate alternative representations of themselves through media outlets available to them. Academics and researchers, including those who might identify or be identified as Latino Muslims, should provide more details regarding the context, diversity, and complexity surrounding issues of representation. Although such reforms require much from many, failure to do so will increasingly threaten our already fragile democratic project in America.

CONCLUSIONS

When I asked Marta Galedary about a story for the *Los Angeles Times* we had both been interviewed for, she said the reporter had changed the angle to something about how odd it is for Latinos to participate in Ramadan fasting. "It was, you know, this sensational thing. So I told the reporter I didn't want to do the interview anymore." The story never ran. Having been soured by previous interview experiences, even some academics have been denied interviews and access to Latino Muslim communities. In a footnote to his monograph *Latina/o y Musulmán*, Hjamil A. Martínez-Vázquez writes:

> Weeks after I started contacting the leaders of the different Latina/
> o Muslims organizations across the United States to ask for their help
> in the development of my research project, I received an email from a
> member of the community warning me that an email has been sent out
> to other members asking them not to participate in my research. The
> email, as it was forwarded to me, read: "I have received more than one
> time a message from H. Mrtinez-Vasquez, who is doing a research study
> about Latinos/as converting to Islam. This professor works for an Ultra
> Christian University in Texas. LALMA has declined to participate in
> this research study. We believe that the information gathered from this

research will be used against us in the future. . . . Please, investigate this person and the type of University where he teaches, and warn our brothers and sisters not to participate in this research study. I just wonder, Why a Christian University will be so interested in learning about Latinos/as converts?"[63]

The research project ran. Despite LALMA's critique and without its blessing and participation, Martínez-Vázquez was able to procure twenty interviews to produce the first monograph on Latino Muslims. In my assessment, Martínez-Vázquez was not villainously trying to slander the identity group and was conducting scholarly research independent of his workplace's views of Muslims. On the other hand, his research requests came on the heels of negative experiences the group had had with journalistic representations of the group. LALMA's response therefore also seems understandable given these experiences. The episode reveals just how difficult it is for groups like LALMA to assess the efficacy of participating in interviews. In addition to underscoring the complex negotiation that occurs between scholars and the individuals they work with, negotiations between individual agents and their broader democratic institutions, including the news media cycles that they participate within, are also revealed to be complex and often dauntingly so. Nevertheless, we would fail to engage in these processes to our own detriment and that of our fragile democratic processes.

The increased news media attention that Latino Muslims have received forms part of broader media cycles and a post-9/11 context. Although not overtly negative, news reports on the group have nevertheless been mostly sensational and have myopically focused on conversion. To the question, why do Latinos convert to Islam, answers vary but usually include issues regarding doctrine, social equality, and marriage. The focus on conversion identity and question of why do Latinos convert to Islam presents problematic implications. In addition to covering up the diversity and complexity that exists among Latino Muslim populations, it also implicitly frames the decision to embrace Islam as a senseless multiplication of marginality. Latino Muslims nevertheless continue to provide interviews for these reductive news stories with the hope that they will be able to procure legitimization and recognition and increase their numbers, social capital, and access to broader networks with vital resources.

Such negotiation seems less reasonable when the group is not only reduced to issues of conversion but are overtly represented negatively. And as we have seen, this is precisely what has happened in many interactions with Spanish language media in the United States. Latino Muslim leaders and organizations have responded by forming petitions against media institutions that slander their identity and by more carefully screening journalists prior to granting interviews. For their part, LALMA is much more careful when granting interviews. They and other Latino Muslim leaders have in effect become the gatekeepers for journalists seeking to cover the Latino Muslim beat. These leaders will need to carefully weigh the benefits and costs of working with mass media institutions. If and when they choose to refuse to grant interviews, they will have to navigate the challenges that arise from doing so, including the possibility of having no voice or a significantly reduced one in public representations of their identity. If and when they, on the other hand, choose to grant interviews, they will have to consider the possibility of being reduced to issues of conversion or of even being represented negatively as oppressed or, as we will see in the next chapter, even as potential terrorists.

CHAPTER FIVE

RADICALS

LATINO MUSLIM HIP-HOP AND THE "CLASH OF CIVILIZATIONS" THING

Our most precious asset in the face of such a dire transformation of history is the emergence not of a sense of clash but a sense of community, understanding, sympathy, and hope, which is the direct opposite of what Huntington provokes.

—Edward Said, "The Myth of 'The Clash of Civilizations'"

From the now defunct MySpace.com/M-Team social media page, a digital flag of Puerto Rico fades in to initiate a series of flash-animated graphical images (see fig. 5.1). Then the *shahadah*, the Islamic proclamation of faith, "there is no god but God," and a red revolutionary fist superimposed onto the flag's blue triangle take form on the screen. Images of Hamza and Suliman Pérez, each passionately speaking Islamic protest-poetry into a microphone frame the flag on either side. A shadowy silhouette emerges with a flaming machete raised in hand. He lights fire to all of the color images until all that is left are the ashes of the Puerto Rican flag. The ashes then color a new instance of the *shahadah* now in a sharp-edged modern Kufic calligraphy. The font is a reference to an Islamic identity redesigned for a contemporary hip-hop context. Here, it is part of a logo, a creative and strategic fashioning of Remarkable Current's brand identity, the graphical representation of a record label company. New, less gritty and in-color images then replace the previous black and white action poses of the Pérez brothers. The brothers are calm but project a critical gaze. They sport shades and leather jackets. The image behind them is raw and frenzied, but they are cool. It is a cacophony of signifiers, digital representations

FIGURE 5.1.

Three sequential screenshots of Adobe Flash animated introduction to
M-Team's MySpace website. http://myspace.com/mteam/.

of the Mujahideen Team (aka M-Team, aka Pérez brothers) who wage
a media battle against competing images of Islam.

In 2005, the Pérez brothers released their album *Clash of Civilizations*
and in 2009 *My Enemy's Enemy*. Both musical productions employed
militant and violent rhetoric in their severe critiques of American politics, society, and culture. Then in 2009, PBS broadcast the documentary film *New Muslim Cool*, which focused on Hamza Pérez's social
service work and family life while mostly ignoring the violent content
of his and his brother's hip-hop. The stark contrast between the Pérez
brothers' hip-hop and the *New Muslim Cool* film highlights pervasive
media practices that reduce Muslims to an "either with us or against

us" framework. Critical protest from a Muslim's perspective is, within this framework, largely understood as an "outsider's" attack on a particularly imagined and passionately guarded American culture. Thus, when Latino Muslims appear in mass media they are framed as either harmlessly bizarre or as threateningly villainous. The previous chapter demonstrated how mainstream news media adopted the former approach and Spanish language media the latter. Although most mainstream news articles on Latino Muslims reduce the ethno-religious group almost exclusively to issues of conversion, Latino Muslims have generally not been represented as a threat within this genre. There have been several exceptions to this general trend however. Jose Padilla prompted the first of these exceptions as the first post-9/11 American citizen to be tried as an enemy combatant. And when he attempted to detonate a fake bomb supplied by undercover FBI agents posing as Muslim terrorists, Antonio Martinez prompted the latest news media connection between Latino and a so-called radical Muslim nature.

This chapter is a critical appraisal of media practices that assume conflict rather than peaceful coexistence. I begin by first introducing the "clash of civilizations" thesis, the view that the next world conflict will be fought over cultural values rather than ideological divisions. My examination of the clash of civilizations thesis is prompted by the Pérez brothers' hip-hop album by the same title. The assumption of a culture war has not only contributed to the reduction of Latino Muslims into simplistic binaries, it also infects broader discourses regarding the character of American civilization and the treatment of its so-called minorities. The second part of the chapter therefore deals with news coverage of Antonio Martinez's arrest, which forms part of the ongoing perception that Islam is a threat, but then links "radical" nature (i.e., violent behavior and ideology) to both Muslim and Latino identities.[1] Coverage of Martinez extended its arms to include and move beyond and also echoed biological concepts of race: as if saying that all Latinos are by nature radicals and therefore potential terrorists. Latino Muslim leaders and organizations responded with media campaigns of their own waged on two fronts: one against post-9/11 Islamophobic images, the other internal, against a brand of Islam they understand to be radical. This, however, is a war that cannot be won. Instead, it is a media conflict whose very existence should be denied, or at the very least, overshadowed by much more diverse and complex visions of being. This is because if it is adopted, though it need not be, the clash of civilizations thesis articulated by the likes of Samuel Huntington must and has assumed a vision of conflict over one of peaceful coexistence and constructive relationships.

The Clash via Hip-Hop

In 1993, Samuel P. Huntington published his article "The Clash of Civilizations?" in *Foreign Affairs* and in 1996 expanded it into a book titled *The Clash of Civilizations and the Remaking of World Order*.[2] Here, Huntington argued that the Cold War conflict was essentially between communist and capitalist ideologies. And that when the Cold War came to an end with the collapse of the Soviet Union, global politics has and will continue to be characterized primarily by cultural and religious conflict in its stead. The clash of civilizations thesis aligns itself with the assimilation model for dealing with so-called minority groups or foreigners in the United States. In the opening to his *Clash of Civilizations* book, Huntington identified the 1994 Los Angeles demonstrations against California's Proposition 187 as one important example of the assimilation model he has in mind. The proposed law sought to prohibit so-called illegal aliens from accessing California state services like public education and emergency health care. When protesting Prop 187, many marchers used Mexican flags and not US ones. Journalistic coverage focused much of its attention on the Mexican flags as a sign that the Latino protestors were un-American, asking why they were not holding US flags instead. In response to the negative news media representations, protestors defiantly waved US flags purposefully arranged upside down. The gesture seemed to have worked against the protest movement when in November 1994 Prop 187 was approved by 59 percent of Californian voters.

"In the post–Cold War world," Huntington writes regarding this episode, "flags count and so do other symbols of cultural identity, including crosses, crescents, and even head coverings, because culture counts, and cultural identity is what is most meaningful to most people."[3] After identifying culture and religion as the primary causes of current and future conflict in global politics, Huntington makes several prescriptions. First, foreign policy should "exploit differences and conflicts among Confucian and Islamic states to support in other civilizations groups sympathetic to western values and interests."[4] Second, domestic policies, according to Huntington, should drastically reduce legal immigration to the United States so that those who are already here can "adequately assimilate."[5] For Huntington, and many other influential voices in public discourse, Latinos and Muslims who do not assimilate in such a way as to embody "western values and interests" represent a threat to American civilization and should be dealt with strategically as enemies of the state.

In their highly influential work *Racial Formations in the United States*, Michael Omi and Howard Winant formulate culture as a definitive element of the ethnicity paradigm of race. Ethnicity paradigms that characterized race as cultural constructs displaced the prominence of biologistic paradigms of race, though these continue to play a prevalent role in public discourse today. Ethnicity came to be understood as the result of "a group formation process based on culture and descent."[6] Accordingly, culture was theorized as consisting of language, arts, customs, and, significantly, religion. Despite the progressive move away from biologistic paradigms of race, the ethnicity paradigm failed to promote democratic equality for America's racialized groups in both its assimilationist and multiculturalist forms.

Assimilationists like Huntington and others seek a domestic policy that promotes the integration of so-called minority groups to dominant forms of American society. Assimilationists maintain that if these so-called minority groups would only abandon their culturally distinctive characteristics (e.g., Spanish and radical or different religiosity) and adopt those of the dominant culture, they could gain access to all the freedoms and rights offered by the United States.[7] Latinos, many of whom are also brown or black, present a conundrum to the assimilationist paradigms. Early twentieth-century immigration programs that encouraged farmworkers from Mexico to move to the Southwest were designed to import a temporary and cheap labor force. This paved the way for a perpetual framing of Latinos in public discourse as undesired foreigners. Policies such as these have not only rejected Latino assimilation into American society, but have also worked against it.

When so-called minorities, including Latino and black identity groups, failed to achieve democratic and economic equality despite the shift toward the ethnicity paradigms of race, culture and heredity were often blamed instead. "If Chicanos don't do so well in school," it was argued, "this cannot, even hypothetically, be due to low-quality education; it has instead to do with Chicano values."[8] Latino inequality was, in other words, framed not as the result of failed state policies, but instead as the result of an inherited set of cultural values. Despite the lip service paid to ethnicity as socially constructed, intellectual, religious, and other such characteristics were attributed to values causally transmitted by descent as they had been in the biologistic model of race.

Although not all Latinos constitute an immigrant population, all Latinos are subjected to dominant stereotypes of Latinos as undesired immigrants. Latino ethnicity is in this conception constructed not only by the dominant discourse but also in response to it by Latinos themselves. Rather than taking the position of victimization, economic and political inequalities are reformulated as common foes with the potential to create a unified Latino identity in opposition to them. Likewise, the experience of ethnic marginalization by Latino Muslims has been discursively used to rationalize the development and dissemination of a unified Latino Muslim identity in opposition to marginalization of Latino Muslims.

On January 1, 2005, nearly a decade after Huntington's publication, the Pérez brothers released an album titled *Clash of Civilizations*, self-described as "a conflict of ideas. A combat of visions. A war of words."[9] Both Huntington and the Pérez brothers, in their own ways, articulate a vision of violent conflict between competing cultural and religious traditions, between a Christianity from the West and an Islam from the East. Each articulation not only describes the conflict but also clearly sides with one camp over the other and thus become combatants in a culture war that they have helped to prop up.

The following examines mediations by and of the Pérez brothers.[10] First, I look at discourse within the Pérez brothers' hip-hop and highlight the ways in which it both imagines clear divisions between "us and them" and also renders the Pérez brothers as "outsiders," as enemy combatants in the so-called clash of civilizations. Second, I look at the *New Muslim Cool* documentary film and its contrasting vision of Hamza Pérez, not as an enemy but as a father, a husband, and a "good" moral citizen. Both visions of the Pérez brothers, however, support an "either with us or against us" reduction of not only Muslims but also of more broadly imagined groups of so-called minorities, including Latinos.

MILITANT MEDIA?

As the Mujahideen Team, or the "doers of *jihad*," the Pérez brothers' hip-hop prose expresses militant critiques of America. Like their digital personas, the Pérez brothers regularly included flaming machetes in their live stage performances. "*Machete*," Hamza Pérez explains in an interview, "it's a Puerto Rican custom, ya know, the *macheteros*." "This is a finely crafted art that we have here that we add to our stage performance," adds Suliman, "and when we have interactions and discussions with people after the shows, you know, we're able to relay that to them and let em know a little about what it symbolizes so they don't think we're just two crazy Puerto Ricans on the stage with machetes."[11] In the following scene, the M-Team is introduced to a crowd in a dimly lit venue. As the crowd chants "Mujahideen Team" over and over, the Pérez brothers walk onto the stage with flaming machetes. "We don't care about no Patriot Act! We don't care about surveillance! We don't care about no FBI agents in the crowd, this is for y'all." The camera cuts to several Muslims, diverse in many ways, but all are young and all nod their heads in agreement with Hamza's pronouncements. "Bin Laden didn't blow up the projects" the M-Team raps while using lines and beats from a track titled 911 by Immortal Technique, Mos Def, and

Eminem. The Pérez brothers then break away from the established lyrics offering another set of lines: "Saudi Arabia's in bed with America! Israel, England's in bed with America! No Vaseline when you sleep with the predator. Only one God and Muhammad is his messenger! Cocaine business controls America! Zionist business controls America! Masonic business controls America! . . . yo," the beat comes to an end before they continue "that was for the FBI right there," a critical ending in the tradition of Malcolm X to which the crowd responds to with cheers and applause.

The performance of Puerto Rican identity through props like flaming machete swords and album titles that reference academic arguments contribute to and are better understood through a complex web of signifiers. Rather than simply critique their hip-hop as promoting violence or praise it as an accurate reflection of marginalization, the duo understands their work primarily as a form of *dawah*. Although there is disagreement within various Muslim communities as to whether music in general is a permissible way of calling others to Islam, in keeping with old and new traditions (including Sufi and American) and on the advice of their *sheikh* (religious mentor), the Pérez brothers performed *dawah* through their protest poetry or Islamic hip-hop (also referred to by others, including Five Percenters, as God Hop).[12] They seek to "speak the truth" in the way of Malcolm X, to critique the roots of injustices as they see them. It is a form of protest poetry and a call to action against such injustices. Their protest poetry is situated within a historically specific and complex framework, one performed through a diverse set of symbols. In relation to others, these symbols reference an edgy tension, a strategic cultural consciousness, and a militant critique of American neocolonialism.[13]

The Pérez brothers' album art forms an important part of this web of signifiers. The front cover of the *Clash of Civilizations* album features cropped portraits of the Pérez brothers' faces stylized to resemble the iconic Korda negatives of Latin American revolutionary Ernesto "Che" Guevara.[14] The reference includes a red background, black and white negative stylizing and revolutionary stars. There are also hip-hop elements including graffiti font spelling out "M-Team" and thick white vertical lines bleeding down over the red background resembling a freshly painted mural. The inner case graphics features a photograph of several hands holding up assault rifles and handguns in the air, this time edging closer to visual stories having more to do with "gangster rap" than with Latin American revolutionaries. Written on the inner portion of the foldout is a manifesto:

> The Clash of Civilizations is a conflict of ideas. A combat of visions. A war of words. This clash has ignited the hearts of those who love truth and justice. Those who strive to free themselves from the shackles of oppression, ignorance, and hate. This Clash of Civilizations serves as a warning to the merchants of darkness everywhere: mend your ways or prepare to reap what you have sown. On the frontlines of this clash you will find the Mujahideen Team. A team of strugglers, striving against their own lusts. Soldiers who battle tirelessly against the "Kuffar." By "Kuffar," we mean any person, being or system that attempts to cover the Light and Mercy of the all encompassing Divine Reality. . . . Those who wish to subject humanity to the tyranny of their greed and thirst for worldly power. . . . Those who wish to frustrate the unfolding of a global unity that binds together all humans under the banner of peace through submission to the Creator of all things. In this clash the lines are clearly drawn. What side are you on?—Mujahideen Team.

Despite the machete swords and guns, the M-Team's battle is an ethical one. Their *jihad* or struggle is against their own lusts. The clash is against "the merchants of darkness" and against injustice. In this worldview, a clash of civilizations' worldview, the "lines are clearly drawn." What is clear from their manifesto is that the M-Team has adopted and promoted an "us versus them" worldview.

Much of the album's lyrical sound images are also militant in character. In "Sonic Jihad" scholar SpearIt argues that the most radical rhetoric in the United States is not by Muslim inmates as some have hypothesized, and as will be discussed later in this chapter, instead it is found within the hip-hop genre in general: "hip hop lyrics represent some of the most extremist [or radical] speech at play in American society" writes SpearIt after referencing lyrics by the M-Team. "In this arena, Muslim artists have emerged as leaders against a foe that continues to swallow individuals and communities whole. In this struggle, rappers need no assistance from their religious brethren abroad; they bring a history of rapping over beats rooted in slave spirituals that stretches all the way to Africa."[15] The "foe" that SpearIt here refers to is US structural racisms that include police brutality and the mass incarceration of black and brown people. And rather than fear "foreign" influences or radical ideologies severely critical of US structural injustices, SpearIt points to an "indigenous," sonic, and severe critique of the US' moral standing including the practice of slavery on which much of America was built. If understood as a form of endemic and ubiquitous social injustice, we may find severe criticisms of such practices to be reasonable. Here, the line between reasonable critiques and radical rhetoric may have to do with who we believe is justified in the use of violence or violent rhetoric and who is not (e.g., US military forces and their governing bodies versus Muslim rappers and their producers). And this line between the justified and unjustified has become entangled with our representations of Muslims and Muslim rappers as either "good or bad."[16]

Within the dominant good versus bad and justified versus unjustified binaries, it becomes easy to characterize the M-Team's lyrics as radical. On the "Dead Have Risen'" track, for example, the Pérez brothers repeatedly chant: "Mujahideen Team wear your flag of the *deen* [religion or faith], busting AK's with banana magazines." On their "Gun Fire Sound" track, they rap: "This gun fire sound, it got you ducking down, afraid to come around, it make you hit the ground, your heart it starts to pound, we gonna fire rounds, this gun fire sound, blah!" And on their "FTG" (Flag the Government) track, they declare: "If these *kafirs* [unbelievers] want beef, we can take it to the streets on the battlefield, *jihad* [struggle], you got guns we got guns . . . on the battlefield, *jihad* . . . face the facts, *jihad* is part of this *deen*, it's either with yourself or an M-16. It's either the sword, the gun, the war of the *nafs* [ego], shootouts, death, prison or handcuffs." Lyrical references to battles fought with guns such as these are found throughout the album's sixteen tracks. "Sometimes I don't like the music," the mother of the Pérez brothers complains in an interview, "Sometimes I do. Some songs I like, some songs I don't like. The words are kind of tough sometimes."[17]

In lyrics like these, the Pérez brothers adopt a fairly straightforward understanding of Huntington's clash of civilizations thesis. They seem to agree that Western values are at odds with Muslim mores. Rather than side with Huntington's prescriptions for continued Western domination over Muslim majority societies, however, the Pérez brothers promote Islamic ideals as the best hope for achieving social justice. In their track "Threnody," for example, the Pérez brothers continue to portray themselves as cultural warriors engaged in a fierce battle, one in which they will most likely be killed: "If I fight and I die and they murder me, pray that heaven got a spot for me." The mournful tone of the track not only frames the potential cost of fighting against cultural norms but also sets the tone for the M-Team's ethical worldview:

> The unheard cries of a border child's grave," the track continues ". . . the pain of poor people puts a weight on my chest, the lifestyles and conditions of the poor and oppressed, only thing holding me up from falling down is when my hands and my forehead touch the ground. I hear politicians lying, my little baby crying . . . but their so-called freedom is disguised with lies. My people are locked up, my people are shot up, my people are caught up and raised in handcuffs. The amount of our paychecks is never enough, trying to explain to my child why this life is so rough.

Here, the Pérez brothers articulate their grievances: it is an analysis of unjust conditions produced by a so-called Western civilization. According to this analysis, political leaders render nothing more than lip service to the pervasive problems of discriminatory border practices and class divisions, the problems of unstable and dangerous social conditions, and of a prison industrial complex that is racist by design. As if fighting a losing but nevertheless important battle, the lyrics offer one form of solace, one source of inspiration to continue the struggle: *salat*, prayer, a physical and spiritual prostration before God. It is by falling down in recognition of their own limitations while simultaneously recognizing the omnipotence of God that the Pérez brothers are able to make sense of their inevitable defeat in the war of words that they are engaged in. They believe it is not their place to change the tide. Instead, it is their duty to simply submit to the will of God. Their hip-hop is their *jihad*, it is their struggle. And their struggle is their devotion to God.

The *Clash of Civilizations* album promotes pan-Latino revolutionaries as allies in this struggle. The album's opening track, "Clashtro," begins with the invocation *basmala*, in the name of God, and is followed by a slow steady beat punctuated by an occasional church bell and a Spanish guitar, jazz piano, and trumpet in the background. But the track's main content is the overlay of a Spanish language speech given by Che Guevara to the United Nations General Assembly on December 12, 1964:

> There is no small enemy nor insignificant force, because there are no isolated villages. As stated in the Second Declaration of Havana: No nation in Latin America is weak, because it is part of a family of two hundred million brothers, who suffer the same miseries, who harbor the same feelings, have the same enemy, dream about the same best destination and the solidarity of all honest men and women in the world.[18]

Here, Guevara identified similar experiences rather than biology or even ethnic heredity as the ties that bind together hundreds of millions of people throughout Latin America.[19] And the similar set of experiences that Guevara has in mind are the negative effects of neocolonialism, "the co-option and exploitation of underdeveloped countries through monopolistic capital."[20] Latin Americans are bound together by a common enemy: US imperialism, which has imposed "distorted development" or singular markets utterly dependent on and subservient to the

United States.[21] It is this Pan-Latin American vision, a frontierless Latin America, that informed Guevara's revolutionary action in Cuba and Bolivia even though he was born and raised in Argentina. And it is also a Pan-Latin American vision that, in part, informs the Pérez brothers' self-understanding as "other" to America, as victims of US neocolonialism.

The M-Team's hip-hop articulates a unified, urgent, and revolutionary theme. The "Axe and the Machete" track, for example, begins with a sample from Puerto Rican salsa singer Héctor Lavoe's song "Hacha y Machete" and promptly transitions to a funkier set of sounds and rhymes: "Mobilize . . . we're Colombians, and Peruvians, Puerto Ricans, Blacks and Andalusians," they proclaim in English before switching to Spanish:

> y el Profeta sigue brillando.
> Una cosecha, M-Team está ganando . . .
> hacha y machete, café con leche, cuando llegara el día de mi suerte?
> Revolution, hasta la muerte!
> mi gente . . . Jesucristo, la Virgen María,
> Profeta Muhammad, la luz de la vida

> and the Prophet keeps shining.
> A harvest, the M-Team is gaining . . .
> The axe and the machete, coffee with milk, when will my day arrive?
> Revolution, till the day I die!
> my people . . . Jesus, the Virgin Mary,
> Prophet Muhammad, the light of all life.[22]

Diverse people who have experienced injustices are here called to mobilize and to commit to revolution. But this is not just Guevara's revolutionary vision. Instead, it also, and importantly, draws from other *gente* (people): from Jesus, the Virgin Mary, and the Prophet Muhammad. This is to be a moral and religious revolution, one that overturns Western values with Islamic ones. One which envisions two sides, the forces of good and those of evil. It is a "cosmic war" being played out as a media campaign.[23]

A "CLOSER VIEW OF HUMAN DECENCY"

The Pérez brothers' hip-hop articulates a militant critique of America and is framed as a media attack on so-called Western values. As such, they risk being reduced to Muslim radicals, outsiders and enemies within our post-9/11 media context. However, most media consumers are not introduced to the Pérez brothers through their self-produced hip-hop. A much more widely consumed representation of the Pérez brothers aired on June 23, 2009, in the form of a Point of View documentary film on PBS. What had begun as a project focused on Muslim youth culture and hip-hop by documentary film producer Jennifer Maytorena Taylor ended up focusing instead on the life of Hamza Pérez. In stark contrast to their violently militant protest poetry, the *New Muslim Cool* film focuses on Hamza Pérez's intersecting identities as a Latino and Muslim, as a father and husband, as a brother and son, and as a morally conscious individual and law-abiding citizen.

The same day that the film aired, the *New York Times* published an article titled "New Muslim Cool: Islam, Hope and Charity Inspire Dealer Turned Rapper" by Ginia Bellafante.[24] The article began with an almost thankful tone that the film "has no investment in cool at all." Bellafante from the *Times* is happy to share that the film focuses instead on the character of Puerto Rican Muslim rapper Hamza Pérez and thereby provides "an opportunity to access a closer view of human decency."[25] Bellafante recalls Hamza's opening words in the film: "I would always have two consistent dreams my whole life. One that I was going to experience death at twenty-one. The other one that I was going to be in jail. And then, both of them came true." Both dreams symbolically came true for Hamza at age twenty-one when he converted to Islam, died to his old way of life and found himself in prison working as chaplain. "New Muslim Cool," writes Bellafante, "possesses a kind of beauty that sneaks up on you: it is in Hamza's humility, in the dignity with which he confronts so much of his misfortune, in his commitment to rehabilitating drug dealers because, in his mind, no one else will."[26] Taylor had begun filming Hamza because of his hip-hop, but the film does not linger long on this dimension of Hamza's identity.

This is not the machete-wielding Muslim revolutionary who references an arsenal of firearms when waging his war of words. Instead, those who are introduced to Hamza Pérez via the *New Muslim Cool* film learn much more about his family life and social service work than they do about his militant hip-hop.

The camera closes in on a street sign of Malcolm X Boulevard in New York. Hamza is wearing a black T-shirt with a Puerto Rican flag. He and his brother Suliman Pérez walk up the street and into the Mosque of Islamic Brotherhood Inc., the "lineal descendant" of the Muslim Mosque Inc. founded by Malik el-Shabazz (Malcolm X), in 1964 after his departure from the Nation of Islam.[27] The Pérez brothers sit in a radio studio wearing headphones and lean into a microphone. Hamza Pérez is introduced on WHCR Harlem community radio (from the campus of the City College of New York):

> We have here in the studio my favorite Muslim rap artists, brothers Suliman and Hamza Pérez . . . and they are otherwise known professionally as the Mujahideen Team. And a mujahid is a person who engages in *jihad*. In the post September 11 world, this is a very ah, I mean y'all picked a very strong name.

To which Suliman responds:

> *jihad* doesn't mean holy war, you know, we tell 'em it's struggle. You know, we struggle everyday with our nafs, our inner self, our lower desires. We kind of teach the people what it means and what the word means to us. We're not afraid to use that word.

The radio host then continues:

> So now, brother Hamza, you were a single dad, now you're married. So you're a married man, you're a Muslim, you're American, you're Puerto Rican, you're from the hood, you're an artist, you're a rapper, you're a, you know, ha, you sound like America's worst nightmare![28]

Hamza's intersecting identities defy simplistic categorization and expectations. And this difficulty is underscored as a very American problem rather than as a democratic strength. In another scene within Suliman's home kitchen, the two brothers further discuss their intersectional identities, again in a joking manner:

HAMZA: "We don't know full Arabic, but we know, Arabic-Spanglish-Ebonics."

SULIMAN: "We don't know English well, we don't speak English well, we don't Speak Spanish well or Arabic."

HAMZA: "So we're translating the language of . . ."

SULIMAN: " . . . Puerto Rican Ebonics, Puertoronics!"

HAMZA: "Puertoronics!"

The English, Spanish, and Arabic words he speaks, the Puerto Rican flags, *kufis* (skull cap), Islamic prayer beads, and hip-hop attire he wears, the biological family he communes with and the religious one he prays with, and the life he lives "off and on" media representations articulate specific instances of inter-cultural contact between Latinos and Muslims.

The camera follows Hamza from one domestic scene to another, usually appearing with one or more family members: with his brother, his mother, his children, or his wife Rafiah. Hamza and Rafiah first met on Naseeb.com, a dating website for Muslims. Rafiah tells the audience that she liked the online process because "it eliminated anything, it eliminated any, like, lust or attraction where you get distracted and you don't ask the important questions." The audience is given a glimpse of the wedding that follows Hamza's and Rafiah's courtship. Prior to the wedding, Hamza describes the upcoming ceremony to his barber as a meeting between his Latino and mostly Catholic family and his wife's black and mostly Muslim family as a form of inter-cultural contact. The ceremony takes place in a mosque. Hamza's mother and non-Muslim family are awkward in the unfamiliar Islamic space and do not know exactly what to do. The bride and groom pledge themselves to each other with exuberant smiles and all present celebrate the union with cheers. The newlywed couple move in together where they will raise their children from previous relationships. Hamza and his two children and Rafiah and her daughter are now a family.

In addition to focusing on his domestic life, quite a bit of attention is given to Hamza's social service work in the film. While working as a prison chaplain, Hamza is asked about people who accept your apology for wronging them but nevertheless seek out revenge. Hamza responds:

> You reap what you sow.... If I hurt somebody, right, I go stab somebody, right, I can't just go repent to God and leave it like that. How many of us we've done something to people, and inside we're not at peace with ourselves cause we done hurt this person.... You can't just repent to God and think that everything's all honky-dory, you all set, you chillin now. You repent no doubt, but you have to ask them for forgiveness too, you understand? To gain the complete healing.

Hamza is not merely preaching from theory here, it is from his own direct experiences. He feels he has been given a second chance, that he has hurt people in his past and is now supposed to be dead or locked up as a consequence. He has repented, no doubt, has fundamentally changed his life away from violence, drugs, and crime . . . but he is also asking for forgiveness. It is a penitent and grateful spirit along with a love for people who grew up in similar socioeconomic conditions as his that animates Hamza's social service work.

"I believe that there's stuff that I did on the streets, sometimes it's on me and I feel a responsibility to go and try to rectify that and change it," Hamza explains in a narrative voice as the camera captures him driving toward a community meeting. He stands before a group of young men and their mothers in a rec center: "We're gonna look at hustling like a corporation . . . it's American business, where's there's crack, where there's Nikes, where there's Walmart, it's all pimpin and ho'in." Hamza's narrative voice then returns to explain the scene to the film's audience even as the camera continues to capture his lecture:

As a Muslim, you need to know what's going on in society. . . . We have to deliver in the strongest form possible our message. This is the way of Malcolm X, 'cause Malcolm X didn't care how people felt. He was going to speak the truth, he was going to tell them how it is, and he was going to deliver it by any means necessary.

His lectures in prison and community outreach take the form of protest. This protest, or critical focus on American injustices, provides Hamza with an attentive audience. The hip-hop crowds, the prison inmates, and those who had gathered in the rec center all nod their heads in agreement over and over again as they soak in Hamza's words. And though his hip-hop is part of this protest, a protest poetry, it falls to the wayside in the film. Instead, the focus of *New Muslim Cool* is on Hamza's struggle to be a good father and husband, a good brother and son, a law-abiding citizen and a moral person trying to rectify American injustices. There is one important caveat, however, he is doing so as a Latino Muslim in a post-9/11 America.

After representing Hamza as primarily concerned with his family, community, and with social justice, Hamza ominously narrates, "when things are too good, I start to worry." A few scenes later, the film is interrupted with video clips from what was then breaking news coverage. Hamza's mosque was raided by FBI agents during a Friday *Jummah* prayer. Various theories as to why the mosque was raided by the FBI are explored in the film. Perhaps they were searching for ex-convict Larry Williams who had stayed at the mosque the night before. Or perhaps, Williams had given the FBI an excuse to search the mosque and its members who had, as it turns out, been under surveillance long before Williams stopped by. "I start thinking about my kids you know what I'm saying," Hamza narrates, "where would they go, who's gonna stay with them if I get locked up." After some time and reflection, Hamza offers a new interpretation of the raid: "I just looked at it like, as a, you know, just waking me up a little bit. Letting me know the state of and the reality of being Muslim in America." The film prods its audience to conclude that though some Muslims like Larry Williams are "bad," to treat all Muslims as such is unjust. The film represents a counterexample, it both portrays Hamza as a so-called good Muslim and also criticizes government surveillance and counterterrorism practices that discriminatorily infringe on the rights of such good Muslims.

Within a media war, *New Muslim Cool*, its producers, and its proponents have chosen a side: to combat negative stereotypes of Muslims by increasing representations of so-called good Muslims in public discourse. In *Rebel Music: Race, Empire, and the New Muslim Youth Culture*, Hisham Aidi identifies a dispatch from the American embassy in London recommending the screening of the *New Muslim Cool* film as one example of broad, well-funded, and ongoing attempts by state actors to counter "radical" forms of Islam by promoting media that present moderate or "good" forms of Islam instead.[29] In the film and state endorsement of the film, Hamza is therefore represented as "good," that is, if we are willing to overlook the complexity conjured up by his violent media and protest poetry.

EVALUATING LATINO MUSLIM RELIGION?

In his article "Good Muslim, Bad Muslim: A Political Perspective on Culture and Terrorism," later expanded into a monograph, Mahmood Mamdani offers a critique of the reductive and problematic binary between so-called good and bad Muslims. Here, Mamdani argues that our current "culture talk" or ways of discursively formulating the category of "culture," produce ahistorical and erroneous links between religion and politics.[30] That is, he critiques the idea that if a Muslim's political activism is extremist, then it is her or his religion that is to blame and in need of reform. A focus on Hamza's music as Islamic political activism would, in the good versus bad Muslim binary, move the signification of Hamza into hostile territory (i.e., into a field where all forms of political Islam that refuse to remain within a religious or private sphere are represented as radical, extremist, and anti-American).[31] Instead of a "good family focused Muslim," Hamza's flaming machete, militant lyrics (e.g., "on the battlefield of *jihad*, you got gun we got guns"), and pan-Latino and pan-Muslim call for *jihad* against America's imperialist diffusion of materialistic ideals could be easily used to frame Hamza as a radical Latino informed by a "bad" kind of Islam.[32]

The good versus bad Muslim binary reasoning implies that good Muslim religion would instead result in good Muslim politics (i.e., non-activist or at the very least not "extreme" in their activism); and that in order to thwart a perceived rise in Latino conversions to extremist forms of Islam, a culture war is needed that promotes a "good" or moderate form of Islam in mass media. In response to negative representations of Islam such as Huntington's, media productions like *New Muslim Cool* have made it a point to introduce "good" Muslims to American media consumers in order to both discourage Islamophobia and to encourage so-called good forms of Islam and lessen the threat of terrorism. Although there may be merit to such an approach and may appear admirable at first glance, such an approach embraces a good versus bad Muslim binary reasoning that is not only reductive and misleading when it comes to complex phenomena but is also supported by and supporting of broader discriminatory practices that are also misleading and damaging.

In the remaining section of this chapter, I explore the intersection between post-9/11 media and racist representations of Latinos. First, I critically engage the exceptional instances in which mainstream media has represented Latino Muslims as potential terrorists. In their coverage of would-be bomber Antonio Martinez, journalists mostly focused on the role that internet technologies play in spreading so-called radical brands of Islam. One news story, however, stood out in that it also questions whether Latino nature itself favors radical forms of religion that are conducive to terrorist activities. When the news media links internet technologies, radical Islam, and terrorism to Latino nature, it is extremely problematic and demands critical engagement. Second, I review how Latino Muslim leaders and organizations have responded to these problematic linkages in the media. Although perhaps admirable goals, like those of the *New Muslim Cool* film, these responses may also be similarly involved in a culture war framework. With an eye to how their current and younger or future communities will respond to stories about Latino Muslim radicals like Antonio Martinez, Latino

Muslim concerns over the direction that their faith is taking is understandable. Nevertheless, if Latino Muslim communities uncritically adopt a culture war framework, they do so at their own peril.

LATINO MUSLIM TERRORISTS

In the winter of 2010, Antonio Martinez was arrested for attempting to blow up a military recruitment center in Catonsville, Maryland. Media coverage in general focused on the role that internet technologies had played in the radicalization of Martinez. His online activity had been closely monitored by FBI officials. He was then engaged by undercover agents posing as terrorists. And finally, Martinez was arrested by the FBI for allegedly attempting to detonate what turned out to be a fake bomb. He had never traveled outside of the United States or had face-to-face contact with terrorist organizations. His relationship to the seedy underground of terrorist organizations consisted entirely of virtual associations, of surfing through and occupying *jihadi* websites and of performing a particular form of Islam on social media. It was indeed his digital performance on Facebook that caught the attention of counterterrorist officials who had vested interests in allowing the show to go on beyond an internet stage and onto real vehicles filled with hyper real props. The truck that Martinez had been given by the undercover agents held a fake bomb made to resemble images of homemade bombs found on Google image searches.

"He wasn't very sophisticated," said former terrorism prosecutor Patrick Moran in reference to Antonio Martinez, "but that's maybe what you would expect from a person who has come about his views via the Internet." Patrick Moran's statement reflects a popular view and merits a few comments. First, the phrase "Internet technologies" better describes the diversity of media forms and content referenced by the ambiguous and overreaching term "the Internet." Scholarly content is, of course, available via internet technologies, but perhaps Moran had social media in mind. Yet here again, the critique is problematic: social media includes a range of views some more clearly reasoned and supported than others. Some scholars are increasingly making their research insights and arguments available via social media, and so it is perfectly possible that someone can come to sound conclusions via social media platforms like Facebook, Twitter, and so on.[33] Second, Moran's ad hominem attack of Martinez is indicative of an even more concerning issue: news media's attempt to provide a link between an individual's mediated biography and the "newsworthy" action that individual took. That is, a mediated snapshot of an individual's biography is presented as an explanation or understanding of why that individual took the action they did. It is a similar kind of quick and dirty linking that informs surveillance and counterterrorism officials who mine social media biographies to preemptively intercept potential acts of terrorism.

In a *Religion Dispatches* article titled "For God or for Fame: The Making of a Teenage Bomber," Islamic studies scholar Kambiz GhaneaBassiri argued that in cases similar to Martinez's the FBI left itself open to critiques of entrapment, "An act by the police or their agents, such as informants, to induce a person to commit a crime for the purpose of prosecuting that person for that induced crime."[34] Mohamed Mohamud, dubbed the Christmas Tree Bomber, made headlines a little over a week prior to Martinez for "allegedly attempting to trigger a bomb at a crowded Christmas tree lighting ceremony in downtown Portland, Oregon." Like Martinez, FBI agents monitored Mohamud's use of social media. Then, posing as terrorists, agents approached Mohamud and offered him what turned out to be a fake bomb. Both Mohamud and Martinez appeared to be "all virtual talk" until they were pressured and persuaded by FBI officials to be "real" and act on their militant rhetoric. They were presented with a false choice, one limited to either remaining "all talk" or becoming active bombers. And in this way, GhaneaBassiri accuses the FBI of converting virtual radicals into real-life decision-makers of false dichotomies. An off-line situation without FBI involvement may have never presented itself in this manner to Mohamud or Martinez. Perhaps they would not have acted on their militant rhetoric had the US government not encouraged them to do so.[35] While the FBI and news media focused on an either-or view of Latino Muslim radicals either as "all talk" or as active (hyper-real) terrorist, a third option exists. Whether online or off, militant rhetoric and severe critiques of American injustices may be encouraged as both constructive social service work and political activism.

The use of mediated biographies to explain or understand human decisions is problematic. When practiced by counterterrorist government agencies, as we have seen, it opens up the possibility of entrapment allegations. When practiced by news media, it opens up the possibility of miscommunication and misunderstanding in the public sphere. Ad hominem attacks of identity character like those pronounced by Patrick Moran and his linking of "people who come about their views via the Internet" and people who are "not very sophisticated" produce confusion rather than better understandings in the public sphere. References like Moran's are far too frequent. The same news story that featured the Moran reference also mentioned a linkage between Latino identity and radical religiosity. It was an NPR story by counterterrorism correspondent Dina Temple-Raston titled: "Officials Worry about Some Latino Converts to Islam." The news radio story referenced a possible pattern consisting of four Latino Muslim radicals: Jose Padilla ("the former Chicago native who pleaded guilty to training with al-Qaida"), Daniel Maldonado ("a Latino-American who was one of the first U.S. citizens to join an al-Qaida affiliate group in Somalia"), Bryant Neal Vinas ("a Latino from Long Island who found himself in al-Qaida's inner circle"), and now, Antonio Martinez.

Juan Zarate, a former deputy national security adviser in the Bush administration, was interviewed for the NPR story. In it, Zarate said: "What has got people's attention is the nature of individuals who have been caught in this web. . . . It's both the nature of these individuals but also their case studies."[36] The article stood out from most others in that rather than focus on the "Internet's" role in radicalizing Martinez, it questioned the role Latino "nature" had in his radicalization. In fact, the very title indicates that the story is primarily concerned with linkages or connections that "officials" are making between Latino nature, conversion to Islam, and radicalization. This linkage, between "Latino nature" and traits or tendencies that are heavy with negative connotations reflects the persistence of a biologistic understanding of race still active in public discourse today.[37] That is, the news story implies that Padilla, Maldonado, Vinas, and Martinez present evidence that there is indeed a connection between Latino nature, radical religiosity, and terrorism.

In *Prophesy Deliverance: An Afro-American Revolutionary Christianity*, Cornel West identifies three major historical processes that helped to shape biologistic formulations of race and white supremacy: the scientific revolution, the Cartesian transformation of philosophy, and the classical revival (i.e., "humanist studies through Greek ocular metaphors and classical ideals of beauty, proportion, and moderation").[38] These three historical processes eventually informed the study of humans in terms of both scientific inquiry and Greek definitions of humanity. And this in turn informed the scientific inquiry of questions such as: do different physical features (such as skin color or hair type) lead us to conclude that there are different human species who are predisposed to certain types of behaviors? West notes that by the time of the enlightenment, the intellectual legitimacy of race and white supremacy was so pervasive that many prominent thinkers like Voltaire, Hume, Jefferson, and Kant accepted the tenants of white supremacy without feeling the need to justify it.[39] Regarding the biological paradigm of race Omi and Winant write:

> Race was equated with distinct hereditary characteristics. Differences in intelligence, temperament, and sexuality (among other traits) were deemed to be racial in character. Racial intermixture was seen as a sin against nature which would lead to the creation of "biological throwbacks." These were some of the assumptions in social Darwinist, Spencerist, and eugenicist thinking about race and race relations.[40]

Biologistic paradigms of race draw from Enlightenment ideals and Darwinian doctrines to define race as determining not only skin pigmentation but also physical, intellectual, and religious characteristics and consequently, sovereignty and individual rights as well. Although no longer "politically correct" in public discourse, biologistic conceptions of race continue to be articulated in contemporary speech, including in news media reports on Latino Muslim radicals.

The attempt to connect a racial, biological, or natural understanding of Latino identity to radical religiosity is not new. Indeed, much work has been accomplished to raise critical awareness of this problem by numerous scholars. Postcolonial and lived religions approaches have in particular focused on the diverse religious practices that have been marginalized by previous scholarship. Previously marginalized, over-looked, and ignored, precisely because such practices took place outside of the institutional models of religion. Sometimes pejoratively referred to as folk, superstitious, *brujería* or witchcraft, apostasy, heresy, and so on; it is difference itself that is constantly under attack in these link-ages between race or ethnicity and religiosity. The European colonial friars who followed the military conquests of Latin America with an attempted spiritual conquest were frustrated time and time again, only to too frequently conclude that there was something about the popula-tion's nature that inhibited them from understanding and practicing "proper" religiosity. Scholars like Jennifer Hughes, Timothy Matovina, Orlando Espin, and others compellingly critique the prevalence of similar racialized conclusions in more contemporary contexts.[41] Latino Pentecostals have been regularly labeled "radical" in pejorative ways, and many embrace the term "radical" to positively describe the level of their religious commitment to living in the Spirit, speaking in tongues, and being emboldened by the Holy Ghost.[42] Latino populations have not been spared the label "radical" prior to Martinez. Instead, the implied link between Latino nature or race or ethnicity and radical religiosity in Dina Temple-Raston's NPR story echoes biologistic for-mations of race that continue to underlie too much of American public discourse today.[43]

Immediately following news of Martinez's arrest, LALMA held a special meeting to discuss interpretations of the news story and to draft an official response. Some argued it was entrapment, while most, including LALMA president Marta Galedary, agreed with the major-ity of media stories that the "Internet" is indeed leading to an increase in radical forms of Islam. In the wake of the attempted bombing,

LALMA's first public response was made on its website, in a written statement coded as text larger than any other on their homepage:

> The Los Angeles Latino Muslim Association LALMA, *La Asociacion Latino Musulmana De America*, 210, unequivocally condemns all acts, or attempted acts, of terrorism by any Latino who identifies himself or herself as a Muslim. LALMA rejects literature or propaganda that violates the peaceful core of mainstream Islamic teachings. We, the members of LALMA, are part of the American Muslim community and we strive to be productive, law abiding citizens.

Part the statement's purpose was to distance the community from radical or bad forms of Islam. The statement must be understood within a context in which American Muslims across the nation have been incessantly asked to publically condemn acts of terror by other Muslims or risk being categorically lumped alongside them, again reflecting an either with us or against us worldview.[44]

During the same special meeting held to discuss the Martinez story, LALMA also agreed to become more active in promoting a "moderate" form of Islam among Latino communities and especially to new Latino Muslims. "The new convert," Marta warned, "is especially vulnerable to radical forms of Islam." Toward the goal of entering a media war against the ideology of radical Islam, LALMA's publishing branch, *Luz de Islam*, began working on a Spanish-language translation of Khaled M. Abou El Fadl's book *The Great Theft: Wrestling Islam from the Extremists* in which I also participated. I had heard Abou El Fadl give a talk on the book at UCLA, during which he referenced the numerous languages in which the text had been translated to, Spanish was not one of them. LALMA's hope was that the translation would help to deglamorize radical, or in the words of Abu El Fadl, puritanical forms of Islam while promoting a moderate form instead. LALMA hoped to distribute the publication as widely as possible through their website and as printed hardcopies for those without access, focusing especially on Spanish-speaking prisoners looking into Islam.[45]

Although more research is needed to better understand the complex processes regarding Latinos who embrace Islam while in prison, SpearIt offers several important insights regarding the matter in his article "Muslim Radicalization in Prison: Responding with Sound Penal Policy or the Sound of Alarm?" Here, SpearIt argues that the hypothesis that imprisoned Muslims are particularly vulnerable to radicalization, voiced by state actors and Latino Muslim leaders, is largely without basis. "According to a Congressional Research Service," writes SpearIt, ". . . only one case definitively involved violent extremism that was connected to a U.S. prison."[46] In order to help reduce violence within prison and reduce recidivism, SpearIt encourages prison policy stakeholders to adopt and promote religious pluralism in prison instead of sounding false alarms regarding radicalization in prisons. Such religious pluralism may include: broadcasting live prayer services from diverse Muslim communities, offering Arabic language classes, creating imam-certification programming, lowering barriers for religious leaders to enter (rather than rely on prisoner imams), and offering religious studies programs for the largely underserved Muslim populations in prisons as compared to Christian ones. Rather than remaining "all talk" or becoming terrorists, LALMA members sought out a third option: to help convert radical discourse into constructive social service work and political activism, including in their service to imprisoned Latino Muslims.

Regretfully, however, this third option is too often approached through a media war framework. LALMA, for example, concluding that the "Internet" was to blame for Martinez's radicalization, "fought back" via a Spanish language translation of a book: media versus media. Latino Muslim organizational websites are used with regularity to combat negative stereotypes of Muslims in the media but also to join the battle over which brand of Islam will become dominant in their communities. For his part, Latino Muslim hip-hop artist Hamza Pérez had no qualms representing this media battle in militant and *jihadi* terms. The perceived "culture war" by Muslim and non-Muslim media in America has helped prop up the highly reductive and highly problematic binary between good and bad Muslims, the "either with us or against us" divide that leaves little room for positive representations of politically active Latino Muslims. Too often, the third option is approached through a media war framework by Latino Muslims. Too often, but not always.

A closer examination of the Pérez brothers' media, for example, reveals that their significations of the clash of civilizations thesis are unstable and complex. In some instances, the clash is expanded to include pan-Latin American, pan-Islamic, and pan-black American unity in conflict with Western hegemony. Yet, in other instances, the Pérez brothers provide contrasts to Huntington when "clash" is used to signify a positive and creative result of intercultural contact. In an interview published by their record label, Remarkable Current, the Pérez brothers described the *Clash of Civilizations* album not as a physical or ideological conflict but rather as a creative meeting of various individuals from different cultural backgrounds.[47] "I think with this album," reported Hamza, "we're bringing a side of hip hop that's dying out, and it's a diversity . . . it's reviving the thing that brought and created hip hop, it was a combination of American, African and Latino culture." Suliman then followed up, "*Clash of Civilizations*, it kind of symbolized that. It was just a clash. We just came together with Anas [Canon], Remarkable Current [the M-Team's recording label], and everything just kind of clashed together, you know, just to make a big jumbo, gumbo, you know, soup."[48] Here, rather than violent conflict, a culture clash is meant as a meeting of cultures that results in positive and creative sounds, ideas, and relationships.

Further, in addition to Guevara's United Nations speech celebrating the unity of Latin America against American neocolonialism, the Pérez brothers' "Clashtro" intro track features a second sampled speech following the first. The second speech is by renowned philosopher, linguist, political anarchist, and activist Noam Chomsky. The steady beat of the track is disrupted by a scratch mix and ends with a standalone sample of Chomsky's talk in which he says: "now, let's get back to this clash of civilizations thing."[49] The "Clashtro" mix ends and the album begins. Chomsky's unedited lecture however goes on to critique Huntington's theory as weak, unsupported by facts, and as logically contradictory to US foreign policy currently aligned with Islamic states such as Saudi Arabia.[50] The sample of Chomsky's critique reveals the possibility of a more nuanced engagement with Huntington's thesis by the Pérez brothers. And it is precisely this possibility that may still be adopted by groups like LALMA and others, so long as their media productions are envisioned with the goal of promoting pluralism as a democratic strength rather than promoting representations of "good Muslims" as a combative counterattack to negative ones.

CONCLUSION

A popular perception links the proliferation of post-9/11 depictions of Muslims, usually using negative stereotypes, to increased "conversion" to radical forms of Islam, including by Latinos. Many Latino Muslims have produced their own media representations of themselves that are far too often launched in direct response to such perceptions. These productions are often combative responses formulated within a perceived culture war. In his album *Clash of Civilizations*, Hamza Pérez of the M-Team adopts Samuel Huntington's articulation of the culture war as a clash between Islam and the West. A framework like this, one that colors political activism (and militant critiques of America by Muslims) as radical attacks against the West, props up a simplistic, problematic, and unfortunately too prevalent binary between good and bad Muslims in our public discourse. Simplistic binaries like these flatten the complexity and diversity of lived experiences, they lead to confusion and misunderstanding in the public sphere, and they inform ineffective policies that are morally suspect if not egregiously illegal.

News of the FBI's arrest of Antonio Martinez, for example, was immediately critiqued by many as entrapment. Even more troubling, news of arrests like that of Martinez's on charges of terrorism, further corroborate prevalent formulations of Latino and Muslim nature as radical, that is, as too different to be anything other than an enemy of America and its values. Rather than embrace simplistic and problematic binaries such as those between the so-called East and West and between good and bad Muslims, we should struggle to formulate much more complex visions of diversity, engaging specific actions, and issues instead of assuming that certain identity groups are predisposed somehow to violence.

Hamza Pérez should not be understood simply as a "good" Muslim husband, father, social worker, or American. These identifiers are important, no doubt. Nevertheless, Hamza is much more complex than this. As he struggles to pay for the "sins" of his past, he also struggles to understand the sources of injustice and in his hip-hop often finds these sources are rooted in the structural failures of America rather than in individual choices. Hamza Pérez identifies and is identified as a Latino, a Muslim, and a Latino Muslim. But he is also so much more than the sum total of these and other labels. Rather than simply struggle to place Hamza into categories that might help anticipate certain kinds of behaviors, we should struggle to engage mediations available to us, such as his music persona and domestic life, as historically specific articulations that prompt more diverse and nuanced engagements of each.

In which way does Hamza's media problematically participate in and endorse simplistic and violent binaries between Islam and the West? How does he push back against Huntington? In what ways does Hamza's hip-hop articulate an artistic and peaceful contact between difference? How, if at all, does this peaceful contact create spaces for inclusion while at the same time pushing others (e.g., polytheists and atheists) to exclusion? What are the grounds for Hamza's critiques of American neocolonialism? Are they well supported, overreaching, misguided, or nihilistic? It is the difficult, critical, deep, and sustained dialogue roused by such persistent questioning that is so desperately needed in our public discourse in order to correct our current states of confusion and misunderstanding.

This critical dialogue is necessary if we are to expand the "democratic control over the major institutions that regulate lives in America and abroad" and "promote personal development, cultural growth, and human freedom."[51] Our engagements with so-called minorities like Latino Muslims should not simply attempt to explain away their experiences and responses to marginalization, but rather, we should participate in critical dialogue in order to try to enhance and enrich the lives of everyone in our democracies, including those under the yoke of white supremacy. In a better working democracy, it is the responsibility of not just our officials and journalists, of specialists and group leaders, but of all citizens to commit to the difficult work of such dialogue if we are to move beyond sensationalized, simplistic, and problematic mediations of so-called minorities in the United States.

CHAPTER SIX

THE THIRD WAVE

CONSOLIDATIONS, RECONFIGURATIONS, AND THE 2016 NEWS CYCLE

Think your life is challenging? Then try being both Muslim and Latino as Donald Trump has ginned up the hate against both communities during his campaign.

—Dean Obeidallah in "Donald Trump's Nightmare Voter: Muslim and Latino!"

On Friday, March 11, 2016, the *Washington Post* reported that a Wichita State University student who identifies as a Latino Muslim was assaulted while at a gas station. According to the *Post*, a "white male in his 20's or 30's" had been circling the gas station on a motorcycle harassing an African American man saying "lazy ass . . . You guys don't work." The harasser then turned to the Latino Muslim Wichita student and yelled out "Hey you brown trash, you better go home," to which the student responded, "It's my country. Who the hell are you to tell me, Go home?" The words between the two escalated into a physical altercation and ended with the young Latino Muslim on the floor, kicked, bruised, and beaten. "He was shouting, Trump!" a witness reported. "Trump will take our country from you guys!" The man got back on his motorcycle and drove around in circles chanting "Trump! Trump! Trump! . . . Make America great again! You guys are the losers! You guys, we'll throw you over the wall!" The *Post* article's author Justin Moyer concluded that "after outbreaks of violence at Trump rallies and elsewhere—and unheeded calls for the candidate to try to stop them—the alleged attack in Kansas again suggests how violence is becoming associated with Trump's White House bid."[1] This violence and the xenophobic rhetoric that shapes it are part of a historically specific context in which a third wave of Latino Muslims is emerging.

A little over a month prior to the hate crime in Wichita, on January 30, 2016, the Islam-in-Spanish group celebrated the grand opening in Houston, Texas, of what was being advertised as "the first Spanish speaking Islamic center in the United States." Given the increased interest in all things related to Islam after September 11, 2001, and even more so after the rise of ISIS and its connections to terrorist activities in France, Lebanon, and San Bernardino, and also the politicized villainizing of both Muslims and Latinos in public discourse during the 2016 election cycle, the late January 2016 grand opening of "the first Spanish speaking Islamic center in the United States" was sure to attract media attention. And it did! Several news organizations including Agence France-Presse (AFP) and Vivala published articles prior to the event based on press releases by Islam-in-Spanish. Telemundo, Univision, and others sent reporters to cover the event. The "first Spanish speaking Islamic center in the United States," it is an interesting story to be sure. It is a story not only about Latino Muslims growing in numbers, which so happens to be a common theme in news coverage of the group, it is also about Latino Muslim roots, about their setting down roots in Latino communities like those in Houston and about having the resources to do so. It is a story, however, that is also riddled with issues regarding membership numbers, power, and access to public discourse.

As the crowds gathered for the grand opening of the Latino Muslim Islamic center, old friends greeted each other and new ones introduced themselves to one another. By noon, there were over one hundred and fifty people—a mixture of Latinos, Muslims, one or the other, both, or neither. Jamal, who migrated to the United States from Jordan, told me that he was learning to speak Spanish, including *el acento*: "It's good to learn about the diverse Hispanic community, because we always think it's one culture, but it's actually multiple cultures. There's a lot to learn there, you know, especially with the Muslims in Andalusia." Al-Andalus (Islamic Spain), the *convivencia* or working together between Jewish, Christian, and Muslim communities that was intermittently achieved during nearly eight centuries and other linguistic and artistic connections between multiple and diverse Latino and Islamic cultures were referenced several times throughout the event. Brandon Berrios, a young Latino muralist who is not Muslim but who had been studying the intricate geometric patterns of Andalusian mosaics, had graciously volunteered to paint a mural for the center.[2] The center's references to Andalusian aesthetics and *convivencia* is a strategic attempt to highlight the Islamic roots of present-day Latinos in the United States in a positive accent.

The grand opening officially began with an invocation, *Bismillah al Rahman al Raheem*, "in the Name of God, Most Gracious, Most Merciful," which was promptly followed with several Qur'anic recitations by the children of the Islam-in-Spanish group's leadership. "Todos los mensajeros que envié," one of the children recited in Spanish, "hablaban el lenguaje del pueblo para así decirles claramente el mensaje," "AND NEVER have We sent forth any apostle otherwise than [with a message] in his own people's tongue, so that he might make [the truth] clear unto them" (Qur'an 14:4, English translation by M. Asad).

The recitations were then followed by nearly two hours of speeches. A representative for the FBI's community outreach program was there, she had been invited and gave a speech. Alfredo Ruiz, a civil rights attorney, news analyst, and Spanish language director for the Council on American-Islamic Relations (CAIR) gave a speech. A leader from the Latino Muslim community in New Jersey gave a speech. A spokesperson from a small Indonesian Muslim community in Houston gave a speech. Islam-in-Spanish leaders gave speeches. Two hours of speeches, and then the crowd moved to the ribbon-cutting ceremony that would inaugurate "The First Spanish speaking Islamic Center in the United States." But it was not the first!

A few days after the grand opening Yahya Abdul Latif Figueroa, a leader from New York's Latino Muslim community, wrote that "in 1987 a small Latino group of Muslims formed Alianza Islámica and its nucleus of members gathered and set forth a plan to incorporate and open a mosque/cultural/dawah center." Echoing Figueroa's words, Omar Abdur-Rahim Ocasio, another leader of the New York community, said "The Alianza Islámica, there's a whole other story just about that name, the name was a resistance!" The Alianza's Islamic center and its name, he explained, was in part a response to both Muslim and non-Muslim institutions that persistently marginalized the group and its efforts to help the Spanish Harlem communities they served including, and perhaps especially, those suffering from the AIDS epidemic. Since the Alianza, Latino Muslim groups have been accused of being divisive, of further dividing so-called minority communities, both Latino and Muslim, which already struggle for scarce resources. The Alianza Islámica attempted to address such accusations by pointing out the tendency within so-called minority groups to overlook or dismiss specific requests by those on the margins of the already marginalized. The Alianza's celebration of Latino ways of being Muslim was itself a form of resistance.

Regardless of whether the 2016 ceremonies in Houston inaugurated the first or second Spanish-speaking Islamic center in the United States, the story's hook remains powerful. It is a story about Latino Muslims growing in number, 198,000 across the United States, according to the PEW Research Center's 2011 and 2015 projections.[3] It is a story about Latino Muslim roots in Al-Andalus (Islamic Spain) and in New York's Spanish Harlem and about their setting down roots in New York, New Jersey, Los Angeles, Chicago, Miami, Houston, and other cities with large Latino communities. It is about having resources, the lack thereof, and the struggle to obtain more—including more symbolic capital or legitimization through interviews with various media institutions. And it is a story about something like that of *convivencia*, of working with rather than in absence of or even against difference. "Not only did we dialogue with other faiths," continues Figueroa's response,

we challenged the various ideologies and social movements of the time presenting an Islamic alternative. In its most successful period we served approximately 100 families, many of them single disenfranchised young people. Hundreds of other transients were touched profoundly as well. . . . Our neighborhoods suffered from much of the dysfunction of urban life, discrimination and lack of opportunity, most often the product of discriminatory policies. . . . Alianza is delighted by Islam-in-Spanish's

Centro Islamico and embraces it as an extension of our humble beginning. We hope it enhances the basic message of Alianza, as a force for the unique spiritual culture of historical Andalus and skillfully avoids the excesses and failures of many Islamic movements of our time.[4]

Despite any grievances against the event's organizers for failing to give the Alianza recognition for their pioneering work in the 1980s and 1990s, Figueroa concludes his letter with well wishes to the Islam-in-Spanish group and the emerging community in Houston. Apart from this failure, the 2016 grand opening of the second Spanish-speaking Islamic center in the United States was a well-choreographed media event. It has and will continue to bring attention to the diverse and dynamic Muslim and Latino communities that exist across the United States. And it is through these and its other activities and in relation to other groups and discourses, that the Islam-in-Spanish group has played a dominant role in the emerging third wave of Latino Muslims.

Within a contemporary context that includes the proliferation of reversion stories through internet technologies, post-9/11 news media representations of Latino Muslims, and accusations of Latino Muslims as potential "homegrown" terrorists, a third wave of Latino Muslims is emerging. Although this third wave includes new trajectories by previous organizations and also attempted consolidations of the disparate groups across the nation under a single umbrella organization, it is also characterized by the emergence of the Islam-in-Spanish group, the revival of La Alianza Islámica, and the reconfiguration of LALMA as La Asociación Latino Musulmana de América. Additionally, the third wave of Latino Muslims is being shaped by political discourses around ISIS, immigration, and the 2016 election cycle. These issues have reinvigorated conversations around attempts to unify all of the disparate Latino Muslim organizations that now exist across the nation in isolation from one another. Although the social, political, and media impact of Latino Muslims, as a so-called new minority in America, is yet to be fully realized, it is clear that the identity group will continue to play a significant role in national discourses even as they continue to struggle for their very existence.

In this struggle to further develop and sustain the identity group, internet technologies have played more than a significant role. They have provided a means for carefully and strategically designing, disseminating, and consuming Latino Muslim identity through organizational websites. They have helped to realize and to crystalize the production, amplification, and study of Spanish language media on Islam as one of the group's central activities. In addition to translating literature on Islam from various languages to Spanish, including from English and Arabic, internet technologies have played a crucial role in the proliferation of reversion stories by and about Latino Muslims. Reversion stories and organizational websites present unique opportunities in which, rather than assimilating into existing ways of being Muslim associated with or dominated by other identity groups like Muslims from Saudi Arabia, Egypt, Morocco, and so on, Latino Muslims "carve out" and add their own identity into America's diverse landscape. These self-produced media have also become an important means through which Latino Muslims shape news media representations about themselves. In a post-9/11 news context, coverage of Latino Muslims has exponentially increased but has surprisingly not been overtly negative. It has, however, been characteristically sensational by myopically focusing on issues around conversion. Regarding content for these news stories, Latino Muslim organizational websites provide an initial point of contact for journalists and other researchers. Reversion stories have here become both a news source and a model deployed by Latino Muslims during interviews with journalists.

Despite the careful and strategic development and deployment of these Latino Muslim media and the overall tendency of news media to produce non-overtly negative representations of the group, a new national discourse on Latino Muslims framed in terms of radicalization and security began to emerge after the 2013 arrest of Antonio Martinez on attempted terrorism charges. And it is precisely these concerns, concerns regarding how and by whom Latino Muslim identity will be framed in the public sphere, that have revitalized the internal desire to consolidate the disparate Latino Muslim groups across the nation under a single umbrella organization. The envisioned mission for this umbrella organization would thus be to compete with external visions, often supported by institutions with daunting amounts of material resources and social capital, visions of who Latino Muslims are and what their significance as a so-called minority in America might be.

THE LEAGUE OF LATINO AMERICAN MUSLIM ORGANIZATIONS

Like other pan-Islamic movements, many individuals maintain that gendered, racial, ethnic, and national divisions must be subsumed under a global Muslim identity, and that therefore the promotion of a Latino Muslim identity divisively works against the unity of a universal *ummah*.[5] Puerto Ricans in New York were initially drawn to Islam for its aesthetic appeal, its simplicity (e.g., with regard to the doctrine of the Oneness of God), and its promotion of social equality (e.g., with regard to non-hierarchical social organization during prayer and other prescribed rituals, zakat or charity ideals, and laws prohibiting usury and slavery as forms of exploitation). Their lived experiences within African American, Middle Eastern, and other Asian immigrant Muslim communities did not, however, reflect the Islamic ideal of a universal and inclusive *ummah*. Instead, it was precisely the marginalization of their Latino identity—sometimes by black American Muslims other times by immigrant Muslims from the Middle East and Asia—that animated the creation of specifically Latino Muslim organizations. The Alianza Islámica provided an example of how Latino Muslims could themselves promote social equality by offering educational and martial arts defense training, support for HIV and AIDs victims, food and blankets for the hungry and cold, and other such social services. In addition to improving the material conditions of their neighborhood residents, the Alianza Islámica promoted social equality by producing and disseminating information on Islam in Spanish that emphasized the Islamic roots of Latino ethnicity. By doing so, it was hoped that Latino and Muslim communities could come to accept Latino ethnicity as historically and culturally Islamic. The historical work on Islamic Spain written for a popular audience by T. B. Irving was originally published in Spanish, making it an early and important source for an emerging pan-Latino Muslim vision. The Alianza's relation to Irving's work and subsequent Latino Muslim organizations is demonstrative of the complex networks that gave rise to this vision. Entities such as PIEDAD, LADO, and LALMA have inherited and pushed forward the Alianza's legacy to new directions through their grassroots work and with the aid of internet technologies. These digitized visions have been integral to various other groups and also to dominant discourses on and by Latino Muslims.

Beyond the Alianza, PIEDAD, LADO, and LALMA, many other Latino Muslim groups and voices have emerged, including the California Latino Muslim Association, Alameda Islamica: Latino Muslims of the Bay Area, Latino Muslims of Arizona, the Atlanta Latino Muslim Association, the Chicago Association of Latino-American Muslims, Latino Muslims of New York, Hablamos Islam out of New Jersey, the Tri-State Latino Muslims, and others. Latino Muslims have also gained prominent positions in broader American Muslim organizations. Wilfredo Ruiz, for example, is a civil rights attorney and Spanish language director for CAIR and Nehelia Morales is the National Hispanic Outreach Coordinator for WhyIslam, the *dawah* media production arm of ICNA. The result is a numerous and equally fractured verity of organizational fronts. Although most of these Latino Muslim organizations promote the dominant narratives of ethnic marginalization, ontological reversion to Islam and historical-cultural roots in Islamic Spain, the terms "Latino" and "Muslim" remain highly contested even within Latino Muslim discourse itself.

One Latino Muslim made the following comment regarding the diverse significations of Latino identity and the difficulty in trying to pin it down: "Our meetings usually got stuck around food [and] what cultural dishes would be most appropriate. . . . We have to have rice and beans, but what style beans? Black or Pinto Beans? Central American style, Caribbean style or Mexican Style."[6] Beyond cuisine are concerns around who is and who is not included within the "Latino" and "Hispanic" categories. For example, Brazilians in the United States may identify as Latino but not Hispanic. On the other hand, Spaniards in the United States may have linguistic commonalities with Hispanics but are not from Latin America. The more contested arena has been, however, centered on what forms of Islam are to be adopted and transmitted to the next generation of Latino Muslims.

Various attempts have been made to organizationally overcome ethnic and religious differences. One of the earliest of these attempts occurred in 1979, it pre-dated the Alianza Islámica, included leaders from diverse backgrounds, and represented constituents from Costa Rica, Puerto Rico, Panama, and Brazil. The attempted consolidation was quickly abandoned after meeting considerable resistance rather than support from broader Muslim leaders and communities on the basis that the attempt to form a pan-Latino community was "divisive and damaging to the jamaat (the broader Muslim gathering or community)."[7] A more recent and equally ambitious, despite new developments in communication technologies, attempt to unify Latino Muslims across the nation was the League of Latino American Muslim Organizations, or LLAMO, in 2010. In an interview, Imam Yusef Maisonet, who identifies as being of Puerto Rican descent, described LLAMO as the "brain child" of the late Khadijah Rivera (founder of PIEDAD) and of a few other Latino Muslims. Having worked with Rivera on various other projects, including a missionary trip to visit Muslim communities in Puerto Rico, Maisonet was deeply affected by her death in 2009 and decided to work along with others toward realizing her vision of a nationally united Latino Muslim front. LLAMO's mission statement is published on their Facebook page as follows:

LLAMO's MISSION. Our mission is to disseminate Islamic information within the Latino-American community to promote understanding of Islam and the Muslim community; forming bridges among the multireligious and multiethnic communities in the USA.

OBJECTIVES. LLAMO's principal objective is to bring different Latino Muslim groups together under one name, and become the vehicle through which Latino Muslims will: develop Islamic programs to non Latino/Hispanic Muslim population. To contribute to the social and moral growth of the society we live in, as determined by Islam. Establish multicultural communities that will foster peaceful coexistence by using Islam as their foundation.[8]

Visions for a pan-Latino Muslim organizational front like the one articulated by LLAMO have been shared by many and can be traced as far back as the pre-Alianza's late 1970s group and Rivera and Askia's work in the 1980s. Juan Galvan from LADO also attempted to realize this goal when he joined LADO in 2001:

> When I began revising the LADO mission statement in 2001, one of the initial main points for the mission statement was to unite the Latino Muslim community of the United States. I was not aware of all the complexities of such a goal. . . . You need to understand the methods in which your organization is seeking unity with other organizations.[9]

For Galvan, these complexities included weighing various possible ways to build a substantial unity. One was to dissolve the various organizations and consolidate assets and titles under one of the existing organizations. A second option was to create a new national organization for all assets and titles to be transferred to, and a third was to create a new federation that maintains the autonomy of existing organizations under its umbrella. Regarding the creation of LLAMO, Galvan writes: "Various Latino Muslim organizations, including LADO, attempted to take the third option by developing an organization called the League of Latino American Muslim Organizations (LLAMO). We did not go much farther than selecting a name, a mission statement, and goals."[10] The difficulties of managing various groups under one umbrella has curtailed many of LLAMO's goals. "Currently," continues Galvan,

> Latino Muslim organizations do not have the assets to take on such a great endeavor. Even with assets, decisions regarding details would continue to be the more difficult part of reaching unity. Many difficult decisions must be made. When member organizations maintain all their assets, the new organization suffers due to the lack of contribution that

each member organization could have potentially brought to the new organization. Various organizations working together as LLAMO must be more valuable than various separate organizations. LLAMO would need to be the dominant Latino Muslim organization in the United States. We would need to successfully manage the transfer of some assets to LLAMO from member organizations.[11]

Due to such complications, including the failure to transfer assets into the umbrella organization, the 2011 goal of holding a LLAMO conference in the United States went unrealized, and this is representative of LLAMO's other unrealized activities as well.

LLAMO, as an umbrella organization, has drawn from dominant narratives and local organizations to justify its formation and has been inspired by the life, work, and death of various individuals including Khadijah Rivera. Nonetheless, its digital representation is a reminder that a unified Latino Muslim identity exists more so within mass media networks than in individually and communally lived experiences. As a discursive formation, Latino Muslim identity is, after all, at the margins between lived experiences and hyperreal mediations. Latino Muslims and other identity groups are a discursive hybridity between race, religion, and internet technologies. These margins, it must be noted, have presented opportunities but also challenges to the leaders who seek to nurture a united Latino Muslim community through networking and sharing of resources.

Toward the end of the *New Muslim Cool* film, discussed in the previous chapter, Hamza Perez's clearance to work at a county jail is revoked. Perez is not given a reason for the revocation, and in the early 2000s, as a result of the Patriot Act, we are told in the film that none is needed. Three and half months of FBI silence are finally broken after the ACLU became involved on Hamza's behalf. The FBI cited an interview published on an older version of the M-Team's website as its central reason for pulling Hamza's clearance to work at a federal prison. The film depicts Hamza's case worker with the website in question on her computer screen as she explains the specific quotes from Hamza that had perhaps alarmed the authorities: "The government doesn't give a crap about us, so don't kiss their a** and the situation is just going to get worse" and also "Stop collaborating and sleeping with the snake," the reference here being to the "United Snakes of America."[12] Hamza's ACLU case worker then explains, "I think that the county solicitor recognizes that the jail does have security concerns and so your right to speak at a jail is not going to be as broad as your right to speak outside of a jail. You know you can't say anything you want to the inmates. But when you're talking on your free time outside of that employment context, you have a first amendment right to engage in speech." Hamza's clearance was subsequently returned, and he enthusiastically made his way back to his interfaith work at the prison.

The incident was fraught with issues regarding discriminatory surveillance practices by governmental agencies in a digital age and post-9/11 era. It was also, however, an important lesson for Latino Muslim leaders who rely heavily on internet technologies. "I felt so bad when I watched the *New Muslim Cool* movie," Juan Galvan (director of LADO and web designer of LatinoDawah.org, HispanicMuslims.com, LatinoMuslim.com, and a host of other Latino Muslim websites) told me in an interview. "Hamza asked me to build his website, but I needed content. So I put the interview on the site because he didn't provide me any content." For Latino Muslims in need of websites, Juan Galvan has been an answered prayer. He has single-handedly designed more Latino Muslim websites than any other individual or organization. Today, Galvan is the executive director of one of the most prominent, best connected, and almost completely virtual Latino Muslim organization in the United States. Toward national unity, however, LADO's most important feature is connecting Latino Muslim groups to one another. It provides a networking service rather than a unified mobilization of Latino Muslim individuals and resources.

Internet technologies have provided groups that have limited resources the ability to design and disseminate their identities, to gain a potentially more dominant voice in the public sphere, to create networks with one another, and to mobilize for particular causes (e.g., the translation of Islamic media into the Spanish language). Internet technologies have helped to shape and make possible the creation, dissemination, and mobilization of a pan-Latino Muslim vision characterized by shared narratives of ethnic marginalization, reversion to Islam, and roots in Islamic Spain. These technologies have also, however, facilitated surveillance practices directed at Muslims in a post-9/11 context and have also helped disparate organizations to proliferate in virtual spaces that make it increasingly difficult to create an offline unity. Diversity within America's Muslim and Latino populations further multiplies the challenge of forming a unified Latino Muslim group and identity.

What is at stake in the various attempts to organize a hierarchy of leadership and to consolidate the resources available to the dozens of Latino Muslim groups across the nation is a specific set of practical and ethical questions. What new divisions will be used to create new unities? Will these new divisions be more ethically appealing than previous ones? Will Latino ethnicity be invoked as producing ideal religion or will the identity category instead be grappled with in all of its complex, political, and historical specificity? And will the mediums in which such questions are asked and answered be themselves critically scrutinized? Although these questions may be inapplicable to the now stagnant and defunct LLAMO, neither the dream of nor the attempts to consolidate Latino Muslim organizations have dissipated. Instead, these live on in at least two dominant formations: the Islam-in-Spanish group and the reconfiguration of the Los Angeles LALMA as La Asociación Latino Musulmana de América (with the same abbreviation of LALMA).

ISLAM-IN-SPANISH

On January 15, 2010, Mujahid Fletcher presented his reversion story at the Islamic Institute of Orange County (IIOC). There were over one hundred attendees, the talk was recorded using multiple digital cameras and subsequently posted on YouTube by the IIOC.[13] "I'm originally from Columbia in South America," began Fletcher, "My parents came to this country when I was eight years old." One of his first experiences in the United States was in the third grade at a public school, where his teacher told him not to talk as her policy toward his inability to speak English. "Now, I would categorize that as a culture shock. I went home and told my parents that I never wanted to go back to school." Fletcher went on to narrate even more severe issues that not only threatened his education and physiological well-being but also his physical safety. Latinos would get "jumped" by African Americans at his school Fletcher told the audience. "The Latinos said we have to come together for self-defense. And because we were from Latin America, Central America, so many different places, you know, from Columbia, Venezuela, Costa Rica, Guatemala, so many different places. We titled that gathering, us coming together, as La Familia, meaning the family." Fletcher recounted that the formation of this gang led to violence, murder, police profiling, and prison. "At an age of fourteen [and/or] fifteen, I was visiting my friends in hospitals," friends who had been victims of gang violence or had attempted to commit suicide under the constant pressure of eminent violence.

When, at the age of sixteen, Fletcher narrowly escaped an attempt on his own life, his parents decided to send him back to Columbia. "I thought, you know, if I didn't get killed back in Houston I'm going to die in Columbia." However, instead of the violent stereotypes portrayed in the media, Fletcher experienced "the most well-mannered people" he had ever met. "Living in Columbia at that age, being able to go up a mountain, be in a natural spring river by myself and eat fruits from trees that was something I could have never imagined living back in a place that was nothing but concrete, the concrete streets. So I became kind of inclined to nature." Fletcher also excelled in school while in Columbia. He did not want to return to the United States but his parents told him it was time. Fletcher returned to the United States when he was eighteen years old and eventually fell into another stage of life, one centered on making money as a salesperson at an electronic store. "No matter how much [money] I had around me, I would sit back and think there has to be something else to life. This can't be it, because if this was it then I would be happy and satisfied, but I'm not." As in so many other reversion stories, Fletcher narrated his crisis of meaning. He felt like he was at a crossroad and started to study and seek out answers in different religions. He read about and visited several religious communities including a Kabala Jewish mystical group taught by someone of Mexican descent who had studied in Israel, he visited a Hindu temple, Zen Buddhist centers, and many Christian groups.

While seeking, Fletcher finally met a friend who was Muslim and who described Islam as "the true religion of God." Although the statement made a significant impact on him, Fletcher went on with his life until one day he spoke to his friend's mother who had him watch a video titled "The Qur'an and Modern Sciences" by Jamal Badawi. The video had such an impression on Fletcher that he began reading the Qur'an and he concluded "there's something about this book!" But he was also still going to clubs, parties, and drinking. One night, he and his friends got into a fight with security guards at a club, "it was like twenty against twenty" and while Fletcher was fighting someone else, a police officer hit him in the head with an iron flashlight, and in Fletcher's words, "he broke my head open." Fletcher pointed to the scar still visible on his head through his buzz cut. "I tried to sue, police brutality," Fletcher continued while chuckling, "but I knew things weren't right . . . so I went to a mosque." For a year, Fletcher spoke to a Muslim leader there but had yet another near death experience, a major car wreck, before being completely convinced. "I had to get right with God because I was gonna die, I felt like I was going to die very soon!"

Soon after, Fletcher took shahada. "Allah as my witness," he narrated, "it's as if all this weight came off. And then, it was as if I could hear better, see better and I felt so light. And I felt like everything made sense. . . . When I walked out the masjid . . . the one thing that I wanted to do is call my mother and tell her thank you for even having me, that's the level of thankfulness, I'd never felt that in my life." A week later, Fletcher told the crowd, the woman who had been his girlfriend became a Muslim and a month later they were married. Three months after Fletcher took shahada, his father accepted Islam. Some of his former gang members and even rivals accepted Islam. "My little brother in law," Fletcher went on listing, "at the age of sixteen, embraced Islam. My mother in law embraced Islam. My wife's aunt, before dying from cancer, embraced Islam. My mother embraced Islam. And on, and on, and on."

After narrating his reversion story, Fletcher transitioned to a discussion of his subsequent work as a Latino Muslim in a post-9/11 media context:

> I was blessed with the ability to study in Egypt, especially the Arabic language and the Qur'an. . . . After September 11, brother Isa and myself were put in front of the cameras, you know I embraced Islam three months before September 11. I remember three months later as a new Muslim standing in front of a Church, five hundred people congregated, and telling them about Islam. The sort of response that happened after September 11 made my development quick, dealing with people of knowledge, *alḥamdulillāh* ["praise be to God"] and being able to ask questions. And all of that has led to a lot of trial and error and we realize, especially with the Latino community, it's the last frontier, it's the last people to get this message of Islam due to the issue of language. We came up, *alḥamdulillāh*, with a solution, and we started making audiovisual material, and our material has gone all over the world now. Our website is the number one website now with audiovisual materials.

Fletcher's father had challenged the claim that Islam is universal when it is not available in Spanish. In response to this challenge, the Islam-in-Spanish group was born.[14]

Fletcher sought out multimedia materials in Spanish for his father and other Spanish-speaking Muslims to learn more about Islam but found a lacuna instead. He also concluded that in a post-9/11 context, there was also a need to create educational materials for non-Muslim Latinos who wanted to learn more about Islam. Three months after his father's embrace of Islam, Fletcher, his wife, and his father worked together to produce their first audio compact disc entitled "La Religion de la Verdad" (The Religion of Truth—titled after the manner in which Islam was first described to Fletcher). According to the group's "Our Story" web page, it was this initial media production that introduced Islam to Fletcher's aunt-in-law who finally embraced the religion while on her death bed. The audio recording was hailed as a *dawah* success and has reportedly led to mass education on and even acceptance of Islam across the globe.[15]

These successes led to the development of the Islam-in-Spanish group whose "original mission was to become the trusted source of Islamic Multimedia resources and products to educate Latinos in the Spanish language worldwide."[16] The group has reportedly produced over 500 audio books and 250 video shows. A web video introducing the group features Imam Siraj Wahhaj, from the Al-Taqwa mosque in Brooklyn, who references Spanish as the third most prolific language on the globe. He cites US census figures estimating that "by 2050 there will one hundred million Latinos in this country. Twenty-nine percent of the children in this country will be Latino." This is presented as evidence of the importance of the group's Spanish language media productions on Islam. Filling the gap in media of Islam materials in Spanish is itself understood as a form of *dawah*. It is also, however, envisioned as a historical-cultural return.

In the website's text, the media materials and those who use them are charged with the task of "clarifying misconceptions of Islam and culturally attaching Latinos to their common Islamic roots historically from Al-Andalus or Andulucia to normalize the notion of Islam to Spanish-speakers while encouraging universal principles of a common human good and diversity." Like the Alianza Islámica, T. B. Irving, PIEDAD, LADO, LALMA, and other predecessors, the Islam-in-Spanish group also promotes the connection between Islam in Spain and Latino history and culture as a central identity narrative. The group primarily relies on internet technologies, including its Islam-in-Spanish.org website, YouTube channel, and Soundcloud channel. Beyond its numerous branding elements, including logo, concise textual bios, images, and short promo videos under the *Aprenda Islam* "Learn about Islam" tab, the website contains a "Multimedia Library" with twelve videos on various subjects. One of these is titled *Raices Islamicas en la Cultura Latina* (Islamic roots of Latino culture). The video was published in 2011 and was viewed nearly 1,200 times over a period of about five years and received only four comments, all congratulating Islam-in-Spanish for their *dawah* work.

In contrast to the relatively low number of views that the "Islamic Roots in Latino Culture" video received, other video productions like "Scientific Miracles in the Qur'an" garnered 39,328 views and 488 comments; "The Concept of Worship in Islam" had 16,789 views and 37 comments; "The Religion of Truth" had 14,860 views and 134 comments; "Evolutionary Lies" had 11,023 views and 347 comments; and "Women in Islam" had 10,376 views and 119 comments by 2016. The majority of the Islam-in-Spanish videos are neither hosted nor directly linked on its website and are instead found exclusively on its YouTube channel: youtube.com/c/islaminspanishtv. Here, Islam-in-Spanish maintains about 170 videos. Additionally, Islam-in-Spanish live streams all of its *Jummah kutbas* (Friday sermons). The group also maintains 128 audio tracks on a SoundCloud Channel, a digital audio internet hosting service: soundcloud.com/islaminspanish. The majority of the tracks are *surahs* (chapters) from the Qur'an. There are also 17 tracks that are lectures on various subjects, including on: purification, the ninety-nine names of God, the grand opening of the Latino Mosque in Houston, Texas, educating Latinos on Islam, on God, Islam, and the Qur'an, the forty Hadiths, and on Muhammad, Jesus, and Mary.

Relatively low-cost, for-profit, hosting services like YouTube and SoundCloud provide groups like Islam-in-Spanish the ability to disseminate their self-produced media across the nation and globe. This has also led to the group's website being used primarily as a branding interface rather than an extensive library of media like PIEDAD's website had been and LADO's continues to be. Given Islam-in-Spanish's reliance on services like YouTube and the usage data it makes available, it is again important to note and return to the subject of the "Islamic Roots in Latino Culture" video's relatively low number of views and comments. It is clear in many of the speeches and textual statements made on the organization's brand developing website that the goal is to educate and remind as many people as possible of the historical-cultural connection between Islamic Spain and Latino identity.

Toward the goal of making this connection visually, a previous iteration of the organization's website featured a digital photo of the Alhambra palace dubbed the Red Fort, the last Islamic stronghold in Spain located in Granada. The group's new website features an image of the Great Mosque of Cordoba's interior grid of red and white double horseshoe arches. The "Islamic Roots in Latino Culture" video itself highlights several of Islamic Spain's contributions to Latino culture. The contributions discussed here include various scientific accomplishments like "winged flight" gliders, a water clock, observatory, and the "perfection" of the astrolabe for navigation while at sea and for finding the *Qiblah* (direction of Mecca for prayer). Various infrastructural accomplishments like the Alhambra and other castles, 200,000 houses, 600 mosques, 900 bathhouses, 50 hospitals, and street lights that spanned areas up to 10 miles were also celebrated in the video. Here, a photograph of a bathhouse was used as an example of Al-Andalus' and Islamic Spain's public spaces and services that were open to anyone, Muslim or non-Muslim, and are indicative of the *convivencia* (coexistence) celebrated as an instance of successful pluralism or at the very least of tolerance policies and practices. Lastly, several Spanish language names and words were shown to have their roots in Arabic, including Omar, Guadalajara (the valley of rocks), azucar, arroz, camisa, and so on.[17]

Despite this and other attempts to promote links between Islamic Spain and Latino identity, it seems that the subject is only marginally interesting at best to many Latino Muslims. It is Islam-in-Spanish's multimedia on Islam without direct reference to Latino identity that has instead garnered much attention. Perhaps the language of Spanish itself accomplishes the discursive work of making the connection: Islam by and for Latinos. Regardless of whether Islam-in-Spanish is or will be successful in promoting the link between Islamic Spain and Latino identity as a central identity narrative for Latino Muslims, it is clear that the group has gained a prominent place in Houston through the community's physical presence at the Centro Islamico, as well as in national discourse through its mastery of media technologies. It is well positioned to expand its presence and influence well beyond these physical and virtual borders. It is not, however, the only group to do so.

THE REVIVAL OF LA ALIANZA AND RECONFIGURATION OF LALMA

At the grand opening of the Islam-in-Spanish group's new center in Houston, Texas, Yahya Figueroa stood by a small group of people. He

wore a black leather motorcycle vest with the "Alianza Islámica" letters, a Puerto Rican flag, and shadowy figures meant to signify Taínos
stitched on to it. Neither Yahya Figueroa, Rahim Ocasio, nor anyone
else from the Alianza were given public recognition at the Houston
event. Nevertheless, in those small groups, to those who would listen,
Figueroa talked about his past. He grew up in Spanish Harlem with
the Five Percenters, a breakaway branch of the NOI. According to
Figueroa, the Five Percenters were everywhere in his neighborhood,
he joined when he was just eleven years old. Later, Figueroa had also
joined the Young Lords as they were transitioning from a Latino street
gang to a socially conscious civil rights movement. Islam made sense to
him, at least the kind of Islam he had encountered while in New York's
barrios. It was a socially conscious and active Islam—and for Figueroa
who had grown up during a revolutionary era, it made sense.

Figueroa also talked about the other members of the Alianza, he
described these brothers and sisters as his *Sahaba*, a term usually used
to reference the closest companions of the Prophet. The stories of the
Prophet's companions serve as models for many Muslims but have also
been used to discursively cement divisions between Muslims who try
to live as the Prophet and his companions did and Muslims who inno-
vate from this "traditional" way of living. Although the use of this discursive division is widespread, it has become increasingly associated
with Salafi rhetoric.[18] Figueroa's reference to Alianza members as his
Sahaba, as the spiritual companions of the Prophets who lived in the
here and now and who served as his models for how to live a pious life,
was heavy with passion and critique. Figueroa described having been
scolded by other Muslims at the Houston event for wearing his Alianza
jacket with images of Taínos on it, that this could lead to *shirk*, the association of God with images, and also to divisions among the *ummah*.

Figueroa was especially troubled, however, by his memories of how
certain Muslims, especially those who contracted HIV and died of
AIDS during the 1980s and 1990s, were alienated by other Muslims
in the United States. His *Sahaba*, he exclaimed passionately, were those
Muslims who rather than alienate others helped to bury the brothers
and sisters who were dying during this time despite the risk of being

alienated themselves. Islam made sense to Figueroa because it worked, because he and the rest of the Alianza Islámica put it to work.

Rahim Ocasio, also from the Alianza, had likewise arrived in Houston for the grand opening. Like, Figueroa, he shared several stories about the Alianza's former days with the small groups that would gather around him. His stories, however, also included a positive recollection of the Islam-in-Spanish group's director and founder and of how Fletcher had encouraged him to tell his story and to "get it out there." Either because they felt inspired by the Latino Muslim leaders who had gathered in Houston or concerned by this leadership's failure to provide vitally needed social services like those the Alianza had provided during the first wave of Latino Muslims, Figueroa and Ocasio began to revive the Alianza Islámica, digitally, in the days that followed.

On February 2, 2016, an open letter titled "A Lifetime of Reclaiming Our Islamic Heritage," written by Figueroa and referenced at the outset of this chapter, was distributed widely through email, Facebook, and other internet technologies. Less than two weeks later, this letter and several newspaper articles and encyclopedia entries on the Alianza were posted as entries on the newly minted Alianza Islámica Blog at latinomuslim.com. A month later, another dozen posts had been published on the blog, including posts with only links to other sites, some consisting of only a photo or two and other posts that were paragraph long musings on various topics. Several of the posts, however, were essay-length entries that promptly began to impact discussions among Latino Muslim networks.

On February 16, Jorge "Fabel" Pabon aka Brother Shukriy, who produces the Alianza's leather jackets worn by Figueroa and others, posted an essay titled "What Alianza Islamica Means to Me." In it, Pabon describes his experience at the Alianza's Islamic center:

It seemed as if I walked into an oasis in the middle of El Barrio! I immediately felt a sense of commonality and belonging. . . . My wife and I were married at Alianza Islamica. Several of my close friends took their shahada (embraced Islam) there. It was a safe haven for us. The space was always vibrant and full of activity. Babies were born and brothers

& sisters passed/transitioned. The cycles of life were in motion and revolved around our humble Islamic Center and Masjid. We were/are family in many regards. Although we don't have a physical space at the moment, Alianza Islamica lives in each of the members that continue to hold our mission close to their hearts. We made history by becoming the first Spanish-Speaking Islamic Center and Mosque in Spanish Harlem. We continue to do so. May Allah (swt) guide and protect us throughout our journey and service to our communities.[19]

In addition to essays that remind their readers of the Alianza's legacy and continued work, other blog posts attempt to reorient the direction that contemporary discourse by Latino Muslim leaders has taken. "Reclaiming heritage," writes Figueroa in reference to his earlier posts, "lends itself to the false impression of dwelling on the past. The next few lines are about the future flowing from the past." In their attempts to make the teachings of Islam applicable to their lives, Figueroa recalls having experienced alienation from broader Muslims groups. The alienation was based on the accusation that by gathering as Puerto Ricans and celebrating that particular heritage, they were being separatists. The Alianza's response was to celebrate the unique culture of Andalusia as an important and widely recognized segment of Islamic history and civilizational achievement. "Recall that from our long lost homeland," wrote Figueroa,

came the leadership of Ibn Hazm, Ibn Rushd and Ibn Arabi. Ours was a land of grand jurists, Quran masters, philosophers and perhaps the greatest Sufi masters of all time. Leave for the time the flight of Ibn Arabi and turn to the very sober orthodox message of Ibn Abbad of Ronda and you glimpse the greatness of our past which must not be silenced by the ignorance and fanatics of our post-colonial setting. Andalusia is a heritage we must grasp with courage and leave the crippled version of Islam that has reduced the Muslim world to shambles in so many places.

However, cautions Figueroa, it is equally important to dwell on Andalusia's historical shortcomings in order to not repeat these same mistakes. "The beauty of old Spain," continues Figueroa, "did not pay full attention to peasants and the poor and in time financial instability eroded the fabric of life. These are dangers that we face as well today." In light of these issues, Figueroa's final suggestions or proposals to Latino Muslims today are: (1) to engage in and support reclamation research on Andalusian spirituality and thought; (2) to develop a political-cultural vision for Latino Muslims; and (3) to struggle to reverse social and economic instability among Latinos and others.

The first two of these proposals have been attempted, to varying degrees by a number of organizations. Every Latino Muslim organization since the Alianza has sought to promote the link between Islamic Spain and Latino identity by producing media on Al-Andalus, promoting such media, or both. These media productions, however, have mostly been developed as a response to accusations that Latinos either cannot categorically be Muslim or that they have historically not been Muslim.[20] The reclamation research on Andalusian spirituality and thought that Figueroa is calling for is therefore one that additionally responds to the concern that Latinos too often assimilate to Muslim majority cultures and non-Latino theological developments when they embrace Islam.[21] "An authentic future for us," writes Figueroa,

demands that we reclaim that [Andalusian] heritage and not settle for the models of Islam that seem to only give way to failed states, spiritual death, and finally, suicidal despair . . . we are confronted with a most burning issue—the reality of our direction and the choice of our future. There are two choices: [one] Will we simply jump on the bandwagon of the current troubled Islamic model and poorly translate from one language and culture onto another? In the first image, a few of our brightest will simply go to the Muslim lands and master the formal structure of prayers and religious formalities and bring back with them the current ideals and aspirations of Arabia, Pakistan, or wherever they may happen to go. With this choice, we will attempt to simply poorly imitate the same worn-out failed models throughout the troubled Muslim world uncritically, mechanically, and then expect that it can achieve something for our people other than the misery that surrounds so much of the Muslim world today.[22]

Here, Figueroa echoes concerns by LALMA that Latino Muslim leaders who are trained in Islamic religious universities in Saudi Arabia, Egypt, and so on, are not only regarded internally and externally as more authoritative figures because of their mastery of non-Latino ways of thinking about Islam but also that the kind of Islamic teachings that they return with and propagate among Latino communities are spiritually lacking, morally bankrupt, and socially inefficient.[23]

One response by LALMA has been to help Cesar, one of the group's members and Arabic instructor, receive an Islamic education at the US-based Bayan theological seminary in Claremont, California. Although he is expected to make significant contributions to Latino Islamic thought, it remains to be seen how his and other such work will be received among Latino Muslim communities beyond LALMA and by broader Muslim organizations throughout the United States. "Let us delve into the Quran and Sunnah," proposes Figueroa, "and re-discover their riches as Muslims worldwide did giving birth to all of intellectual diversity that maintained our Muslim people for these centuries." And in a deliberate attack against Salafi thought and its proponents, especially within the Latino Muslim community, Figueroa concludes that "those who claim today to only follow Quran and Sunnah. . . . They simply impose their ignorance unto the Noble sources and cripple themselves and others convinced by their ignorance."[24]

Rather than "simply go to the Muslim lands" and imitate their "ideals and aspirations," writes Figueroa, the group should instead "insist that our path is Andalusian, which is neither East nor West, but a spiritual reality and path to liberation. . . . If Islam among Spanish Cultural groups along with the troubled Andalusian youth in France, Belgium, and the descendants of the sub-continent in England has any authentic future, it can only be by recovering an Andalusian approach and building upon that glorious past." Reclamation research on Al-Andalus, in Figueroa's view, must therefore be developed not only as a response to accusations that Latinos cannot be or have not been Muslim, but as a response and lived attempt to liberate communities from the spiritual and material problems that plague them today. The effectiveness of such reclamation research and development of thought is thus to be measured by its ability offer severe critiques of itself and to inspire, direct, and achieve liberation in a contemporary context. Liberation in these terms, however, was not a central vision upon which Latino Muslims organized around during the second wave of the movement.[25]

Every organization has indeed developed a mission statement based on their particular vision of Latino Muslims. Most of these unifying visions, however, have centered on a shared need for Spanish language Islamic educational media. But as several leaders have pointed out, including Figueroa, not all Latinos speak Spanish. "I made an observation when I attended the recent opening of the dazzling Centro Islamico in Houston," wrote Figueroa,

A meeting was convened of Latino Muslim leaders in a side office. People were there from different parts of the country discussing the dawah efforts in their cities. The discussion, however, was conducted in flawless, un-accented English with the exception of Ruiz from Florida. The irony of this occurring at this auspicious occasion was not lost on me. So far, virtually all questions regarding materials and approaches center on Spanish language books, brochures, CDs and DVDs as if the only ones worth addressing in a Latin-specific way are immigrants [i.e., Latinos who only speak Spanish]. The approach to Latino dawah must be more nuanced and cannot be so narrowly focused. In reality, Alianza was very much a Nuyorican phenomenon as the majority of the converts and members were first generation. Frankly, I don't see much of a difference with the current group of pan-Latino Muslims, first generation English speakers who still hold firmly to their cultural roots. The "Spanish Dawah" and its concomitant materials should be considered a part of an overall "Latino" dawah program which integrates material geared to the first-generation "Latino-American."[26]

Latino Muslim media, according to Figueroa's second proposal, if it is to be relevant must be animated by a vision that includes liberation for all Latino Muslims in the United States, that is, those who develop, embrace, dwell within, and perform Spanish, English, bilingual, or other ways of being Latino.

The visionary component that has been far too absent from Latino Muslim organizational visions since the Alianza, however, has arguably been one that develops, performs, and sustains Figueroa's third and final proposal: to struggle to reverse social and economic instability among Latinos and others. More recent Latino Muslim visions have also focused on engaging in a collective and combative response to negative representation of the identity group, which in Figueroa's view also lacks a clearly articulated path to liberation. Although some social services were provided by PIEDAD and LALMA during the second wave of Latino Muslims, they were not regular practices nor part of these groups' official mission. Instead, organizations developed visions that led to Islamic education centered activities during the second wave. Although this may indeed be understood as a social service itself, one capable of dealing with what may be described as the spiritual root of social injustices, it is clearly not what Figueroa had in mind. In the emerging third wave, however, some leaders have agreed with Figueroa's third proposal that social and economic liberation must be at the center of the identity group's vision and practice.

In 2014, during an interview with the president of what was then the Los Angeles LALMA, Marta Galedary described the social service work of la Alianza Islámica as something she hoped more Latino Muslim groups would start to replicate, including her own. And to her credit, Galedary had indeed pushed LALMA toward greater civic involvement even in the second wave. Under her leadership, LALMA met with interfaith groups and engaged in talks at university classes and forums, public libraries, festivals, and with other such audiences as part of an educational service to American publics in a post-9/11 context. LALMA also met with the Los Angeles Police Department to help improve relations between Muslims and law enforcement in southern California. Finally, Galedary also inspired a few of LALMA's members to attend pro-Palestinian rights protests on one occasion.

Then in late 2012, LALMA underwent a series of organizational reconfigurations. With help from its core members, new talent, and outside consultants, the group created a leadership board with much more formalized democratic processes. LALMA also took several steps to rebrand the group, including a new logo, website, and letterhead. These steps were part of a rebranding campaign that eventually sought to reformulate the organization from a regional one (i.e., the greater Los Angeles area) to a much broader one as La Asociación Latino Musulmán de América (the Latino Muslim Association of America). The renaming of LALMA as an American group rather than a Los Angeles group points to the organization's expansionary vision. Just as significant, the group has reconfigured its mission statement in a way that anticipated Figueroa's third proposal. LALMA's new mission statement, publically available on its revised website at LALMA.net, reads as follows: "LALMA is an organization of Latino Muslims that promotes a better understanding of Islam to the Spanish speaking community and establishes a forum of spiritual nurturing and social support to Latino Muslims, building bridges among the monotheistic community and advocating for social justice in accordance with Islamic values."

Toward the goal of advocating for social justice based on their vision of Islamic values, LALMA began since its reconfiguration to regularly provide social services while also continuing their educational services. One way in which LALMA is living out the social service proposal is in its support of Humanitarian Day events at Los Angeles' skid row where volunteers hand out meals and clothing and provide medical screenings and basic care. The Humanitarian Day services are organized by the ILM (Intellect-Love-Mercy) Foundation and are framed using the Qur'anic ideal here formulated as "Save a Life, Save Humanity" (Qur'an 5:32). Additionally, LALMA began providing educational services on immigration law and for the California Department of Motor Vehicles' written exam for procuring a driver's license.

Moreover, LALMA is extending its vision of Figueroa's third proposal to include participation in attempts to effect public policy. In 2014, LALMA partnered with the LA Voice and the Orange County Congregation Community Organization branches of People Improving Communities through Organizing (PICO) National Network, an interfaith-based civic activism organization. On one of many other occasions, LALMA joined the network in order to advocate for Proposition 47, which sought to reduce what were broadly perceived to be unjustly harsh penalties for various crimes, including illegal drug abuse, and in 2014 the bill passed with over 60 percent of support from voters. LALMA helped advocate for the proposition by "staffing phone banks and canvassing registered voters who didn't cast ballots in the last election" in South-Central Los Angeles. LA Voice was chosen by LALMA precisely because the coalition's interfaith composition represented an opportunity to live out Andalusian *convivencia* in contemporary and relevant ways. At LA Voice's general meeting in July 2016, which began with a list of the group's accomplishments, one individual stood up and recognized the LALMA group: "I wanted to recognize the people sitting at this table as the dream team. When nobody from my organization showed up to canvas voters, these women stepped up to the plate, and in their *hijab* went door to door in South-Central L.A." In addition to their partnership with LA Voice, LALMA has also partnered with several other organizations involved with civic engagement for policy change, including the American Civil Liberties Union, the Inland Congregations United for Change, and the Alliance for Community Transit. [27]

The Alianza's revival and call for Latino Muslim organizations to struggle to reverse social and economic instability among Latinos and others along with LALMA's shift toward greater civic engagement, both in social service and in activism, represent a new development in the third wave of Latino Muslims. The revived Alianza and LALMA's reconfiguration represent a possible path toward what Abdullahi Ahmed An-Na'im terms religious self-determination in *What Is an American Muslim? Embracing Faith and Citizenship*. Here An-Na'im argues that though groups like Muslims, Latinos, and Latino Muslims may be outnumbered and marginalized as such, all individuals have many different and overlapping identities, and all Americans, whether Muslim or not, are part of the majority as American. Rather than engage in politics as minorities, An-Na'im makes an appeal for American Muslims to proactively "exercise their full agency and rights to cultural/religious self-determination" as members of the United States. If American Muslims feel they are being culturally or institutionally discriminated against, it is their right and obligation as Americans (i.e., as part of the majority) to try to realize a more ideal situation.[28]

In an interview with Galedary published in *Religion Dispatches*, Nick Street enthusiastically wrote: "The group's contribution to the larger interfaith effort to pass Prop 47 represented an important shift toward greater civic engagement in immigrant Muslim communities."[29] The revival of civic engagement as a prominent feature of Latino Muslim identity and the emerging prominence of Islam-in-Spanish have not, however, developed in isolation from broader national discourses. Instead, mass media coverage of ISIS and immigration, of law enforcement violence and racial civil unrest, and of the 2016 electoral cycle and the rise of Donald Trump as a viable presidential candidate have all played a significant role in the third wave of Latino Muslims in America.

THE 2016 NEWS CYCLE

Many of the dominant stories in the 2015 news cycle were framed as ongoing threats to national security, including the January 7 Charlie Hebdo attack in Paris claimed by a faction of al Qaeda; the November 13 coordinated attacks in Paris claimed by ISIS; and the December 2 San Bernardino shootings by a Muslim couple in the United States claimed by ISIS to be "supporters" of theirs. Discourse around security also became connected to other discourses regarding immigration, gun control, and racial injustice. A refugee crisis, for example, resulting from the war in Syria prompted numerous stories about mass immigration and the security challenges it presented in Europe and in the United States. Of particular concern to Latino Muslims was the increasingly linked discriminatory discourse against Latinos and Muslims as foreigners and as threats to national security.[30]

By 2016, these stories had been crystalized in Republican presidential candidate Donald Trump's xenophobic speech against Latinos and Muslims. Trump's anti-pluralistic rhetoric included phrases like "I will build a great wall—and nobody builds walls better than me, believe me—and I'll build them very inexpensively. I will build a great, great wall on our southern border, and I will make Mexico pay for that wall. Mark my words"; "When Mexico sends its people, they're not sending the best. They're not sending you, they're sending people that have lots of problems and they're bringing those problems with us. They're bringing drugs. They're bring crime. They're rapists. . . . And some, I assume, are good people"; and with regard to Muslims immigrants "They're not coming to this country if I'm president."[31] This rhetoric, in turn, prompted critical questions about a possible connection between the mass mediation of Trump's xenophobic speech and a perceived spike in hate speech and crimes across the nation.

In the *Washington Post* article referenced at the outset of this chapter, Ibrahim Hooper, CAIR's national communications director, commented on the assault of the Wichita State University student who identified as a Latino Muslim, "I think it's clear," concluded Hooper, "that with this kind of incendiary, inflammatory rhetoric, this kind of thing is almost inevitable. . . . People out there who support him [Trump] take it upon themselves to commit these kinds of acts."[32] Whether or not Trump's mass mediated xenophobic speech prompted the verbal and physical assault in Wichita, it is clear that it helped to shape the historically specific manner in which the events took place. Further, we should ask in what ways is being a victim of physical trauma distinct from being a victim of both physical trauma and of hate speech. And how are these distinct from being both and a victim of hate speech in which the words in question come from a presidential candidate receiving an extraordinary amount of coverage for the very hate speech that is now being uttered by others? Is there an added anxiety when it is understood that these words radiate through invisible airwaves and onto hundreds of millions of digital devices across the nation? Questions regarding the impact of mass mediated hate speech need to be further theorized and empirically researched, nevertheless, it seems clear that coverage of Trump is at the very least shaping the historically specific manner in which hate speech and acts are committed if not prompting an increase in their rate of occurrences.

In addition to fostering and shaping a climate of hate, Trump's xenophobic speech has also ostracized and possibly mobilized significant and growing Latino and Muslim voters. On March 8, the *Daily Beast* published an article titled "Donald Trump's Nightmare Voter: Muslim and Latino!" The article reported that Latino Muslims are worried about a Trump presidency, and that this concern is animating many in the community to vote against and even help campaign against Trump. In addition to or in lieu of public and moral appeals to reduce the level and quantity of hate speech in the public sphere, one pragmatic response has been to underscore the political impact of xenophobic speech (i.e., Trump's "Nightmare Voter").

Given the failure to create an umbrella organization in order to gain more political clout and the number of Latino Muslims relative to the national population, it is difficult to make a rational appeal to political consequences when asking figures like Trump to reduce their hate speech.[33] Rather than just appeal to Latino Muslims as Trump's "nightmare voter," the group has therefore also made symbolic appeals to Andalusian (Islamic Spain's) *convivencia*. Often translated as "coexistence," the term *convivencia* is frequently used as a medieval analogue to contemporary discourse around pluralism. Islamic Spain's *convivencia* is described as an approach to managing difference, an approach in which Muslims, Christians, and Jews not only peaceably lived alongside each other but also worked together to create a civilization referred to as "the ornament of the world" for its academic, scientific, and aesthetic accomplishments.[34] All of the prominent Latino Muslim groups discussed in this book, including the Islam-in-Spanish group, promote the connection between Latino Muslims and Andalusian *convivencia*.

However, Andalusian *convivencia* as a historical approach to managing diversity is best understood as the promotion of mere tolerance rather than a celebration of difference. Religious diversity was managed in Islamic Spain through the taxation of groups claiming a Christian or Jewish identity, the institutionalization of ethnic and religious hierarchical classes, and the encouragement of an often unobtainable assimilation. Further, it is important to keep in mind that mere tolerance was not always practiced throughout Islamic Spain's nearly 800-year rule. Indeed, for several groups, tolerance often gave way to discrimination and even outright persecution.[35] "We must not forget," cautions Figueroa,

> the inherent contradiction of Andalusia, which was a major factor in its eventual decline that was the failure to achieve harmony among the competing ethnic and racial groups that made up our long lost homeland. We observe the same dynamic again today: some racial ethnic group dominates all the others with no concern for the well-being of society. . . . Will our Islam inspired by the unique heritage of Andalusia be a vision, a dream of the highest form of spirituality and social order? Or will it merely be a faulty translation from one failed society to another which we as a minority are already most vulnerable? A choice is ahead of us to create a vibrant future or to the sadly repeat a failed vision.[36]

The pronounced hate speech against Latinos and Muslims leading up to the 2016 news cycle has been extremely concerning to many. Even though Latino Muslims have participated in the public sphere on multiple occasions and in various ways, one of its most significant contributions may indeed lay in its ability to develop a pluralistic vision that improves on Islamic Spain's *convivencia* in order to perform a self-critical and civically active way of being Latino and Muslim in America.

CONCLUSION

The emergence of Islam-in-Spanish and the revived imperative toward civic duties constitute central developments in a third wave of Latino Muslims that is being shaped by both the legacy of its preceding eras and by contemporary developments in public discourse including the xenophobic speech of the 2016 election cycle. Within this context, Figueroa from the revived Alianza Islámica argues that to the extent that Latino Muslim organizations continue to center their vision and resources on developing and disseminating Islamic media translated into Spanish, the identity group will remain stagnant and will likely become irrelevant to English-speaking Latino Muslims who often already identify as Muslim and not Latino. Identity narratives that focus on the history and culture of Islamic Spain and on the concept of *convivencia* have been prevalent throughout all three waves of Latino Muslims and may be one way to generate a unified Latino Muslim vision that is compelling to English-speaking, Spanish-speaking, and bilingual members. However, the group must ask itself why the history of Islamic Spain and the concept of *convivencia* should continue to dominate identity narratives propagated by leadership even when most Latino Muslims are only marginally if at all interested in the reversion framework?

Figueroa's first proposal to engage in and promote research on Islamic Spain here reads as a critique that not enough has been done by leaders to make this connection more relevant to the spiritual and material needs of their various intersecting communities. Indeed, Figueroa's three proposals to: (1) engage in and support research on Andalusian spirituality and thought; (2) develop a political-cultural vision for Latino Muslims; and (3) struggle to reverse social and economic instability among Latinos and others make more sense as a single imperative described in three different ways. Understood as such, or as a cycle,[37] Figueroa calls for the group to (1) gain recognition, legitimization, and subsequently access to social capital and material resources, in order to (2) develop, practice, and sustain visions of liberation directed to their broader Latino, Muslim, and American communities by way of a redeveloped concept of *convivencia*, which itself, if animated by both a sense of religious piety and civic duty, will (3) contribute to a diversity that aims to correct social injustice against the most marginalized before cycling back into an increased sense of recognition and legitimization, "and on, and on, and on."

Figueroa, LALMA, and other diverse Latino Muslims thus offer a self-critique regarding the manner in which they are themselves, as triply marginalized, guilty of marginalizing others (e.g., failing to help AIDS victims because of the stigma associated with the disease and sexual orientation instead of simply helping those in need). They also, however, offer corrective visions toward liberation from these and other injustices. In this manner, Latino Muslim discourse also offers a cautionary and liberationist vision for other groups in the United States and how we, in all of our intersecting identities both broad (e.g., as US citizens) and narrow (e.g., as members of marginalized identity groups), may celebrate our diversity while also critiquing and working against our injustices.

CONCLUSION

LATINO MUSLIM IDENTITY AND SOLIDARITY

In this book, I have attempted to carefully attend to both the stories that Latino Muslims tell about themselves and also to the significance of such stories within broader public discourses. Latino Muslims tell stories about who they are that begin in Al-Andalus, Islamic Spain, the "ornament of the world." In this origin history, Muslim contributions to world civilization are celebrated as part of Latino, Muslim, and Latino Muslim heritage. Although they do not claim a direct or uninterrupted biological link, Latino Muslims articulate having an ontological connection to Islam and a historical-cultural connection to Islamic Spain. In the mid- and late twentieth century, a small group of people began rediscovering, adopting, and disseminating this lost, forgotten, or erased aspect of their heritage.

Within a civil rights and post-immigration reform context that led to increased religious diversity in the United States, Yahya Figueroa, Rahim Ocasio, and Ibrahim González worked to live out, protect and celebrate their Nuyorican, Latino, and Muslim identities by founding La Alianza Islámica. It was in New York's Spanish Harlem that they founded the US's first independent Latino Muslim mosque and Islamic center in 1987. Inspired by memories of Islamic Spain, the Qur'anic themes of charity, their training within other civil rights organizations, and their hunger for community, social justice, and dignity, the Alianza's formulation of *dawah* as both education and social service helped to crystalize a first wave of Latino Muslims in the United States and served as a model to leaders within subsequent waves.

Following the Alianza Islámica, new organizations emerged as dominant voices in a second wave of Latino Muslims. PIEDAD met in New

York and Florida as a women's piety group and procured a profession-ally designed website to disseminate stories about the group's identity and their digitized literature on Islamic beliefs and practices. LADO initially met on AOL message boards then produced their own website that came to host the largest collection of Latino Muslim discourse available through internet technologies and became the most widely connected Latino Muslim network in the United States. LALMA was formed as a Qur'anic study group and relied heavily on Spanish lan-guage translations of Islamic texts produced in Spain and procured through dial-up internet connections.

This second wave of Latino Muslim organizations continued and further developed the Alianza's discursive promotion of ontological and historical-cultural connections between Islamic Spain and Latino iden-tity. However, the second wave also differed from the first in important ways, including in their historically specific emphasis and engagement with gender and women's issues, their focus on *dawah* as education but not social service work, and their willingness to work within rather than separate from broader American Muslim groups. Beyond these new developments and also broader and distinct contexts that included the end of the civil rights era, the prominence of "colorblind" public discourse, the proliferation of internet technologies, and shifts in the US Muslim population, the second wave of Latino Muslims was also shaped in large measure by the development of a Latino Muslim rever-sion story genre and a post-9/11 media context.

During the second wave of Latino Muslims, reversion stories came to be one of the central ways in which the group exercised self-authorship over their identity narratives. These short autobiographies by Latino Muslims focused on an individual's experience and embrace of Islam. Latino Muslim leaders made the stories a prominent feature of their websites and also shared them with journalists and other researchers. The stories invariably began by situating the author as both Latino and Muslim, they provided an account of the spatial, relational, and emo-tional modes in which the protagonist had first encountered Islam, they posited a central or several conflicts that were resolved only by taking *shahada*, and they pointed to possible future work and experiences as

Latino Muslims. The stories drew from broader narrative forms found in religious and American testimonials and also articulated historical specificities. They served as a form of *dawah* or the propagation of Islam and responded to critiques that Latino and Muslim identities are incompatible or foreign to one another by framing Latino identity as ontologically, historically, and culturally linked to Islam and Islamic Spain. They helped to build communities and forge new visions for navigating the challenges encountered in America's cityscapes, they prompted a sense of dignity and produced a social commodity traded for material goods in the information economy. Through these reversion stories, Latino Muslims actively participated in the discursive formation of their own identity.

In contrast to self-authored media like reversion stories, Latino Muslims seldom had editorial control over journalistic coverage of their identity group. These mass mediations were shaped in large measure by a post-9/11 media context that rendered Latino Muslims as perplexing if not outright foolish for choosing to convert to Islam and thereby increasing their marginalization. Spanish language media in the United States additionally formulated the group through orientalist imagery deemed offensive by many. In the wake of such coverage, many leaders began refusing to grant interviews and also formed petitions to call for an end to the defamation of their identity group. Others, however, continued to provide interviews for these reductive news stories with the hope that they would nevertheless be able to procure legitimization and recognition and thereby increase their numbers, social capital, and access to broader networks with vital resources.

These goals were complicated, however, by coverage of Antonio Martinez, which identified the young man as a Latino Muslim radical terrorist. This coverage underscored a broader binary thinking that dominates discursive formations of so-called minorities as being either with or against America. Within this binary, Latino Muslims were formulated as either good or bad. Two very different mediations of Hamza Perez's life and experiences provided poignant examples. The binary rendered Hamza's hip-hop/protest poetry and its severe and rhetorically violent critiques of the United States as evidence that he was a "radical or bad" Muslim. The same binary, however, rendered the *New Muslim Cool* documentary film and its focus on Hamza's domestic life and social service work as evidence that he was a "moderate or good" Muslim. Latino Muslim leaders and organizations responded to this binary with media campaigns of their own waged on two fronts: one against post-9/11 Islamophobic images, the other against a brand of Islam they themselves often refer to as puritanical or even "radical."

During and after the 2016 election cycle, increased representations of Latinos, Muslims, and Latino Muslims as threats played a prominent role in the emergence of a third Latino Muslim wave. Attempts to generate consolidated and unified responses to the negative formulations of Latino Muslims as potential radical terrorists found a new sense of urgency. Members of the Alianza Islámica re-emerged in public discourse to offer a liberationist vision on which such unity among disparate Latino Muslim organizations may be achieved. During the second Latino Muslim wave and its post–civil rights, colorblind politics, and generally non-activist approach to *dawah*, the Alianza's revived call to activism would have seemed out of place. During this third wave, however, one situated within a context of civil unrest, marches decrying police brutality against black populations, protests against Trump and his administration's xenophobic speech and policies directed against women, Latinos, Muslims, and other so-called minorities, and a sense of urgency to participate in providing social services to those in need, the Alianza's revived call to activism, social service, and liberation has resonated with many in the community and may indeed come to be a prominent aspect of Latino Muslim identity.

As Latino Muslim converts or reverts grow older and as new generations of individuals raised within Latino Muslim families continue to grow in number, questions as to what kind of Latino Islam, if any, will be transmitted and preserved trans-generationally also grow in urgency. How will Latino identity be internalized by individuals raised within Latino Muslim families? And where will the source of this identity come from: their Latino Muslim parents, their non-Muslim Latino families, or other communities? Will they be taught Islam in Spanish? Will Arabic displace Spanish as a second language? Will they even identify in any substantial way as Latino? Given the volatile character of religious affiliation in the United States, we might also ask if Latinos raised as Muslims will continue to identify themselves as Muslim throughout their entire lives. Will they raise their children in Islam, and if they do, what forms of Islam? Will it be a Latino form of Islam, or will future Latino Muslims assimilate into broader Muslim communities in the United States that are intertwined with racial, ethnic, or nationalistic identities other than Latino? It therefore remains to be seen if the shared narratives of ethnic marginalization, reversion to Islam, and roots in Islamic Spain will continue to be the hallmark of public representations of Latino Muslims or if these will become more prominent or stagnant or merely a past expression of America's diverse portfolio of religious cultures.

I have thus tried to carefully attend to both these stories that Latino Muslims tell about themselves and to the significance of such stories within public discourse. As such, I have focused on historically specific accounts by and on Latino Muslims but have also engaged several themes and issues that may have broader import. First, Latino Muslims serve as guides between multiple and sometimes competing communities. They introduce Latinos to Muslims and Muslims to Latinos. Similarly, it is my hope that through this work, those interested in Latino religious studies literature have been introduced to Islamic studies scholarship and vice versa. Open and critical engagement with complex and intersecting identity groups like Latino Muslims thus prompts scholars to carefully examine how our fields of specialization both help to illuminate but also at times present disciplinary impediments to our work and reveal how we may rely more heavily on interdisciplinary studies.

Second, Latino Muslim stories flourished in public discourse through internet technologies and post-9/11 media practices and prompted the use of multiple methodologies. Indeed, it was the stories that Latino Muslims themselves told about their communities, including of how they formed groups through AOL message boards, that prompted my study of the group's relation to media technologies and practices in the first place. Nevertheless, it has now become difficult for me to envision a study of any other group that does not employ both ethnographic field work and media analysis. Instead, it seems much more prudent to proceed by examining how lived experiences become mediated and the manner in which the production, dissemination, and consumption of media conversely helps to shape lived experiences.

Third, media on and by Latino Muslims often employ conceptual divisions between religion and culture, a link between culture and ethnicity and complex relations between ethnicity and race that both draw on broader discourses and are applied in specific ways. In addressing accusations that Latino and Muslim identities are categorically incompatible with one another, for example, Latino Muslim discourse has often posited a distinction between a Latino culture that is historically constituted and a universal Islamic religion that is the essence of human ontology. When a Latino Muslim responds to the incompatibility accusation by saying "I'm changing religion, not culture. I still eat tortillas," they challenge the Latino-therefore-Catholic framework and also make certain claims regarding the divisibility between religion and culture or ethnicity. In responding to post-9/11 and other racializing media practices, journalists covering the Antonio Martinez story posited Latino "nature" as radical and as therefore very compatible with radical Islam, thus making a different sort of claim regarding the relation between religion and ethnicity or race. Complex divisions, unifications, and relationships between culture, ethnicity, race, and religion should therefore be approached as dynamic and fluid and critically analyzed in terms of discursive negotiations.

Fourth, discursive negotiations by groups like Latino Muslims prompt us to critically examine the ways in which the "minority" category has served to dominate, negotiate, and liberate. To be identified as a so-called minority may signify a lack of representative power in a deliberative democracy, a subordination of importance, a lack of recognition and of resources, and it may also be a form of discrimination or marginalization. However, to identify as a so-called minority might also signify a political expediency, a timely call for solidarity against white supremacy at time in which the United States is on the verge of becoming a nation whose collective "minorities" will have a numeric advantage over the current majority population.

This raises a final and related issue regarding the particular and the universal or identity and solidarity as it pertains to liberation. If the fact that the nation's so-called minority groups will soon outnumber the majority is to have any political impact toward liberation from marginalization, then these groups will necessarily need to seek out liberation in solidarity with one another. However, what do all of the so-called minority groups in the United States have in common with one another other than the fact that they identify or are identified as "minorities?" What is the common tie upon which a universal group composed of particularities can be recognized as a political challenge? So-called minority groups like Latino Muslims, who consist of less than 200,000 members in a nation with over 300 million, themselves face severe challenges to forming umbrella organizations like the League of Latino Muslim Organizations. If specific organizations fail to unify because of the diversity that exists within the pan-Latino Muslim identity group, then how can we hope to envision solidarity at much larger levels? In the struggle for liberation through recognition politics, diversity appears to be a challenge to solidarity (e.g., between all supporters of the Women's March on Washington, the Black Lives Matter movement, and so on).[1] Categories like "Latino," "Muslim," and even so-called minorities become themselves untenable universals relative to the particularities or diversity that exists within these broader umbrella identities.

In "Revitalizing Hegelian Recognition: Identity Politics and Solidarity," Michael Monahan provides an analysis of the problem between the universal and the particular as it regards liberation movements.[2] The problem of how to reconcile the particular and universal undergirds many of the prominent critiques of identity or recognition politics undertaken by so-called minorities in the United States, including by Latino Muslims. One such critique is that recognition politics essentializes a static identity which experience reveals to be fluid and dynamic instead. Not only is such essentializing contrary to experience, it also has the effect of marginalizing, assimilating, or erasing important differences including those between Latino Muslim men and Latina Muslim women, between first, second, and third generation immigrants, between converts, non-converts, and reverts, between Muslims who are Puerto Rican, Nuyorican, Mexican, Chicano, Central American, and others coded as Latino, and between various understandings of and ways of living out Islamic beliefs and practices.[3] Latino Muslim experiences and articulations of those experiences are not singular nor do they remain the same over time, and yet solidarity between all Latino Muslims has relied on a constant (e.g., the linking of Latino identity to the history of Islamic Spain), which functions to unify the great diversity that exists within all of those who identify as Latino Muslims.

A second critique is that recognition politics reinscribes relations of domination and subordination.[4] Accordingly, Latino Muslim groups seeking recognition will remain dependent on those who provide it. For example, when Latino Muslim groups sought out recognition from broader Muslim groups these attempts were either determined to be successful or not. In the case of La Alianza during the 1980s and 1990s, the failed requests for recognition from mosque communities and groups like the Islamic Party in North America and the Islamic Society of North America would have placed the Alianza members in a position of subordination even if these requests had been granted. They were not granted, however, so the Alianza developed a model of resistance to such groups who failed to recognize their identity narratives. In 1985, Ibrahim from the Alianza organized a Latino Muslim pride event that sought to highlight "Latino culture's Islamic legacy" and to help the community "emerge from the shadows." The group gained recognition from broader Muslim organizations and the campaign was thus deemed a success.[5] Subsequent Latino Muslim groups during the second and emerging third wave have also been successful in procuring recognition from broader mosque communities and Muslim organizations. Nevertheless, Latino Muslim groups are here again reinscribed as dependent on and therefore subordinate to the broader organizations that provided them with such recognition. When Latino Muslims seek recognition from broader groups, whether it be from their Latino or Muslim communities, from journalists, media consumers, academics, or others, it positions them as dependent on providers who can either be gracious or not, but dependent on them nonetheless. When recognition is transacted in these asymmetrical ways, the dominant positionality of those that confer recognition upon others is thus reinscribed.

A third prominent critique of recognition politics is that it presumes discrete and "sovereign" subjects or "independent, self-determining agents."[6] Not only is rational agency a European Enlightenment era construct rather than an ahistorical constitution of humanity, it is one that has produced universal human rights for some while at the same time denying the full humanity and therefore rights of those subjugated by colonialism.[7] Agency has been both a conceptual tool for the self-determination of some and for the domination of others. If liberation for so-called minority groups like Latinos, Muslims, and Latino Muslims is sought out by merely recognizing their agency, then the very humanity of individuals within these groups—in addition to their particular identities—are both essentialized and formulated as dependent and tenuous. In the words of Monahan, "if liberation requires that one receive recognition [of one's agency], then one is left dependent upon the donor of that recognition, so relations of subordination and dependence are simply recapitulated in what is supposed to be a liberatory moment."[8]

The Enlightenment era "sovereign subject" necessarily denies liberation from relations of domination and subjugation, and without a common tie that binds there can be no movements toward liberation in solidarity with others. In response, some philosophers, including Tsenay Serequeberhan in "Amilcar Cabral's 'Return to the Source': A Reading," think about equality in terms of a humanity formulated as fundamentally unknowable or "uncanny" in Heideggerian terms.[9] Drawing from a different set of theoretical sources, political theorist Patchen Markell similarly proposes that all humans are fundamentally unknowable and that this should be understood as the tie that binds.[10] Our unknowability, in Markell's view, is based on a constitution of humanity as fluid and ongoing works in progress. This is a description of humanity that I agree with and have tried to elucidate in this book. It is also, however, a view that may render any propositional definitions of our identity as always "belated."[11] That is, by the time we have stated that there are approximately 198,000 Latino Muslims in the

United States, this number very well might have changed. Or, by the time we say that 'reversion' in contrast to conversion is a vital aspect of Latino Muslim identity, individuals like Juan Galvan from LADO or Marta Galedary from LALMA may have very well changed their minds about the importance of reversion. Although a move like Markell's may indeed avoid the critique of essentialism and of structuring relations of domination and subordination, a constitution of humanity as fluid and ongoing works in progress need not lead us to abandon our knowability or our recognizability and we may thus continue the work of recognition politics.

If our response to these critiques is to abandon recognition politics altogether and instead celebrate particularity rather than universality, then solidarity and collective action becomes difficult if not impossible. When Latino Muslims celebrate their particularity, whether it is at a support group or at a day at the park with *carne asada*, a *piñata*, and prayer toward Mecca, they seek to do so in solidarity with one another. When they seek to combat negative mediations of their identity, they seek to do so as a unified collective by signing petitions and pooling resources. In celebrating their particularity, they are in effect appealing to a universal Latino Muslim identity, albeit one narrower than those of Latino, Muslim, and American. When An'Naim calls for Muslims in the United States to stop participating in public discourse as so-called minorities and to do so instead as US citizens and therefore as members of the majority, what he is in effect doing is appealing to a broader universal. Whether it is an appeal to a national, broader or narrower universal, without solidarity it is difficult to see how liberation can be sought out. Without a common tie that binds, there seems to be no option other than to celebrate ever more fragmented identities that end in particular solipsistic subjects.[12]

Rather than reject particularity for political expediency or reject universality because it essentializes, reinscribes relations of domination, and posits a problematic formulation of the sovereign subject, it may be more fruitful to seek out a reconciliation between the particular and the universal that is itself, like Latinos, Muslims, Latino Muslims, and America: fluid and dynamic. A reconciliation between the universal and the particular as it pertains to recognition politics is possible, argues Monahan, if recognition of self and of others is formulated in terms of practical knowledge rather than propositional, through a "know-how" rather than a "know-that" epistemology. We can recognize Latino Muslim identity groups propositionally as having emerged in New York's Spanish Harlem in the 1980s, as being primarily interested in producing, disseminating, and consuming Spanish language literature on Islam, as living out a "moderate" form of Sunni Islam, and so on and so forth. Such a list of facts regarding Latino Muslims can then be recognized and evaluated as being either true or false, as accurate or inaccurate. However, not only are such evaluations of recognition severely limiting (i.e., you either recognized them correctly or you didn't) but also they constitute Latino Muslims in terms of a static and essentialized identity that marginalizes and ignores important complexities and diversities that exist within Latino Muslim communities and also the way in which they are a work in progress as a community (i.e., constantly reworking their own and our understanding of who they are).

If we recognize Latino Muslim identity groups through practical knowledge instead of propositional, then evaluations of identity can move away from simplistic true or false calculations to much more complex and qualitative judgements. Particular mediations of Latino Muslims can in this way be evaluated as being qualitatively better or worse than other recognitions of the identity group rather than merely being accurate or inaccurate.[13] We therefore need not conclude that we are radically unknowable solipsistic subjects: "Of course you can know yourself and others," argues Monahan, "but you can also always know them and yourself better."[14] Importantly, because everyone "is only in and through others," because no one is an independent sovereign self, a reconciliatory (between the subject-object and particular-universal divides) and practical knowledge of self and others is interdependent on reciprocal relations of recognition between ourselves and others.[15] We can have practical knowledge of ourselves and others, and we can improve and suggest improvement on such knowledge of ourselves and others, but only as interdependent subjects.

We should also realize that the very basis for these evaluations of our practical knowledge is itself always fluid and dynamic. A novice and a virtuoso both know how to do something, but there is also a qualitative difference between their knowing. There are also those who push the very boundaries of what it means to be better or to be able to know someone in a much deeper and meaningful way.[16] Latino Muslims can help broader Latino groups to cultivate deeper and more meaningful recognitions of Muslims and vice versa. During the 2017 month of Ramadan, a "Taco Truck at Every Mosque" campaign received sustained media attention and sought to bring Latinos and Muslims together.[17] The goal was not to just learn facts about each other, but to gain practical knowledge of how to be in relation to one another in daily life and to build solidarity groups in order to collectively seek out liberation. Such work can also help to push the very boundaries of what is meant by the broader more universal categories of Latino and Muslim and also the broader categories of culture, ethnicity, race, and religion themselves. Latino Muslims and those in relation to them can together push the boundaries of what it even means to have a qualitatively better recognition of self and others within the race-religion contexts into which we have been thrust.

Although we have been thrust into a particular context (e.g., we have inherited a history of racialized interactions between each other), this history itself has no singular or static significance. Instead, the meaning of categories like race and religion are dynamic and varied.[18] When we recognize Latino Muslims as reciprocal participants in the constant inheriting and reworking of what it means to be a Latino, a Muslim, a Latino Muslim, an American, of what it means to be a convert or a revert, of what it means that Muslims left an indelible mark on the identity of Spain, Latin America, and the United States, and of what it means to have a racialized religion or a race-religion at the dawn of the twenty-first century, then we avoid the pitfalls of a recognition politics that is based on static, subordinating, and propositional formulations of identity and we come to better recognize ourselves and others as interdependent subjects.

This practical understanding of identity as a dynamic becoming[19] that is reliant upon reciprocal relationships of recognition is a qualitatively better recognition of our own experiences. Further, it does not essentialize humanity as static beings nor does it reinscribe relations of domination. Finally, it formulates humanity as both knowable through a practical epistemology and as interdependent in this knowability, and thus provides a substantial basis upon which solidarity movements can be shaped toward liberation. As Monahan writes: "The task of recognition here, the project of *reconciliation* or as I prefer, *liberation* thus involves self-conscious and deliberate participation in this ongoing process."[20] This is a process of coming from a place in which we have been constituted as racialized subjects and of going to a place where our identity is dynamic and unfixed. It is a process in which we inherit in order to shape the meaning and significance of race-religion in new ways that "open up richer interactions" with each other.[21]

Latino Muslims continue to de-naturalize or de-essentialize, to broaden and to push our varied and unfixed understandings of and relations to Latinos, Muslims, and Latino Muslims, to ourselves and also to the complex ways in which race or ethnicity and religion are entangled in our daily lives and mediated experiences. Although the social, political, and media impact of Latino Muslims as a so-called new minority in America is constantly shifting, it is clear that the identity group will continue to play a significant role in public discourse even as they continue to struggle for recognition, solidarity with one another, and the very existence of their particular ways of becoming. Even as many people view Latinos and Muslims as growing threats, and as mediations of their identities are too often formulated through a propositional epistemology of self, and therefore as essentialized, static, and subordinate, Latino Muslims nevertheless celebrate their intersecting identities in their daily lives and in the mediations of their experiences.

NOTES

INTRODUCTION

1. Pew, "U.S. Religious Landscape Survey: Religious Affiliation," 5.
2. Suárez-Orozco and Páez, *Latinos: Remaking America*.
3. Taylor, Lopes, Martinez, and Valasco, "When Labels Don't Fit: Hispanics and Their Views of Identity."
4. It is important to keep in mind here, as Abdul JanMohamed and David Lloyd write, "minority discourse, is, in the first instance, the product of damage, of damage more or less systematically inflicted on cultures produced as minorities by the dominant culture" ("Introduction: Toward a Theory of Minority Discourse," 7). And that in addition to Marx's description of religion as "the sublimation and the expression of misery," sublimation should be understood as a strategy for survival (8). Lastly, "all minority discourse also derives from the fact that minority individuals are always treated and forced to experience themselves generically," which informs the "strategic nature of minority preoccupation with identity and non-identity" (10). Latino Muslim discourse is thus both the product of damage and also an inhabiting of the "minority" category as a strategy for survival and resistance. Latino Muslim identity is complex, diverse, and fluid in as much as it is both designed to dominate and to also to liberate.
5. An-Naim, *What Is an American Muslim?: Embracing Faith and Citizenship*, 17.
6. Pew, "U.S. Religious Landscape Survey: Religious Affiliation," 22.
7. By 2015 there was an increase by 6 percentage points from the 2007 findings. Pew, "America's Changing Religious Landscape," 33.

8. According to Pew findings, 16 percent of the nation's population identified as having no religious affiliation in 2007, which then climbed to 23 percent in 2015. Ibid., 113.

9. According to the 2015 Pew report, "nearly 13% of all Americans are former Catholics. . . . No other religious group analyzed in the survey has experienced anything close to this ratio of losses to gains via religious switching." Ibid., 35.

10. Twenty-nine percent of all Catholics in the United States identify as Latino or Hispanic in 2007 and 34 percent did so in the 2015 Pew findings. Ibid., 52.

11. Pew, "The Shifting Religious Identity of Latinos in the United States," 37.

12. Pew, "The Shifting Religious Identity of Latinos in the United States," 41.

13. The remaining 10 percent report "self-discovery/other/don't know." Pew, "Muslim Americans: Middle Class and Mostly Mainstream."

14. Pew, "The Changing Global Religious Landscape," 8.

15. Mohamed, "A New Estimate of the U.S. Muslim Population."

16. Pew, "Muslim Americans: Middle Class and Mostly Mainstream," 17, 22–23.

17. Espinosa, Morales, and Galvan. "Latino Muslims in the U.S.: Reversion, Politics and Islamidad," 13–14, 17.

18. The little demographic information available on Latino Muslims is mostly contradictory. A 2007 report by the Islamic Society of North America (ISNA), estimated that there are 40,000 Hispanic Muslims in the United States ("Latino Muslims Growing in Number in the US," ISNA.net, http://hispanicmuslims.com/articles/voanews.html); whereas, the American Muslim Council reported an estimated 200,000 in 2006 (Conci, "Latinos Converting to Islam"). The Pew Charitable Trusts-funded Hispanic Churches in American Public Life national survey (n = 2,060) put the number of Latino Muslims at approximately 52,000 when the percentages were updated per the 2014 US Census data released in 2015 (Espinosa, "Changements démographiques et religieux chez les hispaniques des Etats-Unis"). A 2011 study conducted by the Pew Research Center showed that Latino Muslims accounted for an estimated 6 percent of all Muslims living in the United States. See Pew Research Center, "Muslim

Americans: No Signs of Growth in Alienation or Support for Extremism," August 2011, http://www.people-press.org/files/2011/08/muslim-american-report.pdf. Pew, "The Future of the Global Muslim Population." The Pew Research Center estimated that in 2015 there were about 3.3 million Muslims in the United States. See Mohamed, "A New Estimate of the U.S. Muslim Population." That puts the Latino Muslim population at 198,000. A 2017 report by the Institute for Social Policy and Understanding (ISPU) estimated that 5 percent of Muslims in the United States identify as Hispanic. See Mogahed and Chouhoud, "American Muslim Poll 2017: Muslims at the Crossroads." The report did not produce an estimate of the total Muslim population; if we estimate the total Latino Muslim population using Pew's estimated total U.S. Muslim population of 3.3 million and ISPU's estimate that 5 percent of these are Latinos, then the total Latino Muslim population is closer to 165,000. However, given the low number of Latino Muslim clergy and Spanish-language mosques and my ethnographic experiences, it is likely that there are far fewer Latino Muslims in the United States than both the PEW- and ISPU-based estimates.

19. Pew, "U.S. Religious Landscape Survey: Religious Affiliation," 2.

20. Technological determinism maintains that society is shaped in large measure by technology, including media technologies. Karl Marx and Friedrich Engels, in *The Poverty of Philosophy*, argued, for example, that "the windmill gives you society with the feudal lord: the steam-mill, society with the industrial capitalist" (i.e., technology determines the manner in which social relations are organized). According to this view, public opinion is shaped or determined by mass media technologies. Philosopher, literary and communications scholar, and media determinist, Marshall McLuhan, in *Understanding Media: The Extensions of Man*, for example, famously argued that "the medium is the message" (i.e., a society is not defined by the content of its discourse but by the media technologies that frame and carry such content). Concepts of the self and of democracy are understood here to exist in society only through the technologies that make their articulation possible, and possible only in particular ways.

21. Even if communication technologies determine the messages expressed by a society, a society determines which technologies are

adopted, ignored, or rejected. A society's technologies therefore may be themselves determined by the values of that society. The printing press, for example, was adopted by European societies not simply because it came into existence, but because there was already a demand for texts during the medieval scholastic period. Likewise, mass media technologies not only shape popular opinion, but are themselves shaped by and reflect social values. British cultural studies theorist, Stuart Hall, argued in "Encoding/Decoding" against media determinism. In its stead, Hall advocated a theory that takes the entire media cycle into account where each stage of development, production, dissemination, and consumption retains related though independent interpretations of the communicated narrative event. In his seminal work on the information age, Manuel Castells writes: "Of course, technology does not determine society. Nor does society script the course of technological change, since many factors, including individual inventiveness and entrepreneurialism, intervene in the process of scientific discovery, technological innovation, and social applications, so that the final outcome depends on a complex pattern of interaction. Indeed, the dilemma of technological determinism is probably a false problem, since technology *is* society, and society cannot be understood or represented without its technological tools" (*The Rise of the Network Society*, 5). If society is technology and vice versa, then our racial and religious identities are not only intersections between themselves but also between these and the media technologies through which they are produced, disseminated, and consumed. In the words of Donna J. Haraway's "A Cyborg Manifesto," "we are all chimeras, theorized and fabricated hybrids of machine and organism," creatures of both fiction and lived social realities. We are the airplanes that fly us, the farming tools that help feed us, the computer networks we plug into. It follows then that Latino Muslims identities are hybrid: they are both lived experiences and technological formations, authentic and designed, multiple, complex, and diverse in their lived experiences and mediated representations.

22. See Brasher, *Give Me That Online Religion*; Hoover and Schofield Clark, *Practicing Religion in the Age of the Media*; Eickelman and Anderson, *New Media in the Muslim World*; Nakamura, *Digitizing*

Race: Visual Cultures of the Internet; Campbell, "When Religion Meets New Media."

23. For more on lived religions, see Orsi, Between Heaven and Earth; McGuire, Lived Religion: Faith and Practice in Everyday Life; and Hughes, Biography of a Mexican Crucifix. For more on media and new media studies, see Hall, "Encoding/Decoding" and "Foucault: Power, Knowledge and Discourse"; Castells, The Rise of the Network Society and The Power of Identity: The Information Age: Economy, Society and Culture; Nakamura, Digitizing Race; and Campbell, "Understanding the Relationship between Religious Practice Online and Offline." For more on the interplay between lived experience/ethnography and the mediation of these experiences/media studies, see Starrett, "Muslim Identities and the Great Chain of Buying."

24. Dawah is usually translated as propagation of Islam or calling others to Islam. Others have additionally translated it or explained it as a form of outreach. In Rebel Music, Hisham Aidi writes, "But many [Muslims, including Salafi or conservative Muslims] are active in da'wa (outreach) and in trying to bring Islamic norms to the spaces they inhabit" (49).

CHAPTER 1

1. Castro, The Spaniards: An Introduction to Their History, 232.
2. Berkey, The Formation of Islam.
3. Flood, "Light in Stone: The Commemoration of the Prophet in Umayyad Architecture."
4. Aslan, No God but God.
5. Irving, Falcon of Spain.
6. Irving, The Qur'ān: The First American Version.
7. Irving, Halcon de España.
8. Irving, "Dates, Names and Places: The End of Islamic Spain."
9. Menocal, The Ornament of the World, 61.
10. See Clendinnen, Ambivalent Conquests; and also Hughes, Biography of a Mexican Crucifix.
11. For more on the politicized character of names ranging from Hispania to Andalusia, see Fernández-Morera, The Myth of the Andalusian Paradise.

12. Narbona, Pinto, and Karam, *Crescent over Another Horizon.*
13. Irving, *Falcon of Spain,* 152.
14. Ibid., 149.
15. Menocal, *The Ornament of the World,* 208–209.
16. Menocal, Scheindlin, and Sells, *The Literature of Al-Andalus;* Menocal, "Culture in the Time of Tolerance."
17. Menocal, *The Ornament of the World,* 282–283.
18. Menocal, "Culture in the Time of Tolerance: Al-Andalus as a Model for Our Time," 8.
19. Lane-Poole, *The Muslims in Spain.*
20. Menocal, "Culture in the Time of Tolerance," 2.
21. Carr, *Blood and Faith.*
22. Saada, *Edición y Estudio del Manuscrito Aljamiado-Morisco de la Biblioteca Nacional de Madrid.*
23. See Curtis, *Muslims in America,* 4–5; Smith, *Islam in America,* 50–51; GhaneaBassiri, *A History of Islam in America,* 9–14.
24. Narbona, Pinto, and Karam, *Crescent over Another Horizon.*
25. See Austin, *African Muslims in Antebellum America,* 22; Gomez, *Black Crescent,* 22; Curtis, *Muslims in America,* 4.
26. Castillo, *The Conquest of New Spain.*
27. Casas, *A Brief Account of the Destruction of the Indies.*
28. See Elizondo and Matovina, *New Frontiers in Guadalupan Studies;* Matovina, *Guadalupe and Her Faithful;* and Elizondo, *Guadalupe, Mother of the New Creation.*
29. Martínez-Vázquez, *Latina/o y Musulmán.*
30. Curtis, *Muslims in America,* 15–22.
31. GhaneaBassiri, *A History of Islam in America;* Smith, *Islam in America.*
32. Smith, "Religious Diversity in America," 1; Mann, Numbrish, and Williams, *Buddhists, Hindus, and Sikhs in America,* 8, 45–46, 117.
33. Smith, *Islam in America,* 80–81.
34. Bowen, "Early U.S. Latina/o African-American Muslim Connections."
35. Ibid., 401.
36. Turner, *Islam in the African-American Experience,* 114–117; Lee, "Review of *Black Crescent,*" 252.
37. Turner, *Islam in the African-American Experience.*
38. Curtis, *Black Muslim Religion in the Nation of Islam,* 11, 19, 33.
39. Bowen, "Early U.S. Latina/o African-American Muslim Connections."

40. Ibid.
41. Marable, *Malcolm X: A Life of Reinvention*.
42. Ibid.
43. More research is needed on the Mosque of Islamic Brotherhood in general and its Latino membership in particular. For a reference, see Dannin and Stahl, *Black Pilgrimage to Islam*, 69.
44. Kong, "History Draws Hispanics to Islam"; Muhammad, "A Brief History of 'Latinos' in the Nation of Islam."
45. Nuruddin, "The Five Percenters," 113 and 117.
46. Bowen, "Early U.S. Latina/o African-American Muslim Connections."
47. Haddad and Smith, *Muslim Minorities in the West*, 77–106.
48. Smith, *Islam in America*, 68–70.
49. Galeano, *Open Veins of Latin America*, 65, 71.
50. Whalen and Vázquez-Hernández, *The Puerto Rican Diaspora*, 12–13.
51. Masland, *Through the Back Doors of the World*.
52. The Virtual Pan Am Museum, "Principle Passenger Fares Chart, Latin American Services."
53. Wagenheim and Jiménez de Wagenheim, *The Puerto Ricans*, 236.
54. Noel, *In Visible Movement*, 46, 178.
55. Thomas, *Down These Mean Streets*.
56. Ibid., 85–92.
57. Viscidi, "Latino Muslims a Growing Presence in America."
58. Iqbal, "Hispanics and Islam."
59. Talegani, Mutahhari, Shari'ati, Abedi, and Legenhausen, *Jihad and Shahadat*, 2–3.
60. Wakin, "Ranks of Latinos Turning to Islam Are Increasing."
61. As quoted by Khalid Fattah Griggs in Haddad and Smith, *Muslim Communities in North America*, 97.
62. Curtis, *Encyclopedia of Muslim-American History*, 293.
63. Aslan, *No God but God*, 47–53.
64. Haddad and Smith, *Muslim Minorities in the West*, 97.
65. Aidi, "Latino Muslims are part of US religious landscape."
66. Ocasio, "Alianza Islamica: The True Story."
67. Although many scholarly and journalistic texts cite 1975 as the founding year of the Alianza, these are based on Hisham Aidi's 1999 Africana.com article "Olé to Allah"; Aidi has since then revised the date to "the late 1980's" in his 2016 Al Jazeera article "Latino

Muslims Are Part of US Religious Landscape." In a January 2016 interview with Ocasio and Figueroa, I was given 1987 as the founding date; which was also the date cited in Ocasio's March 2016 *The Islamic Monthly* article "Alianza Islamica: The True Story," http://theislamicmonthly.com/alianza-islamica-the-true-story/.

68. Mathews, "The Latino Crescent."

69. Aidi, "Olé to Allah"; Ocasio, "A Brief History of Alianza Islamica."

70. El-Amin, "Bism Rabbik's Footnote."

71. Mujahid, "Malcolm X = Malik Shabazz: Why Did He Change?"

72. Alianza member, Jorge "Fabel" Pabon, writes, "the multitude of services they [the Alianza Islámica] provided for the community (for both Muslims and non-Muslims) [included]: Islamic studies, spiritual counseling, family counseling, GED programs, self-defense courses, sewing courses, HIV support and awareness, Puerto Rican studies, nutrition courses, survival courses, support for battered women, security services, neighborhood watch (taking a stance against the neighborhood drug dealers), Millati Islami services, administering shahadas, marriages, akikas, jenazahs, Eid celebrations, community events and the list goes on & on. Considering the limited space in the facilities, there was an unbelievable amount of activity going on. Alianza Islamica was a force to be reckoned with." Pabon, "Oasis in El Barrio."

73. Mathews, "The Latino Crescent."

CHAPTER 2

1. Chiorazzi, "From Cross to Crescent."

2. Rivera, "My Hispanic Muslim Legacy."

3. Ibid.

4. Ibid.

5. Ibid.

6. Movements like the Moorish Science Temple, NOI, and Fiver Percenters are often referred to as "proto-Islamic." This moniker, however, reveals a certain evaluative positionality that I do not here adopt. Edward Curtis instead refers to the process of turning away from NOI teachings and practices toward Sunni ones as a *Sunnification*. Sherman Jackson points out that these processes are often referred to

in post-NOI communities as a "Second Resurrection," the first being "during a time which blacks were said to have delivered from the darkness of their slave mentality into the light of their true selves" by the Honorable Elijah Muhammad. Haddad and Smith, *Muslim Communities in North America*, 260; Curtis, *Black Muslim Religion in the Nation of Islam*, 185; Jackson, *Islam and the Blackamerican*, 6.

7. Omi and Winant, *Racial Formation in the United States*, 20–21, 117.

8. GhaneaBassiri, *A History of Islam in America*, 292–295.

9. See Castells, *The Rise of the Network Society*, 5–6; Nakamura, *Digitizing Race*, 1–5; Hafner and Lyon, *Where Wizards Stay Up Late*.

10. Nakamura, *Digitizing Race*, 1–2. Castells, *The Rise of the Network Society*, 5–6.

11. Pew estimates that 64 percent of Latinos have access to internet technologies as compared to the 78 percent non-Latino national average. Brown, Lopez, and Lopez, "Digital Divide Narrows for Latinos as More Spanish Speakers and Immigrants Go Online."

12. Although Brenda Brasher and others cite several instances of innovative online rituals, including among Wiccan practitioners, she concludes that internet technologies have not led to the proliferation of virtual rituals or to the development of innovative digital personas. Brasher, *Give Me That Online Religion*.

13. See Eickelman and Anderson, *New Media in the Muslim World*, 1–18, 45–60. Hoover and Clark, *Practicing Religion in the Age of the Media*, 237–253.

14. Essa, "Interview with LADO/Piedad."

15. Mahmood, *Politics of Piety*.

16. A portion of Askia El-Amin's letter addressing the life and death of T. B. Irving is quoted in chapter 1 of this book.

17. Rivera, "Dr T B Irving—Frontier for Latino Dawah in USA."

18. PIEDAD, "Wise Women."

19. WhyIslam, "Revelando el Misterio del Jiyab."

20. Abu-Lughod, *Remaking Women*.

21. Aisha, Zeina, and Khadijah, "One God, One People, One Belief."

22. Rushdan, "American Muslim Women's Leadership Training, United Arab Emirates (UAE)."

23. "Khadijah Rivera 1950–2009: Heart of the Community," April 2010. https://issuu.com/isnacreative/docs/mar_apr_2010.

24. Alvarado, "The LADO Genesis."
25. Ibid.
26. Ibid.
27. Abeytia, "Curries, Tajeens and Moles: Exploring Culture and Conversion through Food."
28. Bowen, "The Latino American Da'wah Organization and the Latina/o Muslim Identity in the United States," 6.
29. Foucault et al., *Technologies of the Self.*
30. Alvarado, "The LADO Genesis."
31. Galvan, "FAQs about the LADO Group."
32. Griswold del Castillo, *The Treaty of Guadalupe Hidalgo*, 62–86.
33. Lopez, "In 2014, Latinos Will Surpass Whites as Largest Racial/Ethnic Group in California."
34. León, *The Political Spirituality of Cesar Chavez*, 1–34.
35. Leonard, *Making Ethnic Choices California's Punjabi Mexican Americans*, 130.
36. Ibid.; Burg, *Sacramento's Southside Park*, 58–59; Johnson, "Muslim Mosque Association Set to Expand Facilities in Southside Park."
37. Regarding conflicts at these two and other mosque communities in Los Angeles, Ron Kelly writes that "among the factors mitigating against the dream of a locally empowered Muslim solidarity are stresses upon the Muslim family, cultural fragmentation, political fragmentation, religious fragmentation, and gaps between immigrant Muslims and African American believers." Kelly, "Muslims in Los Angeles," 136–140. Latino Muslims have often been accused of being divisive; it seems, however, that Muslim communities in cosmopolitan areas like Los Angeles struggle with forming and or maintaining unity with or without Latino Muslims. This issue regarding the struggle between particularity and solidarity is an important theme throughout this book, one which I address explicitly in the conclusion while offering a model for reconciling the existence of particular identity groups and broader solidarity movements.
38. Ramirez, "New Islamic Movement Seeks Latino Converts."
39. Smith, *Islam in America*, 67.
40. For an introduction to the pillars of practice and tenants of faith within an American context, see ibid., 5–21.
41. Lings, *Muhammad: His Life Based on the Earliest Sources*, 300.

42. al-Kanadee, "Perennialist Poison in Martin Lings' Biography of the Prophet."

43. See Sells, *Approaching the Qur'an*, 16.

44. For a detailed account of the evolution of Las Fiestas Patrias to Fiesta Broadway, see Romo, *East Los Angeles: History of a Barrio*.

45. Kandiyoti, "Bargaining with Patriarchy."

46. There have been a few women (including associate professor of Near Eastern Languages and Cultures at UCLA, Dr. Asma Sayeed) who have given doctrinal lectures and answered questions from the LALMA community but not as long-term sponsors of the group. Also, César Domínguez has regularly provided Arabic classes for LALMA, is completing an Islamic chaplaincy program at Bayan Claremont, and will be a strong candidate for becoming LALMA's first sponsoring Latino Muslim scholar.

47. From LALMA's 2008 document: "Dialogo con Dr. Fathi Osman" (Dialogue with Dr. Fathi Osman), in which the scholar answered several other questions by the LALMA community, including one regarding prayer to which he responded: "Prayer should not be difficult. If the person cannot memorize the prayers for some reason, if they can't memorize al Fatiha, it's fine, they can say "Allahu Akbar." If it is impossible for them to memorize al Fatiha in Arabic, there are some opinions (that are not the dominant opinion) which indicate that it is permissible to recite the prayer in another language [i.e., Spanish]." In another session held years later with another scholar, members were told that it is most certainly not permissible to recite prayers in a language other the Arabic, which was met with resistance from some of LALMA's members who quipped: "That's not what Dr. Osman taught us." It should be noted, nevertheless, that most Latino Muslims do not believe it is permissible to perform the obligatory five daily prayers in the Spanish language.

CHAPTER 3

1. I derive the term "technology of the self" from Foucault who states: "As a context, we must understand that there are four major types of these 'technologies,' each a matrix of practical reason: (1) technologies of production, which permit us to produce,

transform, or manipulate things; (2) technologies of sign systems, which permit us to use signs, meanings, symbols, or signification; (3) technologies of power, which determine the conduct of individuals and submit them to certain ends or domination, an objectivizing of the subject; (4) technologies of the self, which permit individuals to effect by their own means or with the help of others a certain number of operations on their own bodies and souls, thoughts, conduct, and way of being, so as to transform themselves in order to attain a certain state of happiness, purity, wisdom, perfection, or immortality . . . I am more and more interested in the interaction between oneself and others and in the technologies of individual domination, the history of how an individual acts upon himself, in the technology of self." This shift in Foucault's focus from technologies of power to technologies of self is what Ivan Strenski hopes will also represent a move away from the theorizing of religious selves in terms of domination. Strenski proposes that we think of religious doings in terms of work instead: "Work is about the realization of our plans; contest and competition are secondary aspects of work at best" ("Religion, Power, and Final Foucault," 353). Strenski thus concludes that religion should not be studied simply as discursive structures used for the domination of people, but rather, religion should be studied as a way in which people try to work "things" out, i.e., to "attain a certain state of happiness, purity, wisdom, perfection, or immortality" (354). Although it is clear that some discursive formations of Latino Muslim identities are accomplished through the use of discursive power and domination (e.g., journalistic mediations of the group examined in chapter 4 of this book), I approach reversions stories not strictly as the product of technologies of power but also and mainly as the result of our technologies of the self. See Foucault et al., *Technologies of the Self*; Strenski, "Religion, Power, and Final Foucault."

2. Lamb and Bryant, *Religious Conversion*, 164.
3. Rambo, *Understanding Religious Conversion*, 1.
4. Rivera, "My Hispanic Muslim Legacy."
5. Galvan, "How Allah Found Me in Texas."
6. Galedary, "Khadija's Revert Story."
7. Caldwell, *The Puritan Conversion Narrative.*

8. King, *The Iron of Melancholy*; Juster, "In a Different Voice," 35.

9. Sells, *Approaching the Qur'an*, 43.

10. In *Approaching the Qur'an*, Michael Sells writes: "This phrase is frequently translated, 'In the name of God the Compassionate the Merciful,' but traditional scholars have emphasized that the terms Rahman and Rahim are based upon an Arabic etymology linked to the word for womb (rahm). In addition, "mercy" as a quality of forgiveness has been strongly marked by Christian associations with the doctrine of original sin, whereas the Qur'an does not posit the notion of original sin. For these reasons, and for the purposes of euphony and alliteration, I have used the translation "the Compassionate the Caring"' (21). See also Sells, *Early Islamic Mysticism*, 304–320.

11. See Aslan, *No God but God*, 142–173; Esposito, *Islam: The Straight Path*, 165, 178; Sells, *Approaching the Qur'an*, 18–19; Smith, *Islam in America*, 6.

12. Iqbal, "A Separate Muslim State in the Subcontinent."

13. For nuanced examinations of the complex historical relationships between the race or ethnicity and religion of Latino communities, see Busto, *King Tiger*; and León, *La Llorona's Children*.

14. When presented as an account of the causal factors that led up to their embrace of Islam, the authors could be said to describe a necessary set of conditions for their embrace of Islam but not a sufficient or exhaustive explanation.

15. Ali, "A Chicano's Story of Becoming Muslim."

16. Gomez, "Conversion Story."

17. Ibid.

18. Ibid.

19. Galvan, "How Allah Found Me in Texas."

20. Cruz, "Becoming Muslim."

21. Clark and Clanton, *Understanding Religion and Popular Culture*, 172–189.

22. Esposito, *Islam: The Straight Path*, 13.

23. Galedary, "Khadija's Revert Story."

24. Sells, *Approaching the Qur'an*, 40.

25. Qur'an 1:1–7, from Esposito, *Islam: The Straight Path*, 1.

26. Gomez, "Conversion Story."

27. Levtzion, *Conversión to Islam*, 24–29.

28. Lamb and Bryant, *Religious Conversion*, 151.
29. Musaji, "Interview with Prof. T. B. Irving."
30. See John 3:1–15; Romans 8:9; 2 Corinthians 3:18.
31. Galvan, "Reversion Stories."
32. Mohamed, "The Interpretations of Fitrah."
33. In "The Interpretations of Fitrah," Yasien Mohamed references this Hadith and offers an analysis of three interpretations of *fitrah*: "the dual, the neutral and the positive." The dual interpretation maintains the human nature has both good and evil innate tendencies; "the neutral view represents both good and evil as external agents of guidance and [that human nature] is predisposed to neither"; the positive interpretation of *fitrah* maintains that human nature is "essentially good and evil [is] exclusively an external agent of misguidance. Ibid., 129–130. Although the dual interpretation of *fitrah* represents a problem for reversion as a return to an original ontological state of submission to the will of God, this is not the view held by the Latino Muslims who in interviews expressed a positive view of human nature instead while blaming culture for sin an evil.
34. For a critical analysis of "authenticity" in religious discourse, see Chidester, *Authentic Fakes*.
35. Reza, "Embracing Islam, Praying for Acceptance."
36. Sells, *Approaching the Qur'an*, 23.
37. Gomez, "Conversion Story."

CHAPTER 4

1. Nieves, "A New Minority Makes Itself Known: Hispanic Muslims."
2. See Börjesson, *Feet to the Fire*; Altheide, *Terror Post 9/11 and the Media*; and Slocum, "9/11 Film and Media Scholarship."
3. Aidi, "Let Us Be Moors."
4. See "Slowly Escaping New York: The New York Times?"; and US Securities and Exchange Commission, "2010 Annual Report of the New York Times Company."
5. Nieves, "A New Minority Makes Itself Known: Hispanic Muslims."
6. Ibid.
7. Said, *Covering Islam*, 1.
8. Baral, "Hispanic Muslims."

9. Dotson-Renta, "Latino Muslims in the United States after 9/11."

10. See Muftah, "Our Mission," http://muftah.org/about/; and Kilbride, "The Middle East Deserves More Thoughtful Coverage from Major US Media."

11. Dotson-Renta, "Latino Muslims in the United States after 9/11."

12. West, *Prophesy Deliverance!*, 30.

13. Ibid.

14. Elizondo, *Galilean Journey*, 106.

15. I reordered Dotson-Renta's list of "binds" or forms of alienation to better reflect the intensity and frequency of each category as reported by Latino Muslims themselves.

16. Naili, "Akbar Ahmed Explores the Challenges Facing Latino-Muslims."

17. Ponce, "Latino and Muslim."

18. Ibid.

19. Cordova, "Muslim Community Sees Increase in Latinos Converting to Islam."

20. Ruiz, "Islam in America . . . en Español."

21. Naili, "Akbar Ahmed Explores the Challenges Facing Latino-Muslims."

22. Carveth, "More Latinos Turning to Islam"; Pew, "Changing Faiths."

23. Levy, "Another Growing Component of the Muslim Fabric."

24. Aidi, "Olé to Allah."

25. From the reports, it seems that much of the gender-based difference stems from women feeling pressured to veil as a form of piety, whereas men usually pass as non-Muslims at a glance. There may be an additional patriarchal dimension within domestic situations in which daughters are treated more harshly for converting than sons. Future research may yield more conclusive and nuanced understandings of the complex issues raised by the fourth bind regarding gender.

26. Feeney, "Hispanic Woman Who Converted to Islam Experiences Prejudice from Fellow East Harlem Residents."

27. Martin, "Latinas Choosing Islam over Catholicism."

28. Aidi, "Olé to Allah."

29. Reddy, "Even as Islam Booms, Its Many Faces Can Deter Converts."

30. See Wise, "In a New Light—New Faith, Changed Man"; Cusido, "Embracing Islam."

31. Martin, "Latinas Choosing Islam over Catholicism."
32. Ibid.
33. Viscidi, "Latino Muslims a Growing Presence in America."
34. Ibid.
35. Ibid.
36. Pew, "The Future of World Religions."
37. Green, "More US Hispanics Drawn to Islam."
38. Kong, "History Draws Hispanics to Islam."
39. The controversial conclusion that Latinos are converting because of marriage is explored in more detail in chapter 3 of this book.
40. Cervantes, "5 Reasons Why Media Coverage of 'Latina' Converts Does Not Represent Me."
41. Viscidi, "Latino Muslims a Growing Presence in America."
42. Sanchez and Galvan, "Latino Muslims."
43. The term "social capital" is from Pierre Bourdieu's work, which defines it as: "the sum of the resources, actual or virtual, that accrue to an individual or a group by virtue of possessing a durable network of more or less institutionalized relationships of mutual acquaintance and recognition." Bourdieu and Wacquant, *An Invitation to Reflexive Sociology*, 119.
44. Iqbal, "Hispanics and Islam."
45. Butler, "Reshaping One Nation under God."
46. In his seminal book, *Orientalism*, Edward Said formulates the term "Orientalism" as a form of discursive violence perpetrated by Western Scholars of the Orient in their reduction of richly dynamic sets of differences to a static and monolithic whole. Said, *Orientalism*.
47. Aidi, "Let Us Be Moors," 39.
48. Ibid.
49. Regarding iconographic similarities between precolonial Aztec skulls and those found in contemporary *Día de Muertos* practices, Stanley Brandes points out that the function of such icons would have been drastically different from one another. The former would, for example, would be a reference to solemn sacrificial practices and the latter to playful and festive celebrations of life. Stanley H. Brandes, *Skulls to the Living, Bread to the Dead*, 49.
50. Jackson, *Islam and the Blackamerican*, 99–108.
51. Ibid., 102.

52. Abu-Lughod, *Do Muslim Women Need Saving?*, 36.

53. See Kandiyoti, "Bargaining with Patriarchy."

54. Ahmed, "Journey Into America"; Rivera, "Puerto Rican, Muslim and Female."

55. Mora, *Making Hispanics*, 137.

56. Ibid., 127; and "Look Out Oprah: Here Comes Cristina."

57. Said, *Covering Islam*.

58. Rivera et al., "Petition to Protest the Defamation by the Spanish Communication Media against Muslim Women and Islam."

59. Fernandez, "Farewell for 'El Show de Cristina.'"

60. With regard to this moral obligation within democratic societies, Amy Gutmann writes: "The special obligation view focuses attention on the moral obligations of those (more advantaged) people who are ascriptively identified with a disadvantaged group. By so doing, it averts public attention from the far greater moral obligations of advantaged people who are not identified with disadvantaged groups. There is no good reason why obligations to fight injustice should be placed first and foremost at the feet of members of disadvantaged groups." Gutmann, *Identity in Democracy*, 119, 141. I contend that Latino Muslims should be at the forefront of our critiques of injustice against Latino Muslims because it is their lived experiences that are being represented through mass media in this instance and that they are therefore in the best position to improve the representation. I also, however, agree with Gutmann that Latino Muslims are under no "special obligation" to engage in the fight for justice even if they stand to make the most gains if successful. Instead, a general moral obligation remains the case.

61. For an analysis of the efficacy of E-Petitions, see Scott, "Populism and Downing Street E-petitions." Here, Wright argues that e-petitions alone are rarely if ever successful alone. Instead, such tactics seem to work only in conjunction with much more robust networks of support and activities.

62. See chapter 2 on LADO's the *Latino Muslim Voice* and chapter 3 on reversion stories for two examples of Latino Muslim self-produced alternatives to news media representations of their identities.

63. Martínez-Vázquez, *Latina/o y Musulmán*, 6–7.

CHAPTER 5

1. In his article "Muslim Radicalization in Prison," SpearIt describes the etymological development of the term "radical" as follows: "early use of radical was loyal to the etymology of *rad*, which meant 'radish' or 'roots,' hence, a radical connoted one returning to 'roots' of tradition—the origins or essence. Used this way, radical overlaps in meaning with the notion of fundamentalist, which similarly conveys a turn to the basics or fundamentals. Later use of radical, however, would connote a somewhat opposite meaning, as movement away from a particular norm, being 'far out' or 'extreme' with respect to the cultural status quo. Such use is not typically viewed as a pejorative, since radicals were often seen as progressives who contributed to the development of thought, politics, and culture. Today, however, the meaning of radicalization is not typically intended as a positive association. More particularly, it has been something of a code for violent behavior and ideology, despite the fact that violence is the exception among radicals." SpearIt, "Muslim Radicalization in Prison"

2. Before Huntington, Bernard Lewis wrote in his 1990 article "The Roots of Muslim Rage" published in the September edition of the *Atlantic Monthly*, that "it should by now be clear that we are facing a mood and a movement in Islam far transcending the level of issues and policies and the governments that pursue them. This is no less than a clash of civilizations."

3. Huntington, *The Clash of Civilizations and the Remaking of World Order*, 19–20.

4. Huntington, "The Clash of Civilizations?," 49; Huntington, *The Clash of Civilizations and the Remaking of World Order*, 206.

5. Huntington, *The Clash of Civilizations and the Remaking of World Order*, 206.

6. Omi and Winant, *Racial Formation in the United States: From the 1960s to the 1990s*, 15.

7. Huntington, *The Clash of Civilizations and the Remaking of World Order*, 20–21.

8. Omi and Winant, *Racial Formation in the United States: From the 1960s to the 1990s*, 21.

9. The M-Team's previous album was titled *Wretched of the Earth* named after Frantz Fanon's critical analysis colonization. Regarding their album titles, the Pérez brothers made the following statement in an interview: "we name our albums after books so our listeners can check out certain books. Many revolutionaries like Malcolm X, the Panthers, and the Young Lords read the book *The Wretched of the Earth*." Yahsmin and BoBo, "A New Day in Hip Hop."

10. Although there are several other prolific Latino Muslim hip-hop artists including Abu Nurah, there are several reasons why I focus solely on the M-Team. First, an overview of all Latino Muslim hip-hop would not allow for a detailed analysis. Second, most other Latino Muslim hip-hop artists have not received the national attention that the M-Team has. Finally, the mediation by and of the M-Team provides insights that are especially relevant to this study. For an examination of broader Puerto Rican Muslim hip-hop artists, see Ramadan-Santiago, "Insha'Allah/Ojala, Yes Yes Y'all."

11. Taylor, "New Muslim Cool."

12. Aidi, *Rebel Music*, 55–56; Cooke and Lawrence, *Muslim Networks from Hajj to Hip Hop*; Nuruddin, "The Five Percenters."

13. In *Rebel Music*, Hisham Aidi examines the complex cycles and relations between hip-hop, protest, state co-option, and subversion. These models are helpful for understanding Latino Muslim hip-hop in the United States.

14. Kunzle, *Che Guevara*.

15. SpearIt, "Sonic Jihad," 217.

16. Aidi, *Rebel Music*.

17. Taylor, "New Muslim Cool."

18. Guevara, "Discurso del Comandante Che Guevara en la Asamblea General de las Naciones Unidas."

19. Nationalistic formulations of race have offered alternative models to biologistic and ethnic formulations of race in the United States. Eddie Glaude defines the African-American community not as a racial group with shared biological characteristics that are unique to that group, but rather as a group of people who have a shared common experience of being on the underside of white supremacy and thus also share the desire for liberation from the injustices of white supremacy. Glaude, *Exodus!: Religion, Race, and Nation in Early*

Nineteenth-Century Black America, 62; Omi and Winant, *Racial Formation in the United States*, 36–47.

20. Anderson, *Che Guevara: A Revolutionary Life*, 590.
21. Guevara, "Cuba: Historical Exception or Vanguard in the Anticolonial Struggle?." For a detailed analysis of economic dependency/neo-colonialism, see Eduardo Galeano, *Open Veins of Latin America*.
22. The translation is my own.
23. When answering the question: How do you win a cosmic war? Reza Aslan's answer is: you don't, that is, the best response to a cosmic war is to not recognize its existence and to not engage in it as a battle between good and evil. Aslan, *How to Win a Cosmic War*.
24. Bellafante, "Islam, Hope and Charity Inspire Dealer Turned Rapper."
25. Ibid.
26. Ibid.
27. "A Brief History of the Mosque of Islamic Brotherhood."
28. Taylor, "New Muslim Cool."
29. Aidi, *Rebel Music*, 211.
30. Mamdani, *Good Muslim, Bad Muslim*, 17–62.
31. Religion is not an entirely private practice, though it may include elements that are. Religion informs or is manifested in various public practices, including social service, activism, and politics. For a few examples, see Espinosa, Elizondo, and Miranda, *Latino Religions and Civic Activism in the United States*, and Glaude, *Exodus!*.
32. In *Rebel Music*, Hisham Aidi examines how young European and American Muslims "search for a nonracist utopia" through music while critically engaging the ways in which governments seek to co-opt such movements. The mediation of Hamza, I argue, is self-produced and co-opted, reductive and celebratory of intersectionality. In short, it is complex, diverse, and fluid. Aidi, *Rebel Music*, xiii.
33. See Haustein, Sugimoto, and Larivière, "Social Media in Scholarly Communication"; Bar-Ilan, "Beyond Citations: Scholars' Visibility on the Social Web."
34. Hill and Hill, *Nolo's Plain-English Law Dictionary*.
35. GhaneaBassiri, "For God or for Fame."
36. Temple-Raston, "Officials Worry about Some Latino Converts to Islam."

37. See Omi and Winant, *Racial Formation in the United States*, and West, *Prophesy Deliverance!*.
38. West, *Prophesy Deliverance!*, 53.
39. Ibid., 61.
40. Omi and Winant, *Racial Formation in the United States*, 15.
41. See Matovina, *Guadalupe and Her Faithful*; Hughes, *Biography of a Mexican Crucifix*; Espin, *The Faith of the People*.
42. See Sánchez-Walsh, *Latino Pentecostal Identity*; Espinosa, *Latino Pentecostals in America*, 31, 88.
43. Edward Curtis has also voiced his concern with Temple-Raston's coverage of "terrorism" describing it as "underwhelming" and problematic. Curtis, "The Study of Religion and Responses to Terrorism."
44. See Abdalla, "The Murders in Paris and Lebanon"; Tharoor, "Watch: Little Children Apologize for Terrorism"; and Ali, "My Take: Muslims Should Stop Apologizing for 9/11."
45. Echoing LALMA's concern, SpearIt identifies several policy recommendations as possible deterrents to radicalization within prisons, including an increase in pluralistic media that presents diverse understandings of Islam. SpearIt, "Muslim Radicalization in Prison."
46. Ibid., 66.
47. Pérez and Pérez, *My Enemy's Enemy Interview with M-Team*.
48. Ibid.
49. Chomsky, "Noam Chomsky on The Clash of Civilizations."
50. Ibid.
51. West, *Prophesy Deliverance!*, 90–91.

CHAPTER 6

1. Moyer, "Trump! Trump! Trump!"
2. Berrios, "Geometrik Alchemist."
3. A 2011 study conducted by the Pew Research Center showed that Latino Muslims accounted for an estimated 6 percent of all Muslims living in the United States. See Pew Research Center, "Muslim Americans: No Signs of Growth in Alienation or Support for Extremism," August 2011, http://www.people-press.org/files/2011/08/muslim-american-report.pdf. Pew, "The Future of the Global Muslim Population." The Pew Research Center estimated that in

2015 there were about 3.3 million Muslims in the United States. See Mohamed, "A New Estimate of the U.S. Muslim Population." That puts the Latino Muslim population at 198,000.

4. Figueroa, "Reclaiming Our Heritage, part 2."

5. In his essay titled "Raza Islamica," SpearIt describes the prominence of a "colorblind" Islam in which all other identities, racial, ethnic, gendered, and so on, are relegated to the mundane: "Islam is the key ingredient of identity—nothing matters more than the shared belief in Allah and his prophet Muhammad—not even the color of one's skin." He also argues that the trend has been and will continue to be that converts who are initially attracted to Islam as a way of being black or Latino will convert a second time into a colorblind version of Islam which, drawing from Jose Vasconcellos's *cosmic race*, he terms a *raza Islamica*, an Islamic race. SpearIt, "Raza Islamica," 175, 177.

6. Espinoza, "Latino Muslim Cultural Night."

7. Ocasio, "A Brief History of Alianza Islamica."

8. LLAMO, "Mission Statement," https://www.facebook.com/pg/ LatinoAmericanMuslims/about/?ref=page_interna.

9. Galvan, "FAQs About the LADO Group."

10. Ibid.

11. Ibid.

12. SpearIt, "Muslim Radicalization in Prison," 65.

13. Fletcher and Parada, "Journey to Islam."

14. Ibid.

15. Fletcher, "Story of Why Islam-in-Spanish Started."

16. Ibid.

17. Hernandez, "Raices Islamicas En La Cultura Latina."

18. See Aidi, *Rebel Music*; Aslan, *No God but God*; and Fadl, *The Great Theft*.

19. Pabon, "What Alianza Islamica Means to Me."

20. Latino Muslim discourse around "reversion," or a return to Islamic roots is explored in more detail in chapter 3 of this book.

21. This is a similar concern voiced by many black Muslim communities and leaders in the United States, in particular, Sherman Jackson has called for a "third resurrection," whereas the first is envisioned as Elijah Muhammad's intervention via the Nation of Islam, the second is W. D. Mohammed's "Sunnification" of the Nation of Islam,

and the third is a yet to be realized development of independent Islamic thought produced by black American Muslims themselves. See Sherman A. Jackson, *Islam and the Blackamerican.*

22. Figueroa, "An Andalusia of Heart and Soul."

23. It is this specific concern by LALMA with certain strands of Islam, especially Salafi movements explored in chapter 2 of this book that LALMA views as too conservative and unaccepting of difference, which prompted the group's translate and study Fadl's *The Great Theft.*

24. Figueroa, "An Andalusia of Heart and Soul."

25. Outside of Latino Muslim organizational structures, a few young Latinx Muslims are emerging as scholarly, critical, and liberationist voices, including Antonio Lopez's "Ethnopoetic Imagination" performance and "Islamic Liberation Theology" essay presented at Middle East in Latino America symposium held at Duke University on October 21, 2016. I am convinced that it is these, often poetic and intuitive, voices that best capture Figueroa's call to action.

26. Figueroa, "Observations on the Centro Islamico in Huston."

27. LALMA, "La Asociacion Latino Musulmana de America."

28. An-Naim, *What Is an American Muslim?.*

29. Street, "How Muslim Civic Activism Helped Pass California's Prop 47."

30. See Keneally, "Year in Review: 13 Biggest News Stories of 2015," and Griggs, "The 15 Stories That Had You Talking in 2015."

31. Demaria and Gonzalez-Ramirez, "Trump Slams Justice Ruth Bader Ginsburg."

32. Moyer, "Trump! Trump! Trump!"

33. The problem of numeric representation and political clout was also present in the Latino Muslim petition against Univision, see chapter 4 for more details.

34. Rosa Menocal is widely regarded as an optimistic proponent of the theory that Islamic Spain's accomplishments were due largely to its embrace of diversity as an ideal, though she also cautions that there were and are limits to what may now be termed pluralism. See Menocal, *The Ornament of the World,* 282–283, 317.

35. See Fernández-Morera, *The Myth of the Andalusian Paradise*; and Corfis, *Al-Andalus, Sepharad and Medieval Iberia.*

36. Figueroa, "An Andalusia of Heart and Soul."
37. In "Encoding/Decoding," media and critical theorist Stuart Hall argued against a unidirectional theory of media influence or causation and developed instead a cyclical theory that takes the entire media cycle into account where each stage of development, production, dissemination, and consumption retains related though independent interpretations of the communicated narrative event. If at all regarding media, Figueroa's call may more fruitfully be understood in terms of media cycle processes described by Hall. See Stuart Hall, "Encoding/Decoding."

CONCLUSION

1. See Taylor, "The Politics of Recognition," 25–74; Simpson, "Pride March Must Include People of Color in Key Roles"; Gutmann, *Identity in Democracy.*
2. Monahan, "Revitalizing Hegelian Recognition." See also Monahan, *The Creolizing Subject.*
3. Monahan, "Revitalizing Hegelian Recognition," 2. See also Appiah, "Identity, Authenticity, Survivial," 149–164.
4. Monahan, "Revitalizing Hegelian Recognition," 3. See also Fanon, *The Wretched of the Earth*; Coulthard, *Red Skin, White Masks.*
5. Ocasio, "A Brief History of Alianza Islamica."
6. In the words of Monahan, the "sovereign" subject is "the paradigmatic autonomous, independent subject of the European enlightenment—the Kantian rational subject that has been the object of so much sustained critique since at least the 19th century—and very much the focus of critique from feminist theory and critical philosophy of race" ("Revitalizing Hegelian Recognition," 4). See also Markell, *Bound by Recognition*, 179.
7. With regard to the double edged sword of the "sovereign" subject, Monahan writes: "'All men are created equal' in a slave-holding society that denies all women the franchise is true if and only if we take 'men' to be gendered and raced in quite particular ways" ("Revitalizing Hegelian Recognition," 20).
8. Monahan, "Revitalizing Hegelian Recognition," 6.
9. Serequeberhan, "Amilcar Cabral's 'Return to the Source.'"

NOTES

10. Monahan, "Revitalizing Hegelian Recognition," 4. See also Markell, *Bound by Recognition*, 11.
11. Monahan, "Revitalizing Hegelian Recognition," 5. See also Markell, *Bound by Recognition*, 94.
12. Monahan, "Revitalizing Hegelian Recognition," 20. See also Anzaldúa, *Borderlands: The New Mestiza = La Frontera*, 25.
13. Regarding the move from true or false evaluations of recognition to more qualitative ones, Monahan writes: "Likewise, since recognition is better understood as something that I am constantly doing, the important questions are not whether or how much I am recognizing (as in the economic exchange model), but rather how well am I recognizing (or even better: how well we are recognizing each other)" ("Revitalizing Hegelian Recognition," 14).
14. Monahan, "Revitalizing Hegelian Recognition," 13.
15. Regarding Hegelian reconciliation between subject and object and the correlated question of what is the basis for qualitative evaluations of recognition, Monahan writes: "the question we must ask is what exactly is it that recognition is supposed to be *doing*, such that we can subject a given performance to evaluation? In the *Phenomenology*, Hegel begins his discussion of recognition with an account of pure recognition that helps to answer this crucial question. In these paragraphs (¶178–¶185), Hegel credits recognition with being a necessary and crucial moment in the development of self-consciousness. Through pure recognition, the interdependence of our negating, abstract, independent consciousness (for-itself) and our concrete, positive, and dependent aspect (in-itself) is made manifest to us. The unity of our status as both subject and object, to use slightly different terminology, is taken out of the abstract and made *concrete* for us through the moment of pure recognition. A engages her subjectivity as she recognizes B as both subject *and* object. When B is reciprocating this moment, then what is actually happening is that A is recognizing B who is himself in the act of recognizing her as both subject and object, and in this moment of A recognizing B *as* recognizing her, the unity of her self-consciousness is *given back to her* through the act of mutual (pure) recognition" ("Revitalizing Hegelian Recognition," 15).
16. Monahan, "Revitalizing Hegelian Recognition: Identity Politics and Solidarity," 11–15. See also Nietzsche, *Thus Spoke Zarathustra*.

237

17. See Do, "Muslim and Latino Groups Unite during Ramadan"; Stimson and Presha, "#TacoTrucksAtEveryMosque Bridges Muslim and Latino San Diego Communities"; de la Cruz, "Taco Trucks at Every Mosque."
18. I agree with J. Z. Smith who argues that the fact that religion (and we can here include race as well) has numerous definitions should not lead us to conclude that religion cannot be defined, but rather that religion can, has, and will continue to be defined in numerous ways. See Smith, "Religion, Religions, Religious," 281.
19. Monahan, "Revitalizing Hegelian Recognition," 12 and 19. See also Markell, *Bound by Recognition*, 59–60.
20. Monahan, "Revitalizing Hegelian Recognition," 23.
21. Ibid., 24.

REFERENCES

Abdalla, Mohomad. "The Murders in Paris and Lebanon: Why Muslims Should Not Apologise." ABC: Religion and Ethics, November 16, 2016. http://www.abc.net.au/religion/articles/2015/11/16/4352803.htm.

Abeytia, Anisa. "Curries, Tajeens and Moles: Exploring Culture and Conversion Through Food." *The Latino Muslim Voice*, July–September 2006. http://www.latinodawah.org/newsletter/july-sept2k6.html#4.

Abou El Fadl, Khaled. *The Great Theft: Wrestling Islam from the Extremists*. New York: HarperCollins, 2009.

Abu-Lughod, Lila. *Do Muslim Women Need Saving?* Cambridge, MA: Harvard University Press, 2013.

Abu-Lughod, Lila. *Remaking Women: Feminism and Modernity in the Middle East*. Princeton, NJ: Princeton University Press, 1998.

Ahmed, Akbar. "Journey Into America: The Challenge of Islam." https://journeyintoamerica.wordpress.com/about/.

Aidi, Hisham. "Latino Muslims Are Part of US Religious Landscape." Al Jazeera, February 3, 2016. http://www.aljazeera.com/indepth/opinion/2016/02/latino-muslims-part-religious-landscape-160202081705201.html.

Aidi, Hisham. "Let Us Be Moors: Islam, Race and Connected Histories." *Middle East Report*, no. 229 (2003): 42–53.

Aidi, Hisham. "Olé to Allah: New York's Latino Muslims." Africana, November 11, 1999. http://hispanicmuslims.com/articles/oletoallah.html.

Aidi, Hisham. *Rebel Music: Race, Empire, and the New Muslim Youth Culture*. New York: Vintage Books, 2014.

Aisha, Zeina, and Khadijah. "One God, One People, One Belief." PIEDAD, August 10, 2008. http://piedad-latinodawah.blogspot.com/2008/08/one-god-one-people-one-belief-isna-2001.html.

Ali. "A Chicano's Story of Becoming Muslim." HispanicMuslims.com. http://hispanicmuslims.com/stories/ali.html.

al-Kanadee, Aboo Bilaal Mustafaa. "Perennialist Poison in Martin Lings' Biography of the Prophet." May 1, 2013. https://muslimanswersfiles. wordpress.com/2013/05/01/perennialist-poison-in-martin-lings-biography-of-the-prophet/.

Altheide, David. *Terror Post 9/11 and the Media*. Bern: Peter Lang, 2009.

Amir Ruiz, Wilfredo. "Islam in America . . . En Español." HuffPost Religion, November 16, 2011. http://www.huffingtonpost.com/wilfredo-amr-ruiz/latino-muslims-in-america_b_1095672.html.

Anderson, Jon Lee. *Che Guevara: A Revolutionary Life*. New York, NY: Grove Press, 2010.

An-Naim, Abdullahi Ahmed. *What Is an American Muslim?: Embracing Faith and Citizenship*. New York: Oxford University Press, 2014.

Anzaldúa, Gloria. *Borderlands: The New Mestiza = La Frontera*. 4th ed. San Francisco, CA: Aunt Lute Books, 2012.

Appiah, Kwame Anthony. "Identity, Authenticity, Survival: Multicultural Societies and Social Reproduction." In *Multiculturalism: Examining the Politics of Recognition*, edited by Amy Gutman, 149–164. Princeton, NJ: Princeton University Press, 1994.

Aslan, Reza. *How to Win a Cosmic War: Confronting Radical Islam*. Portsmouth, UK: William Heinemann, 2009.

Aslan, Reza. *No God but God: The Origins, Evolution, and Future of Islam*. Updated ed. New York: Random House, 2011.

Austin, Allan. *African Muslims in Antebellum America: Transatlantic Stories and Spiritual Struggles*. Rev. and updated ed. New York: Routledge, 1997.

Baral, Susmita. "Hispanic Muslims: Why Are Catholic Hispanic Americans Converting to Islam?" *Latin Times*, August 21, 2013. http://www. latintimes.com/hispanic-muslims-why-are-catholic-hispanic-americans-converting-islam-130483.

Bar-Ilan, Judith. "Beyond Citations: Scholars' Visibility on the Social Web." *arXiv* 1205.5611 (2012). https://arxiv.org/ftp/arxiv/papers/1205/1205.5611.pdf.

Bellafante, Ginia. "Islam, Hope and Charity Inspire Dealer Turned Rapper." *New York Times*, June 23, 2009.

Berkey, Jonathan Porter. *The Formation of Islam: Religion and Society in the Near East, 600–1800*. New York: Cambridge University Press, 2003.

Berrios, Brandon. "Geometrik Alchemist." January 19, 2016. https://www.instagram.com/eldezine_one91/.

Börjesson, Kristina Borjesson. *Feet to the Fire: The Media after 9/11, Top Journalists Speak Out.* Amherst, NY: Prometheus Books, 2005.

Bourdieu, Pierre, and Loïc J. D. Wacquant. *An Invitation to Reflexive Sociology.* Chicago: University of Chicago Press, 1992.

Bowen, Patrick D. "Early U.S. Latina/o African-American Muslim Connections: Paths to Conversion." *MUWO: The Muslim World* 100, no. 4 (2010): 390–413.

Bowen, Patrick D. "The Latino American Da'wah Organization and the Latina/o Muslim Identity in the United States." *Journal of Race, Ethnicity, and Religion* 1, no. 11 (2010): 1–23.

Brandes, Stanley H. *Skulls to the Living, Bread to the Dead: The Day of the Dead in Mexico and Beyond.* Malden, MA: Blackwell, 2006.

Brasher, Brenda E. *Give Me That Online Religion.* San Francisco, CA: Jossey-Bass, 2001.

"A Brief History of the Mosque of Islamic Brotherhood." http://www.mibnyc.com/index.php?option=com_content&view=article&id=57&Itemid=61.

Brown, Anna, Gustavo Lopez, and Mark Hugo Lopez. "Digital Divide Narrows for Latinos as More Spanish Speakers and Immigrants Go Online: Broadband Use Little Changed in Recent Years among Hispanics." Pew Research Center: Hispanic Trends (2016). http://www.pewhispanic.org/2016/07/20/digital-divide-narrows-for-latinos-as-more-spanish-speakers-and-immigrants-go-online/.

Burg, W. *Sacramento's Southside Park.* Mount Pleasant, WI: Arcadia Publishing, 2007.

Busto, Rudy V. *King Tiger: The Religious Vision of Reies López Tijerina.* Albuquerque: University of New Mexico Press, 2005.

Butler, Kenneth. "Reshaping One Nation under God." *Brownstone Magazine*, February 14, 2006.

Caldwell, Patricia. *The Puritan Conversion Narrative: The Beginnings of American Expression.* Cambridge: Cambridge University Press, 1985.

Campbell, Heidi. "Understanding the Relationship between Religious Practice Online and Offline in a Networked Society." *Journal of the American Academy of Religion* 80, no. 1 (2012): 64–93.

Campbell, Heidi. *When Religion Meets New Media*. Abingdon, UK: Routledge, 2010.

Carr, Matthew. *Blood and Faith: The Purging of Muslim Spain*. New York: New Press, 2009.

Carveth, Rod. "More Latinos Turning to Islam." CT Latino News, July 16, 2012. http://ctlatinonews.com/2012/07/16/more-latinos-turning-to-islam/.

Casas, Bartolome de las. *A Brief Account of the Destruction of the Indies*. Project Gutenberg, 2007.

Castells, Manuel. *The Power of Identity: The Information Age: Economy, Society and Culture*, 2nd ed. Hoboken, NJ: Wiley-Blackwell, 2009.

Castells, Manuel. *The Rise of the Network Society*, 2nd ed. Oxford: Wiley-Blackwell, 2009.

Castillo, Bernal Diaz. *The Conquest of New Spain*. London: Penguin Books, 2003.

Castro, Américo. *The Spaniards: An Introduction to Their History*. Berkeley and Los Angeles: University of California Press, 1971.

Cervantes, Eren Arruna. "5 Reasons Why Media Coverage of 'Latina' Converts Does Not Represent Me." http://www.muslimahmediawatch.org/2014/10/28/5-reasons-why-media-coverage-of-latina-converts-does-not-represent-me/.

Chidester, David. *Authentic Fakes: Religion and American Popular Culture*. Berkeley: University of California Press, 2005.

Chiorazzi, Anthony. "From Cross to Crescent." Busted Halo, May 8, 2007. http://bustedhalo.com/features/from-cross-to-crescent.

Chomsky, Noam. "Noam Chomsky on The Clash of Civilizations." March 2, 2007. https://www.youtube.com/watch?v=qT64TNh059I.

Clark, Terry R., and Dan W. Clanton. *Understanding Religion and Popular Culture: Theories, Themes, Products and Practices*. Abingdon, UK: Routledge, 2012.

Clendinnen, I. *Ambivalent Conquests: Maya and Spaniard in Yucatan, 1517–1570*. Cambridge: Cambridge University Press, 2003.

Conci, Pilar. "Latinos Converting to Islam." *Dallas Morning News*. March 2008. http://religionblog.dallasnews.com/archives/2008/03/latinos-converting-to-islam.html.

Cooke, Miriam, and Bruce B. Lawrence. *Muslim Networks from Hajj to Hip Hop*. Chapel Hill: University of North Carolina Press, 2005.

Cordova, Elisa. "Muslim Community Sees Increase in Latinos Converting to Islam." Cronkite News, October 29, 2013. http://www.tucsonsentinel.com/local/report/110513_latinos_islam/muslim-community-sees-increase-latinos-converting-islam/.

Corfis, I. A. *Al-Andalus, Sepharad and Medieval Iberia: Cultural Contact and Diffusion.* Leiden: Brill, 2009.

Coulthard, Glen Sean. *Red Skin, White Masks Rejecting the Colonial Politics of Recognition.* Minneapolis: University of Minnesota Press.

Cruz, Denise de la. "'Taco Trucks at Every Mosque' Celebrated Latino and Muslim Unity in Garden Grove Last Night." OC Weekly, June 15, 2017. http://www.ocweekly.com/news/taco-trucks-at-every-mosque-celebrated-latino-and-muslim-unity-in-garden-grove-last-night-8187697.

Cruz, Themise. "Becoming Muslim." *The Story of New Muslims.* February 27, 1997. http://hispanicmuslims.com/stories/themisecruz.html.

Curtis, Edward E. *Black Muslim Religion in the Nation of Islam, 1960–1975.* Chapel Hill: University of North Carolina Press, 2009.

Curtis, Edward E. *Encyclopedia of Muslim-American History.* New York: Infobase Publishing, 2010.

Curtis, Edward E. *Muslims in America: A Short History.* New York: Oxford University Press, 2009.

Curtis, Edward. "The Study of Religion and Responses to Terrorism: Paris, Beirut, and Beyond." November 21, 2015. https://soundcloud.com/rsn-aar/the-study-of-religion-and-responses-to-terrorism.

Cusido, Carmen. "Embracing Islam." *New Jersey Monthly Magazine,* February 8, 2010.

Dannin, Robert, and Jolie Stahl. *Black Pilgrimage to Islam.* Oxford: Oxford University Press, 2005.

Demaria, Meghan, and Andrea Gonzalez-Ramirez. "Trump Slams Justice Ruth Bader Ginsburg." Refinery29, July 13, 2016. http://www.refinery29.com/2015/08/91867/donald-trump-offensive-quotes.

Do, Anh. "Muslim and Latino Groups Unite during Ramadan, Breaking Fast with Tacos at Mosques." *Los Angeles Times,* June 4, 2017.

Dotson-Renta, Lara. "Latino Muslims in the United States after 9/11: The Triple Bind." Muftah, April 11, 2011. https://muftah.org/latino-muslims-in-the-united-states-after-911-the-triple-bind/#.WdZH2VtSzIU.

Eickelman, Dale F., and Jon W. Anderson, eds. *New Media in the Muslim World: The Emerging Public Sphere.* 2d ed. Bloomington: Indiana University Press, 2003.

El-Amin, Carl Askia. "Bism Rabbik's Footnote." February 9, 2007. http:// piedad-latinodawah.blogspot.com/2007/02/dr-t-b-irving-frontier-for-latino-dawah.html.

Elizondo, V. P. *Galilean Journey: The Mexican-American Promise.* Maryknoll, NY: Orbis Books, 2000.

Elizondo, Virgilio P. *Guadalupe, Mother of the New Creation.* Maryknoll, NY: Orbis Books, 2013.

Elizondo, Virgilio P., and Timothy M. Matovina. *New Frontiers in Guadalupan Studies.* Eugene, OR: Pickwick Publications, 2014.

Espin, Orlando. *The Faith of the People: Theological Reflections on Popular Catholicism.* Maryknoll, NY: Orbis Books.

Espinosa, Gastón. "Changements démographiques et religieux chez les hispaniques des Etats-Unis." *Social Compass: International Review of Sociology of Religion* 51, no. 3 (2004): 309–327.

Espinosa, Gastón. *Latino Pentecostals in America: Faith and Politics in Action.* Cambridge, MA: Harvard University Press, 2014.

Espinosa, Gastón, Virgilio P. Elizondo, and Jesse Miranda. *Latino Religions and Civic Activism in the United States.* New York: Oxford University Press, 2005.

Espinosa, Gaston, Harold Morales, and Juan Galvan. "Latino Muslims in the United States: Reversion, Politics, and Islamidad." *Journal of Race, Ethnicity, and Religion* 8, no.1 (2017): 1–48. http://www.raceandreligion.com/JRER/Volume_8_(2017)_files/Espinosa%208%201.pdf.

Espinoza, Kathryn. "Latino Muslim Cultural Night." The Latino Muslim Voice, October–December 2004. http://www.latinodawah.org/newsletter/oct-dec2k4.html#5.

Esposito, John L. *Islam: The Straight Path.* Oxford: Oxford University Press, 2011.

Essa, Yasmin. "Interview with LADO/Piedad." MBMuslima, March/April 2010. https://issuu.com/mbmuslima/docs/mbm8.

Fanon, Frantz. *The Wretched of the Earth.* 1st Evergreen ed. New York: Grove Weidenfeld, 1991.

Feeney, Michael J. "Hispanic Woman Who Converted to Islam Experiences Prejudice from Fellow East Harlem Residents." *NY Daily News,* August 31, 2011.

Fernandez, Maria Elena. "Farewell for 'El Show De Cristina.'" *Los Angeles Times*, November 1, 2010.

Fernández-Morera, D. *The Myth of the Andalusian Paradise*. Wilmington, DE: Intercollegiate Studies Institute, 2016.

Figueroa, Yahya Abdul-Latif, "An Andalusia of Heart and Soul." February 17, 2017. http://my.latinomuslim.com/an-andalusia-of-heart-and-soul-part-1.

Figueroa, Yahya Abdul-Latif. "Observations on the Centro Islamico in Huston." 2016. http://latinomuslim.com/?p=66.

Fletcher, Mujahid. "Story of Why IslamInSpanish Started." January 4, 2010. https://www.islaminspanish.org/ourstory/.

Fletcher, Mujahid, and Isa Parada. "Journey to Islam: Latino Muslims Share Their Story." Islamic Institute of Orange County, January 30, 2010. https://www.youtube.com/watch?v=QAjfUWmenBI.

Flood, Finbarr Barry. "Light in Stone: The Commemoration of the Prophet in Umayyad Architecture." *Bayt al-Maqdis. Jerusalem and Early Islam*, Oxford 311 (1999): 59.

Foucault, Michel, Luther H. Martin, Huck Gutman, and Patrick H. Hutton. *Technologies of the Self: A Seminar with Michel Foucault*. Amherst: University of Massachusetts Press, 1988.

Galeano, Eduardo. *Open Veins of Latin America: Five Centuries of the Pillage of a Continent*. 25th anniversary ed. New York: Monthly Review Press, 1997.

Galedary, Marta. "Khadija's Revert Story." 2010.

Galvan, Juan. "How Allah Found Me in Texas." June 6, 2007. http://hispanicmuslims.com/stories/juangalvan.html.

Galvan, Juan. "Reversion Stories." http://hispanicmuslims.com/stories/.

GhaneaBassiri, Kambiz. "For God or for Fame: The Making of a Teenage Bomber." Religion Dispatches, December 14, 2010. http://religiondispatches.org/for-god-or-for-fame-the-making-of-a-teenage-bomber/.

GhaneaBassiri, Kambiz. *A History of Islam in America: From the New World to the New World Order*. Cambridge: Cambridge University Press, 2010.

Glaude, Eddie S. *Exodus!: Religion, Race, and Nation in Early Nineteenth-Century Black America*. Chicago: University of Chicago Press, 2000.

Gomez, Michael Angelo. *Black Crescent: The Experience and Legacy of African Muslims in the Americas.* Cambridge: Cambridge University Press, 2005.

Gomez, Walter. "Conversion Story." http://hispanicmuslims.com/stories/waltergomez.html.

Green, Amy. "More Us Hispanics Drawn to Islam." *Christian Science Monitor*, September 28, 2006.

Griggs, Brandon. "The 15 Stories That Had You Talking in 2015." CNN, December 29, 2015. http://www.cnn.com/2015/12/21/world/top-stories-year-talking-2015-feat/index.html.

Griswold del Castillo, Richard. *The Treaty of Guadalupe Hidalgo: A Legacy of Conflict.* Norman: University of Oklahoma Press, 1990.

Guevara, Ernesto. "Cuba: Historical Exception or Vanguard in the Anticolonial Struggle?" In *The Che Reader*, edited by David Deutschmann, 130–142. 1961. Reprint, North Melbourne, VIC: Ocean Press, 2003.

Guevara, Ernesto. "December 11, 1964 Discurso del Comandante Che Guevara en la Asamblea General de las Naciones Unidas." August 17, 2012. http://www.un.org/content/es/_vidout/video740.shtml.

Gutmann, Amy. *Identity in Democracy.* Princeton, NJ: Princeton University Press, 2003.

Haddad, Yvonne Yazbeck, and Jane I. Smith. *Muslim Communities in North America.* Albany: State University of New York Press, 1994.

Haddad, Yvonne Yazbeck, and Jane I. Smith. *Muslim Minorities in the West: Visible and Invisible.* Walnut Creek, CA: AltaMira Press, 2002.

Hafner, Katie, and Matthew Lyon. *Where Wizards Stay up Late: The Origins of the Internet.* New York: Simon & Schuster, 1996.

Hall, Stuart. "Encoding/Decoding." In *Culture, Media, Language: Working Papers in Cultural Studies, 1972–79*, edited by Stuart Hall, Doothy Hobson, Andrew Lowe, and Paul Willis, 117–127. New York: Routledge, 1991.

Hall, Stuart. "Foucault: Power, Knowledge and Discourse." In *Discourse Theory and Practice: A Reader*, edited by Margaret Wetherell, Stephanie Joyce Ann Taylor, and Simeon J Yates, 72–81. Thousand Oaks, CA: Sage Publications, 2001.

Haraway, Donna. "A Cyborg Manifesto: Science, Technology and Socialist-Feminism in the Late Twentieth Century." In *The Cybercultures Reader*, edited by David Bell and Barbara M. Kennedy, 291–324. New York: Routledge, 2000.

Haustein, Stefanie, Cassidy R. Sugimoto, and Vincent Larivière. "Social Media in Scholarly Communication." *Aslib Journal of Information Management* 67, no. 3 (2015): 1–14.

Hernandez, Abdul Daniel. "Raices Islamicas en la Cultura Latina." IslamInSpanish, 2011. https://www.youtube.com/watch?v=6DxfudTEVew&t=9s.

Hill, Gerald, and Kathleen Hill. *Nolo's Plain-English Law Dictionary.* Berkely, CA: NOLO, 2009.

Hoover, Stewart, and Lynn Schofield Clark, eds. *Practicing Religion in the Age of the Media.* New York: Columbia University Press, 2002.

Hughes, Jennifer Scheper. *Biography of a Mexican Crucifix: Lived Religion and Local Faith from the Conquest to the Present.* Oxford: Oxford University Press, 2010.

Huntington, Samuel P. "The Clash of Civilizations?" *Foreign Affairs* 72, no. 3 (1993): 22–49.

Huntington, Samuel P. *The Clash of Civilizations and the Remaking of World Order.* New York: Simon & Schuster, 1996.

Iqbal, Muhammad. "A Separate Muslim State in the Subcontinent." In *Islam in Transition: Muslim Perspectives,* edited by John Donohue and John Esposito, 71–73. New York: Oxford University Press, 2007.

Iqbal, Sameera. "Hispanics and Islam." ABC News, November 20, 2007. http://abcnews.go.com/Exclusiva/story?id=3871913.

Irving, T. B. *Halcon De España.* Guatemala: Universidad de San Carlos de Guatemala, 1951.

Irving, Thomas Ballantine. "Dates, Names and Places: The End of Islamic Spain." Edited by The Mother Mosque Foundation, 1990.

Irving, Thomas Ballantine. *Falcon of Spain: A Study of Eighth Century Spain, with Special Emphasis upon the Life of the Umayyad Ruler Abdurrahman I, 756–788.* 2d ed. Lahore: Sh. M. Ashraf, 1962.

Irving, Thomas Ballantine. *The Qur'ān: The First American Version.* Beltsville, MD: Amana Publications, 1985.

Jackson, Sherman A. *Islam and the Blackamerican: Looking toward the Third Resurrection.* Oxford: Oxford University Press, 2005.

JanMohamed, Abdul, and David Lloyd. "Introduction: Toward a Theory of Minority Discourse." *Cultural Critique,* no. 6 (1987): 5–12.

Johnson, Dane. "Muslim Mosque Association Set to Expand Facilities in Southside Park." *Sacramento Press,* September 2, 2010.

Juster, Susan. "In a Different Voice: Male and Female Narratives of Religious Conversion in Post-Revolutionary America." *American Quarterly* 41, no. 1 (1989): 34–62.

Kandiyoti, Deniz. "Bargaining with Patriarchy." *Gender and Society* 2, no. 3 (1988): 274–290.

Kelly, Ron. "Muslims in Los Angeles." In *Muslim Communities in North America*, edited by Yvonne Yazbeck Haddad and Jane Idleman Smith, 135–167. Albany: State University of New York Press, 1994.

Keneally, Meghan. "Year in Review: 13 Biggest News Stories of 2015." ABC News, December 29, 2015. http://abcnews.go.com/US/year-review-13-biggest-news-stories-2015/story?id=35852690.

"Khadijah Rivera 1950–2009: Heart of the Community." *Islamic Horizons*, February 2010. https://issuu.com/isnacreative/docs/mar_apr_2010.

Kilbride, Erin. "The Middle East Deserves More Thoughtful Coverage from Major US Media." May 27, 2015. https://qz.com/412537/revolutionizing-mid-east-coverage/.

King, John Owen. *The Iron of Melancholy: Structures of Spiritual Conversion in America from the Puritan Conscience to Victorian Neurosis.* Middletown, CT: Wesleyan University Press, 1983.

Kong, Deborah. "History Draws Hispanics to Islam." *Huron Daily Tribune*, June 16, 2002. http://www.michigansthumb.com/news/amp/History-Draws-Hispanics-to-Islam-7341877.php.

Kunzle, David. *Che Guevara: Icon, Myth, and Message.* Los Angeles: University of California, Fowler Museum, 1997.

Lamb, Christopher, and M. Darrol Bryant, eds. *Religious Conversion: Contemporary Practices and Controversies.* New York: Bloomsbury Academic, 1999.

Lane-Poole, Stanley. *The Muslims in Spain.* Chennai: Goodword Books, 2001.

León, Luis D. *La Llorona's Children: Religion, Life, and Death in the U.S.–Mexican Borderlands.* Berkeley and Los Angeles: University of California Press, 2004.

León, Luis D. *The Political Spirituality of Cesar Chavez: Crossing Religious Borders.* Oakland: University of California Press, 2015.

Leonard, Karen Isaksen. *Making Ethnic Choices: California's Punjabi Mexican Americans.* Philadelphia: Temple University Press, 1992.

Levtzion, Nehemia. *Conversión to Islam.* Teaneck, NJ: Holmes & Meier, 1979.

Levy, Rachael. "Another Growing Component of the Muslim Fabric: Latino Muslims Are Bringing Another Experience to the Muslim American Community." *Islamic Horizons*, January/February 2014.

Lings, Martin. *Muhammad: His Life Based on the Earliest Sources.* New York: Inner Traditions International, 1983.

"Look out Oprah: Here Comes Cristina." ABC News, April 20, 2012. http://abcnews.go.com/2020/story?id=123879.

Lopez, Mark Hugo. "In 2014, Latinos Will Surpass Whites as Largest Racial/Ethnic Group in California." Pew Research Center (2014). http://www.pewresearch.org/fact-tank/2014/01/24/in-2014-latinos-will-surpass-whites-as-largest-racialethnic-group-in-california/.

Mahmood, Saba. *Politics of Piety: The Islamic Revival and the Feminist Subject.* Princeton, NJ: Princeton University Press, 2011.

Mamdani, Mahmood. *Good Muslim, Bad Muslim: America, the Cold War, and the Roots of Terror.* New York: Pantheon Books, 2004.

Mann, Gurinder Singh, Paul Numbrish, and Raymond Williams. *Buddhists, Hindus, and Sikhs in America.* New York: Oxford University Press, 2008.

Marable, Manning. *Malcolm X: A Life of Reinvention.* New York: Viking, 2011.

Markell, Patchen. *Bound by Recognition.* Princeton, NJ: Princeton University Press, 2003.

Martin, Rachel. "Latinas Choosing Islam over Catholicism." National Public Radio, September 24, 2006. http://www.npr.org/templates/story/story.php?storyId=6133579.

Martínez-Vázquez, Hjamil A. *Latina/o y Musulmán: The Construction of Latina/o Identity among Latina/o Muslims in the United States.* Eugene, OR: Pickwick Publications, 2010.

Marx, Karl, and Friedrich Engels. *The Poverty of Philosophy.* New York: International Publishers, 1963.

Masland, William. *Through the Back Doors of the World in a Ship That Had Wings.* New York: Vantage Press, 1985.

Mathews, Lyndsey. "The Latino Crescent: Latinos Make a Place for Themselves in Muslim America." The Brooklyn Rail, September 4, 2009. http://brooklynrail.org/2009/09/local/the-latino-crescent.

Matovina, Timothy M. *Guadalupe and Her Faithful: Latino Catholics in San Antonio, from Colonial Origins to the Present.* Baltimore, MD: Johns Hopkins University Press, 2005.

McGuire, Meredith B. *Lived Religion: Faith and Practice in Everyday Life.* Oxford: Oxford University Press, 2008.

McLuhan, Marshall. *Understanding Media: The Extensions of Man.* Cambridge, MA: MIT Press, 1994.

Menocal, Maria Rosa. *The Ornament of the World: How Muslims, Jews, and Christians Created a Culture of Tolerance in Medieval Spain.* Boston: Little, Brown, 2002.

Menocal, Maria Rosa, Raymond Scheindlin, and Michael Sells, eds. *The Literature of Al-Andalus.* Cambridge: Cambridge University Press, 2000.

Menocal, Rosa. "Culture in the Time of Tolerance: Al-Andalus as a Model for Our Time." Yale Law School Legal Scholarship Repository (2000). http://digitalcommons.law.yale.edu/cgi/viewcontent.cgi?article=1000&context=ylsop_papers.

Mogahed, Dalia, and Youssef Chouhoud. "American Muslim Poll 2017: Muslims at the Crossroads." ISPU. http://www.ispu.org/wp-content/uploads/2017/03/American-Muslim-Poll-2017-Report.pdf.

Mohamed, Besheer. "A New Estimate of the U.S. Muslim Population." Pew Research Center, January 6, 2016. http://www.pewresearch.org/fact-tank/2016/01/06/a-new-estimate-of-the-u-s-muslim-population/.

Mohamed, Yasien. "The Interpretations of Fitrah." *Islamic Studies* 34, no. 2 (1995): 129–151.

Monahan, Michael. *The Creolizing Subject: Race, Reason, and the Politics of Purity.* New York: Fordham University Press, 2011.

Monahan, Michael. "Revitalizing Hegelian Recognition: Identity Politics and Solidarity." Presentation at the John Hopkins University Conference on Race, Recognition and Respect, Baltimore, MD, April 7–8, 2017.

Mora, G. Cristina. *Making Hispanics: How Activists, Bureaucrats, and Media Constructed a New American.* Chicago: University of Chicago Press, 2014.

Moyer, Justin. "'Trump! Trump! Trump!' Attacker Allegedly Yelled as He Beat Hispanic Man, Muslim Student." *Washington Post*, March 14, 2016.

Muhammad, David J. "A Brief History of 'Latinos' in the Nation of Islam." The Final Call, September 4, 2012. http://www.finalcall.com/artman/publish/Perspectives_1/article_9164.shtml.

Mujahid, Abdul Malik. "Malcolm X = Malik Shabazz: Why Did He Change?"

Musaji, Sheila. "Interview with Prof. T. B. Irving." The American Muslim, 2002. http://theamericanmuslim.org/tam.php/features/articles/profile_professor_thomas_ballantine_tb_irving.

Museum, The Virtual Pan Am. "Principle Passenger Fares Chart, Latin American Services." 1949. http://www.everythingpanam.com/images/1949%20Jul%201%20Latin%20Fare%20chart.jpg.

Naili, Hajer. "Akbar Ahmed Explores the Challenges Facing Latino-Muslims." ILLUME Magazine, April 14, 2011.

Nakamura, Lisa. Digitizing Race: Visual Cultures of the Internet. Minneapolis: University of Minnesota Press, 2007.

Narbona, Maria del Mar Logroño, Paulo G. Pinto, and John Tofik Karam. Crescent over Another Horizon: Islam in Latin America, the Caribbean, and Latino USA. Austin: University of Texas Press, 2015.

Nietzsche, Friedrich Wilhelm. Thus Spoke Zarathustra. Cambridge: Cambridge University Press, 2006.

Nieves, Evelyn. "A New Minority Makes Itself Known: Hispanic Muslims." New York Times, December 17, 2001.

Noel, Urayoan. In Visible Movement: Nuyorican Poetry from the Sixties to Slam. Iowa City: University of Iowa Press, 2014.

Nuruddin, Yusuf. "The Five Percenters: A Teenage Nation of Gods and Earth." In Muslim Communities in North America, edited by Yvonne Yazbeck Haddad and Jane I. Smith, 109–132. Albany: State University of New York Press, 1994.

Ocasio, Rahim. "A Brief History of Alianza Islamica." December 22, 2016. http://latinomuslim.com/brief-history-alianza-islamica-official-story.

Ocasio, Rahim. "Alianza Islamica: The True Story." The Islamic Monthly, March 14, 2016. https://www.theislamicmonthly.com/alianza-islamica-the-true-story/.

Omi, Michael, and Howard Winant. Racial Formation in the United States: From the 1960s to the 1990s. 2d ed. New York: Routledge, 1994.

Orisi, Robert A. Between Heaven and Earth: The Religious Worlds People Make and the People Who Study Them. Princeton, NJ: Princeton University Press, 2005.

Pabon, Jorge Fabel. "Oasis in El Barrio." February 17, 2017. http://my.latinomuslim.com/alianza-islamica-oasis-in-el-barrio.

Pérez and Pérez. "My Enemy's Enemy Interview with M-Team." March 28, 2009. https://www.youtube.com/watch?v=4-Oj84aSM9I.

Pew. "America's Changing Religious Landscape." May 15, 2015. http://www.pewforum.org/2015/05/12/americas-changing-religious-landscape/.

Pew. "Changing Faiths: Latinos and the Transformation of American Religion." April 25, 2007. http://www.pewforum.org/2007/04/25/changing-faiths-latinos-and-the-transformation-of-american-religion-2/.

Pew. "The Changing Global Religious Landscape." April 5, 2017. http://www.pewforum.org/2017/04/05/the-changing-global-religious-landscape/.

Pew. "The Future of the Global Muslim Population." January 15, 2011. http://www.pewforum.org/interactives/muslim-population-graphic/.

Pew. "The Future of World Religions." April 2, 2015. http://www.pewforum.org/2015/04/02/religious-projections-2010-2050/.

Pew. "Muslim Americans: Middle Class and Mostly Mainstream." May 22, 2007. http://www.pewresearch.org/2007/05/22/muslim-americans-middle-class-and-mostly-mainstream/.

Pew. "Muslim Americans: No Signs of Growth in Alienation or Support for Extremism: Mainstream and Moderate Attitudes." August 30, 2011. http://www.people-press.org/2011/08/30/muslim-americans-no-signs-of-growth-in-alienation-or-support-for-extremism/.

Pew. "The Shifting Religious Identity of Latinos in the United States." May 7, 2014. http://www.pewforum.org/2014/05/07/the-shifting-religious-identity-of-latinos-in-the-united-states/.

Pew. "U.S. Religious Landscape Survey." http://www.pewforum.org/religious-landscape-study/.

PIEDAD. "Wise Women." http://piedadislam.org/wisewomen/.

Ponce, Audris. "Latino and Muslim: A Growing Minority." The Venture, August 22, 2011. https://www.theventureonline.com/2011/08/latino-muslim/.

Presha, Brie Stimson, and Alex Presha. "#Tacotrucksateverymosque Bridges Muslim and Latino San Diego Communities." NBC Bay Area, June 24, 2017. http://www.nbcbayarea.com/news/california/Tacos-at-Every-Mosque-Unites-Two-Disparate-Cultures-During-Ramadan--430638203.html.

Ramadan-Santiago, Omar. "Insha'allah/Ojala, Yes Yes Y'all: Puerto Ricans (Re)Examining and (Re)Imagining Their Identities through Islam and Hip Hop." In Islam and the Americas: New World Diasporas, edited by Aisha Khan, 115–140. Gainesville: University Press of Florida, 2015.

Rambo, Lewis R. *Understanding Religious Conversion*. New Haven, CT: Yale University, 1993.

Ramirez, Margaret. "New Islamic Movement Seeks Latino Converts." *Los Angeles Times*, March 15, 1999.

Reddy, Mrinalini. "Even as Islam Booms, Its Many Faces Can Deter Converts." News21, August 23, 2007. https://news21.com/story/2007/08/22/even_as_islam_booms_its.

Reza, H. G. "Embracing Islam, Praying for Acceptance." *Los Angeles Times*, October 29, 2005.

Rivera, Khadijah. "My Hispanic Muslim Legacy." 2009.

Rivera, Khadijah. "Dr T B Irving—Frontier for Latino Dawah in USA." February 9, 2007. http://piedad-latinodawah.blogspot.com/2007/02/dr-t-b-irving-frontier-for-latino-dawah.html.

Rivera, Khadijah. "Puerto Rican, Muslim and Female." January 3, 2009. https://www.youtube.com/watch?v=rDVOhEiePOY.

Rivera, Khadijah, Liliana Parodi, Samantha Sanchez Ngem, Nicole Ballvian, and Marta Galedary. "Petition to Protest the Defamation by the Spanish Communication Media against Muslim Women and Islam." 2002. http://www.petitiononline.com/petitions/Muslimah/signatures?page=3.

Romo, Ricardo. *East Los Angeles: History of a Barrio*. Austin: University of Texas Press, 1983.

Rushdan, Malika. "American Muslim Women's Leadership Training, United Arab Emirates (UAE)." January 29, 2009. http://piedad-latinodawah.blogspot.com/2009_01_01_archive.html.

Saada, Miriam Medhat. "Edición y Estudio del Manuscrito Aljamiado-Morisco de la Biblioteca Nacional de Madrid." PhD diss., University of California Los Angeles, 2011.

Said, Edward W. *Covering Islam: How the Media and the Experts Determine How We See the Rest of the World*. New York: Vintage Books, 1997.

Said, Edward W. *Orientalism*. London: Penguin, 2003.

Sanchez, Samantha, and Juan Galvan. "Latino Muslims: The Changing Face of Islam in America." *Islamic Horizons Magazine*, 2002, 22–30.

Sánchez-Walsh, Arlene. *Latino Pentecostal Identity: Evangelical Faith, Self, and Society*. New York: Columbia University Press, 2012.

Scott, Wright. "Populism and Downing Street E-Petitions: Connective Action, Hybridity, and the Changing Nature of Organizing." *Political Communication* 32, no. 3 (2015): 414–433.

Sells, M. A. *Early Islamic Mysticism: Sufi, Qur'an, Miraj, Poetic and Theological Writings.* New York: Paulist Press, 1996.

Sells, Michael. *Approaching the Qur'an: The Early Revelations.* 2d ed. Ashland, OR: White Cloud Press, 2007.

Serequeberhan, Tsenay. "Amilcar Cabral's 'Return to the Source': A Reading." In *A Luta Continua: (Re)Introducing Amilcar Cabral to a New Generation of Thinkers*, edited by P. Khalil Saucier, 69–85. Trenton, NJ: Africa World Press, 2016.

Simpson, Anika. "Pride March Must Include People of Color in Key Roles." *Blade*, February 25, 2017. http://www.washingtonblade.com/2017/02/25/pride-march-must-include-people-color-key-roles/.

Slocum, David. "9/11 Film and Media Scholarship." *Cinema Journal* 51, no. 1 (2011): 181–193.

"Slowly Escaping New York: The New York Times?" April 20, 2011. http://politicalcalculations.blogspot.com/2011/04/slowly-escaping-new-york-new-york-times.html#.

Smith, Jane I. *Islam in America.* 2d ed. New York: Columbia University Press, 2010.

Smith, Jonathan Z. "Religion, Religions, Religious." In *Critical Terms for Religious Studies*, edited by Mark C. Taylor, 269–284. Chicago: University of Chicago Press, 1998.

Smith, Tom W. "Religious Diversity in America: The Emergence of Muslims, Buddhists, Hindus, and Others." *Journal for the Scientific Study of Religion* 41, no. 3 (2002): 577–585.

SpearIt. "Muslim Radicalization in Prison: Responding with Sound Penal Policy or the Sound of Alarm?" *Gonzaga Law Review* 49, no 1 (2014): 37–82. https://papers.ssrn.com/sol3/Delivery.cfm/SSRN_ID2387928_code1504583.pdf?abstractid=2387928&mirid=1.

SpearIt. "Raza Islamica: Prisons, Hip Hop & Converting Converts." *Berkeley La Raza Law Journal* 22, no. 9 (2012): 175–202. http://scholarship.law.berkeley.edu/cgi/viewcontent.cgi?article=1243&context=blrlj.

SpearIt. "Sonic Jihad: Muslim Hip Hop in the Age of Mass Incarceration." *FIU Law Review*, 11 no. 201 (2015): 201–219 https://papers.ssrn.com/sol3/Delivery.cfm/SSRN_ID2767194_code1504583.pdf?abstractid=2767194&mirid=1.

Starrett, Gregory. "Muslim Identities and the Great Chain of Buying." In *New Media in the Muslim World: The Emerging Public Sphere*,

2nd ed., edited by Dale F. Eickelman and Jon W. Anderson, 80–101. Bloomington: Indiana University Press, 2003.

Street, Nick. "How Muslim Civic Activism Helped Pass California's Prop 47." Religion Dispatches, November 6, 2014. http://religiondispatches. org/how-muslim-civic-activism-helped-pass-californias-prop-47/.

Strenski, Ivan. "Religion, Power, and Final Foucault." *Journal of the American Academy of Religion* 66, no. 2 (1998): 345–367.

Suárez-Orozco, M. M., and M. Páez. *Latinos: Remaking America*. Berkeley and Los Angeles: University of California Press, 2008.

Talegani, Ayatullah Mahmud, Ayatullah Murtada Mutahhari, Ali Shari'ati, Mehdi Abedi, and Gary Legenhausen. *Jihad and Shahadat: Struggle and Martyrdom in Islam*. North Haledon, NJ: Islamic Publications International, 2005.

Taylor, Charles. "The Politics of Recognition." In *Multiculturalism: Examining the Politics of Recognition*, edited by Amy Gutman, 25–74. Princeton, NJ: Princeton University Press, 1994.

Taylor, Jennifer Maytorena. "New Muslim Cool." *Point of View*, Public Broadcasting Service, 2009. DVD.

Taylor, Pual, Mark Hugo Lopes, Jessica Martinez, and Gabriel Valasco. "When Labels Don't Fit: Hispanics and Their Views of Identity." Pew Research Center: Hispanic Trends (2012). http://www.pewhispanic.org/ 2012/04/04/when-labels-dont-fit-hispanics-and-their-views-of-identity/.

Temple-Raston, Dina. "Officials Worry About Some Latino Converts to Islam." National Public Radio, December 9, 2010. http://www.npr.org/2010/ 12/09/131916271/officials-worry-about-some-latino-converts-to-islam.

Tharoor, Ishaan. "Watch: Little Children Apologize for Terrorism." *Washington Post*, February 6, 2015.

Thomas, Piri. *Down These Mean Streets*. 30th anniversary ed. New York: Vintage Books, 1997.

Turner, Richard Brent. *Islam in the African-American Experience*. Bloomington: Indiana University Press, 2003.

US Securities and Exchange Commission. "2010 Annual Report of the New York Times Company." 2016. http://www.sec.gov/Archives/edgar/ data/71691/000119312511042247/d10k.htm.

Viscidi, Lisa. "Latino Muslims a Growing Presence in America." Washington Report on Middle East Affairs, June 2003. https://www.wrmea.org/ 2003-june/latino-muslims-a-growing-presence-in-america.html.

Wagenheim, Kal, and Olga Jiménez de Wagenheim. *The Puerto Ricans: A Documentary History.* New York: Praeger, 1973.

Wakin, Daniel J. "Ranks of Latinos Turning to Islam Are Increasing." *New York Times,* January 2, 2002.

West, Cornel. *Democracy Matters: Winning the Fight against Imperialism.* New York: Penguin Books, 2004.

West, Cornel. *Prophesy Deliverance!: An Afro-American Revolutionary Christianity.* Louisville, KY: Westminster John Knox Press, 2002.

West, Cornel. *Race Matters.* New York: Vintage, 1993.

Whalen, Carmen Teresa, and Víctor Vázquez-Hernández. *The Puerto Rican Diaspora: Historical Perspectives.* Philadelphia: Temple University Press, 2005.

WhyIslam. "Revelando el Misterio del Jiyab." http://d1.islamhouse.com/data/es/ih_articles/single/es_revelando_misterio_del_Jiyab.pdf.

Wise, Lindsay. "In a New Light—New Faith, Changed Man." *The Houston Chronicle,* June 13, 2008.

Yahsmin, and Nikkol Binti BoBo. "A New Day in Hip Hop: Interview w/ Mujahideen Team." March 21, 2006. http://halalstyle.blogspot.com/2006/03/new-day-in-hip-hop-interview-w.html.

INDEX

Printed in the USA
CPSIA information can be obtained
at www.ICGtesting.com
CBHW051349021223
2301CB00002B/4